CONSTITUENT POWER BEYOND THE STATE

The concept of constituent power plays a major part in modern political and legal theory—in how we think about the political. This book tackles the two-fold issue of public authority, and public autonomy in the modern conception of the political by analysing the concept of constituent power, its function in the modern political apparatus, and debates about its meaning and function in our own context.

Focusing on contemporary debates on constitutionalism beyond the state, Geneviève Nootens assesses the prospects for recasting the notion of constituent power in a polycentric setting that challenges state sovereignty as embodying the autonomy of the political. She argues that constituent power belongs with the conceptual apparatus of a theory of government peculiar to a statist way of knowing, and being into, the world, and that it is too much dependent upon the statist framework for it to have critical purchase on the new mappings of public authority. Nootens stresses the critical need to frame public authority appropriately if we are to conceptualize a conception of collective political agency that can sustain public autonomy in the current era.

Constituent Power Beyond the State will be of interest to students and scholars of political theory, democratic theory, law, and constitutionalism.

Geneviève Nootens is Full Professor of Political Science at the Université du Québec à Chicoutimi, Chicoutimi, QC, Canada. Her research interests are mainly concerned with the redeployment of democratic practices and the diffusion of sovereignty; majority and minority nationalism; and plurinational societies.

CONSTITUENT POWER BEYOND THE STATE

Democratic Agency in Polycentric Polities

Geneviève Nootens

Routledge
Taylor & Francis Group
NEW YORK AND LONDON

Cover image: © Getty Images
First published 2022
by Routledge
605 Third Avenue, New York, NY 10158

and by Routledge
2 Park Square, Milton Park, Abingdon, Oxon, OX14 4RN

Routledge is an imprint of the Taylor & Francis Group, an informa business

Library of Congress Cataloging-in-Publication Data
A catalogue record for this title has been requested

ISBN: 978-1-032-11833-8 (hbk)
ISBN: 978-1-032-11832-1 (pbk)
ISBN: 978-1-003-22172-2 (ebk)

DOI: 10.4324/9781003221722

Typeset in Bembo
by KnowledgeWorks Global Ltd.

CONTENTS

ACKNOWLEDGEMENTS

The work on which this book builds has benefited from the support of two research units: the *Groupe de recherche sur les sociétés plurinationales* (GRSP), led by Prof. Alain-G. Gagnon, and the *Centre de recherche interdisciplinaire sur la diversité et la démocratie* (CRIDAQ), led by Prof. Dominique Leydet. I wish to thank them both for their financial support and for the intellectually stimulating environment they offer. I am especially grateful to Alain-G. Gagnon who is always particularly keen to foster and promote his colleagues' work, including mine. He has kindly read and commented on a preliminary draft of the book. I also warmly thank Prof. Stephen Tierney, who commented on the preliminary draft as well. His intellectual rigor and his support are invaluable.

Two anonymous reviewers have contributed to significantly improve the manuscript. They have rightly and consistently pointed to its weaknesses in both content and form. Without their rigour and scrutiny, the argument would have been a lot less consistent. I am very grateful to them for their rigorous, yet benevolent, reviews. Of course, all remaining weaknesses and flaws are my responsibility.

I am also very grateful to Routledge's editorial team, and particularly to Natalja Mortensen. Her professionalism, kindness, and enthusiasm have encouraged me to proceed systematically, yet swiftly, with the thorough revision of the manuscript, and to complete this project on which I have been working for a while.

Finally, I wish to stress the support of the ones I love and share my life with. I am certain that at times they have been wondering how someone can spend so much time working on abstract theoretical notions. Yet they always have been confident that I would be up to the task I set myself. For this (and all the rest) I am deeply grateful.

INTRODUCTION

At first sight, constituent power seems to be a highly theoretical notion, remote from the everyday life of people in liberal democracies. It is rarely invoked in daily debates about the political, especially in contexts in which most of politics is routinized—namely, contexts in which the polity and its constitution are not significantly challenged. The issue of constituent power seems to arise only in exceptional circumstances, such as when a constituent assembly meets to create a new constitution; and such events most often are seen to bear the threat of instability and chaos, at least from a liberal democratic perspective.

Yet, the concept of constituent power plays a major part in modern Western political and legal theory—in how we think about the political. It actually is one of the most basic concepts of the conceptual and normative apparatus we use to frame the political. For the concept of constituent power

> captures the radically democratic promise for citizens to be able to make a new beginning, to refound their polity if they so desire [...] It offers an attractive possibility to provide constitutional legal orders with a basic norm, a *Grundnorm*, from which they derive their validity. It provides a justification for the superiority of the constitution in the hierarchy of norms, and a legitimacy basis for constitutional review over parliamentary legislation.
>
> (Krisch 2016, 661)

As a "pure" concept, the idea of constituent power explains why ordinary legislation must conform to the constitution (Tushnet 2015). It also helps to solve a puzzle about constitutional amendments accomplished by means short of convening a new constituent assembly (an exercise delegated to the legislature

DOI: 10.4324/9781003221722-1

or a referendum process in the original exercise of the constituent power). As a concept, though, it "cannot tell us when the constituent power has been exercised" (Tushnet 2015, 646); this we can know only "when a successful constitutional transformation has occurred. That is, identifying exercises of constituent power is possible only in retrospect" (Tushnet 2015, 647).

More specifically, the modern idea of constituent power embodies the collective political agency of the persons who belong to a polity and the idea that they (both as individuals and as a group) are to be the source of the arrangements peculiar to a specific regime[1]. Constituent power is a way of expressing public autonomy. It embodies the idea that authority must have a democratic pedigree (citizens as a self-authorizing source of valid claims) and that the constitutional form must ensure fidelity to the interests, goods, and values associated to it (Walker 2006; Walker 2008). Therefore, it also is significant as the symbolic reconstruction of a multitude as a collective political agent. This reconstruction is crystallized in specific representations of the people. These specific representations generally are established retrospectively, but they also have a prospective function[2]. These representations always are the result of the empirical and discursive dominance of peculiar interests, but their function nonetheless is to represent the body politics as such.

Constituent power as the symbolic pole of reference of the subject of the constitution is a modern concept. It is related to the secularization and rationalization movement of 18th-century European thought (Loughlin 2014, 219). The first formulations of constituent power occurred during the debates on the English Revolution in the mid-17th century (Loughlin 2007)[3]. The term was used in the 18th century to refer to the right of the people "to instruct, and be obeyed by, representatives" (Colón-Riós 2014, 307), and was then "frequently deployed to point toward a sovereign people (as opposed to a sovereign Parliament or King)" (Colón-Riós 2014, 308). Constituent power rests on two conditions: the recognition that the ultimate source of political authority derives from an entity known as "the people", and the acceptance of the idea of a constitution as something that is created. Hence, the concept of constituent power is closely related to the modern significance of agency (Krisch 2016). It has been a revolutionary concept from the start, because it granted people the right to make and remake government, so that constitution-making allows "for the radical realization of the idea of agency" (Krisch 2011, 49). It rested on the modern idea "that government and society were subject to intervention and human agency [...] and concentrated the claim to agency in the people, the 'nation'" (Krisch 2016, 659). With its emphasis on agency, constituent power hence "provides a very distinctive foundation for a legal and political order, very much in contrast with substantive moral, autocratic or theocratic foundations and historically characteristic of a certain period in which a democratic ideology found a particular form in the modern nation-state" (Krisch 2016, 661–2). By connecting the idea of legitimation to collective agency in some founding act, the idea of constituent power makes the idea of legitimation within such systems quite specific (Krisch 2016, 672).

The notion of constituent power, therefore, expresses the conviction that power vests ultimately in "the people", a persistent theme in modern constitutional thought since the late 18th century (Loughlin 2014, 218). But despite its basic significance in modern constitutional though, the concept of constituent power remains a disputed, contested one, "whose meaning is bound up with deeper disputes concerning the nature of legal, political and constitutional ordering" (Loughlin 2014, 218–9). Scholars do not agree on what it does mean exactly, nor on what it implies specifically. In other words, although most scholars acknowledge the normative resonance of the concept, they disagree about specific dimensions of its meaning and function in political and legal theory[4]. Such disagreements relate (amongst other things) to how scholars conceive of the status of constitutions (are they constitutive or regulative?), of the exact meaning of the reference to constituent power (e.g., is it a self-reference, internal to the polity and the act of constitution-making, or does it need to look like an ascription from the outside in order to actualize its legitimating function?), and more generally, of the paradigmatic role of sovereign statehood and of the nature of public law. These differences, therefore, also impact significantly on the core issue of this book: does it still make sense to use the category of constituent power to express public autonomy and to symbolize democratic authorization, in a post-Westphalian context?[5]

This is a significant issue, for it points both to the challenge of legitimating new types of governance arrangements and to (what I take to be) the inherent limitations of the notion of constituent power. These limitations were already noticeable in the "domestic" context, but they were most often overlooked. The consequences of globalization processes have made them more obvious. The modern notion of constituent power actually raises issues in at least four significant contemporary settings, both in the "domestic" and global/transnational domains: the EU; global/transnational regimes; multi- or plurinational states; and settler states. These examples show the difficulties involved in the issue of constituent power, at a variety of levels (from substate to global ones). Let me explain briefly the type of issues the modern notion of constituent power raises in each of these contexts.

The context of the EU has been particularly fruitful for discussions about constituent power and constitutionalization beyond the state[6], because of the peculiar character of the EU and of its high degree of integration when compared to other supra- or transnational polities and regimes. Debates as to the nature of the EU certainly are not settled. For example, there is no consensus on the kind of polity it actually is, nor on the approaches that are appropriate to deal with it. Neither is there a consensus on whether processes of constitutionalization (that should be distinguished from legalization processes) are going on. Therefore, it is not obvious whether the EU needs a constituent power or whether it can actually have one—and if so, how such a constituent power is to be conceived. One could argue that a European constitution does not need a constituent power; or, alternatively, that a constituent power is a necessary feature of any constitution, but that the necessary conditions will never be met in the EU; or that there is no European constituent power right now, but that such a constituent power could develop in the future. For example, an interpretation of the EU focusing on intergovernmentalism certainly clashes with some of the public narratives discussed in Chapter 6, narratives on the basis of which citizens challenge an executive-centred approach of the Union by claiming some kind of constituent power for the people. This clash of the people's claim to constituent power with an approach centred on executives and treaty-making has been particularly highlighted by the referenda in France and the Netherlands in 2005. But even when we take a closer look at these narratives (as does M. Patberg[7]), we realize that these public narratives vary on how they frame such a constituent power of "the people"—or, more exactly, on who "the people" is: is there one, cross-border constituent power composed of European citizens? Is there a plurality of constituent powers? Or maybe there is no delineated subject of constituent power but rather merely a multitude of individuals that resist supranational governance? Let me stress that I do not intend to discuss the case of the EU at length in this book. However, some of the approaches I discuss do focus on the EU; hence, here and there, there will be references to the case of the EU. As I will explain, I take the EU to be a *sui generis* case, but also as a case in which the discussion of constituent power does not actually need to depart significantly from the modern notion. Hence, it may not be as useful as expected when debating about constituent power beyond the state.

When we talk of global or transnational regimes, of transnational social movements, and of transnational democratization, the possibility of a constituent power seems even more remote and dubious than in the case of the EU. One significant reason for this is that constituent power usually has been associated with a demos. If we make democratic authorization dependent upon some prior "socio-cultural facts concerning identity, solidarity, and allegiance", then there can be "no real prospect of a full constitutionalism beyond the state" (Walker 2010, 294)—and hence, no prospect for constituent power nor for democratic authorization (for it is the former that embodies the possibility of the latter in the state). Yet, approaches such as constitutionalism from below and democratic constitutionalism, as well as some scholars working in the field of political sociology, have proposed ways in which democratic authorization may be reframed in such contexts. For example, S. Bailey and U. Mattei have argued that the common goods movement (in Italy) is part of an oppositional global constituency made up of transnational social movements (Bailey and Mattei 2013, 1008ff). They take this movement to be an example of the way in which social movements are emerging as an important form of constituent power by enforcing weakened constitutional public interest protections, by challenging the assumption of private property that underpins the liberal constitutional form, and by providing an alternative channel for politics (Bailey and Mattei 2013, 969). G. Anderson argues that social movements represent a constitutionalism "from below" that can reveal "the always-existing noninstitutional dimension of constitutionalism" (Anderson 2013, 881); taking into account these forms of mobilization allows for "a fuller and more representative account of contemporary legal and political struggle" (Anderson 2013, 904). But such approaches still have some way to go if they are to propose how these movements can frame alternate symbolic poles of democratic authorization. As I will explain in Chapter 5, the idea of democratic authorization conveyed by constituent power is not confined to resistance, dissent, or mere consent. It also points to a prospective (constructive) dimension and a jurisgenerative capacity. But then, in order to frame public authority and autonomy in the current context, we need to be able to grasp a complex world of fluctuating and overlapping constituencies—a world in which state and non-state polities coexist, in which authority does not comply with the "command" model (Krisch 2016), and in which some state capabilities are redirected to a disassemblage of the national (Sassen 2006). At the end of the day, constituent power, as it is closely intertwined with statehood, may not be the right category to use when we try to frame democratic authorization beyond the state.

One must stress, though, that even in the state context, constitutionalism (and therefore, constituent power) never has been an unequivocal achievement[8]. The existence of a single constituent power is paramount of statehood. Yet, in multi- or plurinational states, its existence has been challenged for a while by minority nations. The latter claim a constituent power of their own, and a primary right to self-determination. Let us think for example of the claim of Quebec, Catalonia, and Scotland to have the right to decide on their own of their future as polities. Such a claim usually is denied by the wider constituency and state institutions, for it challenges the very existence of the state. Some degree of (lenient) recognition is sometimes granted (one that has no consequence on political and juridical institutions), but it often stops short of renegotiating the terms of the state in a way that could meet minority nations' claims. Most often, the dominance of the overarching constituency builds upon the denial of the very claim of a minority nation to be a "nation". For example, in the *Reference on Quebec Secession* (1998), the Supreme Court of Canada recognizes only one nation, the one created in 1867 (namely, Canada), and makes Quebec a cultural and linguistic minority rather than a minority nation (Nootens 2019b).

The case of minority nations still is different from the ones of First Nations in the context of settler states, though. For minority nations usually aim at achieving self-rule on the model of statehood, whereas First Nations challenge the sovereign territorial (settler) state. This challenge points to constituent power as a building block of a modern conceptual apparatus (the sovereign territorial state) that entails culturally specific assumptions. K. Shaw (2008) has explained how such assumptions have been excluding First Nations from the very realm of the political. However, as sovereignty serves as a precondition for politics in the contemporary world, "any effort by indigenous people to engage with settler state officials in the political arena requires them to conform to the cultural entailments of sovereignty—a set of assumptions about the nature of space, time, knowledge, and sociality that is intimately bound with the state form—on risk not being heard at all" (Nadasdy 2017, 3–4). Therefore, First Nations face two issues, as to constituent power: it belongs with a (statist) framework that right from the beginning framed them as the "outside" of sovereign statehood, but now requires them to conform to its assumptions if they are to negotiate some self-rule arrangements with settler states; yet, they had their own ways of providing for the authorization of authority, more in line with what Tully refers to as "embedded" or "ancient" constitutions (Tully 1995)[9].

In all these cases, what is at stake is the issue of democratic authorization, public autonomy, and collective political agency in heterogenous/divided societies—namely, societies in which relationships are not framed by only one constitutional norm, or in which the existence of a single norm is challenged. In all these cases, sovereign statehood as embodying the autonomy of the political narrowly frames the expression of public autonomy by making the existence of constituent power dependent upon the very existence of the state and by making the one overarching constituency the subject of democratic authorization. It hence constrains the possibilities for expressing public autonomy. This book argues that constituent power belongs with the conceptual apparatus of a theory of government peculiar to a statist way of "knowing, and being into", the world (Loughlin, 2003); it belongs with a world in which public power is equated with state power, based on the pivotal role of sovereignty. This means that in the context of new mappings of authority that challenge the sovereign state as embodying the autonomy of the political, the modern notion of constituent power may not be appropriate to capture democratic agency and authorization at post- and non-state levels.

The book also builds upon a broader normative argument that shall be mentioned, although it is not its main focus: the challenges raised in the context of these new mappings of authority also are an opportunity to reconsider how, in the state, struggles for civic freedom have been subordinated to state sovereignty. I have argued (Nootens 2013; Nootens 2015) that in predominant, statist views, "the people-as-the-governed" are subsumed under a structure of public law that disempowers them and makes them "invisible". Constituent power is assumed to be unformed and unbounded unless framed by a conception of the state that actually owes much to the thesis of absolute regal power[10]. Although constituent power is deemed to symbolize democratic authorization by a people, it participates in a structure of public law that ensures the domination of certain interests; and most of the time it does so without the actual participation of those to whom it has been ascribed[11]. In some way, then, debates on constituent power in the EU and in transnational regimes underscore tensions that have belonged with the statist paradigm for a while, and that were already palpable and apparent in plurinational societies and settler states. The claims of trans- and post-state constituencies, as well as those of First Nations, allow to understand even better these tensions and the asymmetries in power relationships, because such claims challenge the modern state itself, whereas minority nations usually claim some form of statehood. I am aware that it is very difficult to consistently think beyond the state, both because states still are major actors (and can be expected to remain so in a foreseeable future), and because, as Krisch has stressed, we try to chart these new spaces "with the maps we possess" (Krisch 2016). Yet, it is necessary to do so, both because the statist framework limits our capacity to think democratic agency in a way appropriate to the transformations of public authority, and because struggles for civic freedom have been unduly subordinated to state sovereignty.

As I said, although a broader normative argument about the subordination of struggles for civic freedom to state sovereignty is present in the book, I focus on the issues related to the challenge of framing a conception of collective political agency that can embody democratic iteration in a polycentric setting of governance (what I also refer to as mixed polities, namely, polities combining state and non-state forms of public power). More precisely, this book tackles the twofold issue of public authority and public autonomy in the modern conception of the political embodied in the state by analyzing the notion of constituent power, its function in the modern apparatus, and debates about its meaning and function in our own context. As Krisch (2016, 658) has argued, an inquiry into whether there is a place for constituent power in the postnational order should help us both to elucidate the continuing role of this concept, and to assess the promises and limitations of transferring constitutionalist ideas beyond the state.

The argumentative thread of the book is the following: new mappings of public authority challenge the sovereign state as embodying the autonomy of the political; in this context, the classical notion of constituent power may not be appropriate to capture democratic agency and authorization, at least at post- and non-state levels. Constituent power is too much dependent upon the statist framework for it to have critical purchase on these new mappings. There are particularly three dimensions that have accounted for the normative resonance of the concept of constituent power: the way the modern notion of agency is shaped in the notion of constituent power, the idea of a foundation, and a holistic ambition. All of these dimensions build on statehood. Constituent power embodies the idea of the people acting together as equals to found a polity; this depends upon statehood because it is made possible by the fact that it is the state that makes the unity of the people. Constituent power also provides for a specific structure of justification of legitimate authority, one in which a comprehensive founding of self-government is attributed *a posteriori* to a people; this was made possible "by the comprehensive ambition of the absolutist state" (Krisch 2011, 54). Finally, it relates with a holistic ambition: the one of the public sphere as offering a comprehensive and authoritative expression of the world, and hence, as being autonomous. This holistic ambition also is closely dependent upon state sovereignty, because it is the latter that embodies the "autonomy of the political".

By assessing the meaning and relevance of the notion of constituent power, this book hopes to contribute to debates on collective political agency and democratic authorization in the context of new mappings of public authority—ones that challenge significantly the way Western modernity has framed the political. As to constituent power, this context (particularly when connected to the normative argument I briefly outlined above) raises significant issues, because the modern notion of constituent power embodied a radical idea of agency, namely, the claim to a comprehensive founding through self-government as a way of expressing public autonomy. This nested relationship between foundationalism and agency actually leads to a significant conundrum in approaches discussing constituent power beyond the state: scholars who rescue a significant part for agency usually also translate (explicitly or not) foundational constitutionalism at non-state levels, while those who acknowledge that the latter move is not warranted nor desirable have a hard time rescuing a part for agency that can account for a positive, constructive dimension (one that does not fall back on resistance or dissent). I hope to contribute to the resolution of this conundrum. From my point of view, the fact that the postnational order is not a sphere of constitution strictly speaking does not imply that we have to resign ourselves to see it as a mere sphere of fate[12]—forfeiting the radical promise of democratic agency. We somehow need to have the analysis journeying through foundation, contestation, and transformation. Foundationalism is intertwined with statehood, and hence is inappropriate in the context of heterogenous or divided societies—namely, societies in which relationships are not framed by only one constitutional norm, or in which the existence of a single norm is challenged. Contestation has been basic to the democratization of public politics, but it stops short of a prospective and jurisgenerative dimension. A possible third way can be expressed, at least tentatively, by the idea of transformation as embodying the idea that institutions are nonetheless for us to (re)design, rescuing the idea that the persons who belong with a polity are to be the source of arrangements peculiar to a specific regime (and hence, a sense of democratic authorization).

This book addresses the issue of the meaning and relevance of the notion of constituent power in the current context by analyzing contemporary debates on constitutionalism and public law beyond or after the state. As I said, constituent power is part to a specific political apparatus, the one of constitutionalism as a theory of government that developed in peculiar polities—the Western sovereign state. Debates about constitutionalism and public law beyond (or after) the state allow to assess the meaning and significance of the modern notion of constituent power as a building block of a specific political edifice, as well as possible options as to its future. The field of debates on constitutionalism and constituent power beyond the state is a rich one. Brilliant, thorough, and diverse approaches run through it, contributing significantly to pondering the unique nature of the framing of public autonomy as constituent power. This monograph builds on a discussion of these contributions. Right from the start my intention was to not go back to the classics—for example, the reader will not find any discussion of what Sieyès did really mean by the distinction between *pouvoir constituant* and *pouvoir constitué*. Of course, there will be, here and then, a reference to some of these classics, when it seems necessary to understand the stance of contemporary scholars on contemporary issues; but this is not the focus of this book.

As I just said, the field already is a prolific one, and diverse approaches have contributed to it. To get a broad picture of the field of the debates on constituent power beyond the state, I have decided to include scholars from different theoretical backgrounds. I could have chosen to focus on scholars building on a classical liberal background. However, from my point of view, the discussion would then have been partial at best. I do not think one can offer a compelling analysis of the prospects for constituent power beyond the state without discussing scholars like G. Teubner and C. Thornhill, for they (each in their own way) significantly challenge constituent power as a conception of agency. I am aware, though, that many of the scholars discussed build on institutional conceptions of constitutionalism. I hope the chapters will make clear that this is not because I agree with an unduly restrictive conception of democracy as being limited to representative institutions. Rather, there are three good reasons to focus on such approaches. First, these approaches are inescapable, when discussing constitutionalism and constituent power beyond the state; and they actually contribute significantly to the field, even if from my point of view, they also convey important shortcomings. Second (and relatedly), they allow to highlight the continuing and pervasive part played by statehood in these debates. Third, I think we should be rather cautious of anti-juridical conceptions of constituent power, for these significantly underestimate the part played by institutions in social and political life[13].

As to these different approaches discussed, I have kept the discussion of their theoretical backgrounds short, except when it seems necessary in order to understand why they frame constituent power as they do. For example, I spend a bit more time mentioning the basics of Teubner's approach because some readers may be less familiar with systems theory; a broader presentation was necessary in order to understand the shortcomings of how he proposes to recast constituent power beyond the state. The same comment applies to the few references to debates about public law that have been included. It is for example difficult to grasp correctly M. Loughlin's perspective without alluding to his conception of public law as not being merely a subset of positive law, but rather as *droit politique*[14].

References to conceptions of constitutionalism play an important part, of course, because constituent power plays a specific part in the constitutional apparatus. Conceptions of constitutionalism and of the constitution are basic in understanding how scholars tackle the issue of constituent power (and *vice-versa*). Debates on constituent power beyond the state cannot be properly assessed if one does not also analyze how scholars debate post-state constitutionalism[15]. Actually, it is generally when discussing constitutionalism beyond (or after) the state that these scholars happen to discuss constituent power. That also means that when one tackles the issue of constituent power, one has to deal with complex debates both in political and legal theory, for as N. Walker stresses, the question of constitutionalism (with which constituent power belongs) is one both for political and legal theory. The significance and meaning of constitutionalism arise at the juncture of political and legal theory. But it is important to stress that this is not a book about constitutionalism *per se*.

To give an example of the implications pertaining to legal theory, let me briefly recall the differences between normativism, decisionism, and relationalism in what regards the basic grounds of constitutional authority, as discussed by Walker and Loughlin. As Walker has explained, normativists understand law as a system of norms. They tend either to indicate some norm, norm-giver, or social convention whose source of authority simply is presupposed (in a positivist perspective), or to focus on the evolution of legality as a practice with its own moral integrity (in an anti-positivist perspective) (Walker 2017, 907). In a normativist perspective, the foundation is a pure act of representation, and constituent power is entirely absorbed into constituted power (Loughlin 2014). Normativism, actually, "typically has little need or appetite for an independent foundational concept of constituent power" (Walker 2017, 907)[16]. For example, I will explain in Chapter 1 that D. Dyzenhaus argues that the notion of constituent power is inconsistent with liberal theories, and rather belongs with theories that deny that law possesses intrinsic normative qualities that make it authoritative. From his perspective, it is the very idea of legality that "is basic to understanding the authority of law [...]" (Dyzenhaus 2012, 234).

Decisionism sees normativism as seeking to remove the space of the political from constitutional discourse. Decisionists rather affirm constituent power "as a vital expression of sovereign will underwriting the political unity of the people and so necessarily preceding their 'constituted' legal authority" (Walker 2017, 907)[17]. Such accounts acknowledge "that a constitution-founding power is a political undertaking [...] Constitutions are not purely normative constructions: they are bound up with the historical processes of state-building" (Loughlin 2014, 227). Hence, decisionists insist on the rooted authority of the sovereign state (Walker 2017, 907). From this perspective, "Constitutional legality is not self-generating: the practice of legality rests on political conditions it cannot itself guarantee" (Loughlin 2014, 223). When one enquires into the conditions that sustain constitutionality, the issue of how political authority is generated within the political domain actually becomes critical.

However, decisionism fails to recognize that representation is a pivotal issue: "once representation is invoked for the purpose of generating political power, 'the people' must itself be regarded as a representation" (Loughlin 2014, 228). This is why Loughlin argues that the concept of constituent power can only be appreciated by adopting a relational method (Loughlin 2014, 218). From a relational perspective, "Political power is generated only when 'the people' is differentiated from the existential reality of a mass of particular people (the multitude)" (Loughlin 2014, 228). Power "is created through a symbolic act in which a multitude of people recognize themselves as forming a unity, a collective singular: we the people" (Loughlin 2014, 231). In other words, political power "is generated through symbolic representation of foundation and constitution and then is applied through the action of government. Power thus resides neither in 'the people' nor in the constituted authorities: it exists in the relation established between constitutional imagination and governmental action" (Loughlin 2014, 231). Therefore, constituent power "expresses the generative aspect of the political power relationship" (Loughlin 2014, 231). It is the symbolic act by which a multitude recognize themselves as forming a unity that generates political power[18]. Constituent power "cannot be equated to the actual material power of a multitude", contrary to what decisionists claim, because this reduces constituent power to fact (Loughlin 2014, 231). It builds on a dimension of symbolic representation without which it cannot be (Loughlin 2014, 232). Constituent power is a "boundary" or "limit" concept: it is located on the boundaries of legal knowledge and "enables us to specify the constitutional form assumed by a political regime" (Loughlin 2014, 218). For the democratic potential of the modern shift in the source of authority to be retained, "the political space must be recognized as incorporating an unresolved dialectic of determinacy and indeterminacy, of closure and openness" (Loughlin 2014, 228). The foundation is not a pure act of representation, though: constituent power cannot be absorbed entirely into the constitutional order, nor can it be equated with some founding norm (Loughlin 2014, 232). This is why, according to Loughlin, relationalism allows for a full appreciation of how constituent power generates political power, "by exposing the tension between unity and hierarchy in constitutional foundation and the tension between the people-as-one and the people-as-the-governed in the course of constitutional development" (Loughlin 2014, 218).

These distinctions are significant because they bear on the meaning and function of constituent power. They will arise every now and then in the following chapters. For example, they are part of the background explaining the disagreements between statists and post-nationalists as to the proper locus and distribution of constitutional authority: normativists tend to be more readily open to the prospects of postnational (global) constitutionalism, whereas decisionists and relationalists tend to insist on the rooted authority of the sovereign state (Walker 2017, 907). This also impacts on how they conceive of the futures of constituent power.

As I have said earlier, core to constituent power is the idea of a democratic process of constitutional politics initiated by free and equal persons. Such normative resonance builds upon three dimensions (agency, foundation, and holism) that are closely dependent upon statehood. Hence, understanding the implications of the new mappings of public authority on the notion of constituent power first requires to clarify the meaning and function of the notion of constituent power in our political, legal, and constitutional apparatus. Chapter 1 focuses on the dimensions that account for the normative significance of the concept: agency, foundation, and holism. These dimensions make constituent power a peculiar way of expressing and embodying public autonomy. By making a constitution, the people create themselves as a collective political agent vested with the right to make and remake government; legitimation is "connected to collective agency in the founding act" (Krisch 2016, 672). The foundation of a comprehensive system of self-rule is attributed to the people and provides for a specific structure of justification of legitimate authority. In other words, foundation embodies the claim to ground the entire system of government. This in turn explains and sustains the holistic nature of constituent power's ambition. Constituent power is related to a holistic ambition because it is related to the public sphere as offering an authoritative expression of the world (and hence, as being autonomous).

As I will explain, there is a broad consensus on the normative import of the concept of constituent power, even if a close analysis reveals significant differences in interpretations and conceptualizations; these differences pertain to disagreements about the status of the sovereign state and public law, about constitutions[19] and constitutionalism(s), and about what it actually means to summon constituent power. However, there also are approaches that challenge either some of the dimensions that account for the normative import of the concept or this normative import *per se*. Hence, after having discussed the three dimensions that account for the normative resonance of the concept, Chapter 1 turns to such challenges to the normative resonance of the concept of constituent power by way of a discussion of three approaches: Teubner's focus on functional differentiation and self-foundation as a communicative process "with no formal organization of the whole system" (Teubner 2012, 67); approaches building on the claim that constituent power is a reductionist conception of democratic agency and implies a public law bias; and Dyzenhaus's claim that constituent power is inconsistent with liberal theories and belongs with theories that deny that law possesses intrinsic normative qualities that make it authoritative. The first approach (Teubner's) entails a multiplication of constituent powers establishing themselves through self-referential processes, a process that downplays the claim to be able to remake the political system and achieve self-government (Krisch 2016, 673). The second type of approach does not allow for a systematic understanding of how claims translate into lasting transformations of the political and does not assess appropriately the part played by institutions in socializing, in sustaining impersonal forms of reciprocity, and in limiting free-riding. The third one (Dyzenhaus's) tries to solve the inherent tension between constituent power and the rule of law by downplaying the significance of the former, and neglects norm-generating processes.

Statehood is core to the three dimensions emphasized in Chapter 1. Statehood has made possible the ascription of constituent power to an uncontested collective. State sovereignty embodies the autonomy of the political that is assumed in the foundational dimension; and it is the state that made possible the comprehensive reach of the founding of self-government (and hence the holistic ambition of constituent power). Therefore, Chapter 2 turns to the nested relationship between sovereign statehood and constituent power. Constituent power actually depends upon the sovereign state as embodying the autonomy of the political. As I said, it is the state that had allowed to presume of the political unity of the people. Emphasizing this close, and intricate, relationship allows to explain why there are few possibilities for translating constituent power to non-state polities. Chapter 2 stresses the enduring and pervasive presence of the statist paradigm in approaches of post-state constitutionalism, and the impact of such pervasiveness on attempts to translate or rescue constituent power in mixed polities. It discusses three approaches that exemplify the challenges faced by attempts to translate constituent power in mixed polities. It argues that it must be explicitly acknowledged that state sovereignty is integral to modern constitutionalism, and that a failure to do so impacts upon our very ability to propose a fruitful reflection on democratic authorization beyond the state—which from my perspective is an undertaking that is absolutely necessary, both normatively and practically[20].

As constituent power depends upon the state as a sovereign entity embodying the autonomy of the political, the shift in regulatory activity cannot but have a significant impact on constituent power. Chapter 3 focuses on such a shift. It does not intend to provide a full portrait of what is at stake in the current context; this would require a thorough analysis of the ideological and institutional structures of political modernity, as well as a detailed overview of the impacts of globalization—an undertaking that far exceeds the ambitions of this book. I rather wish to stress that the consensus on a shift in regulatory activity actually does not translate in a consensus on the impact such a shift has on public authority. In order to do so, I discuss two different arguments: the argument that there has not been any fundamental change of paradigm yet because there is no conclusive evidence, up to now, that the legal concept of sovereignty (as concerned with authority) has been displaced; and the argument that there has been no significant change because there actually never has been a necessary relationship between the political system in which legitimacy is produced by law itself, on the one hand, and statehood, on the other one—so that public law preserves its defining function in the current context. I then turn to the issue of the impact of this shift in regulatory activity on the three dimensions that account for the normative resonance of the concept of constituent power. This sets the stage for the discussion of approaches that try to recast constituent power in the current context in Chapters 4–6.

A major issue when balancing the democratic ideal conveyed by the notion of constituent power with the circumstances of the global polity is how much of it can, and should, be retained or translated. I argue in Chapter 4 that it cannot simply be swept aside, because it raises the basic issue of political authority, of its narrative(s) and conceptual framework, of public autonomy, and of collective political agency. Discomfort with the democratic deficits and technocratic bias (Möller 2018) of transnational regimes, a sense of usurpation of democratic authorization, and a concern with constitutionalization as a way to re-tighten legitimate decision-making by relating it more closely to collective agency and democratic self-rule have propelled attempts to rescue the idea of constituent power[21]. Chapters 4–6 are devoted to approaches that tackle this issue in different ways. I have chosen to focus on three broad types of approaches: approaches for which constituent power can, or needs to, be contextualized or translated in the postnational domain and for which such a translation does not present seemingly insurmountable challenges (Chapter 4); approaches that challenge the very possibility of collective democratic authorship in a post-state context and rather propose to fall back either on reinforcing domestic constitutionalism or on the notion of destituent power (Chapter 5); and approaches that focus on narratives of protest in order to relate the latter to some sense of political agency akin to constituent power (Chapter 6).

Chapter 4 focuses on approaches for which the translation of the notion of constituent power to the postnational domain does not present seemingly insurmountable challenges. But although they try to retrieve some sense of collective political agency that abides by the ideals of modernity, these approaches actually either stand by the basics of state constitutionalism, or plainly fail to propose a narrative of collective political agency that can account for meaningful democratic authorization. The former stance abides by foundationalism, which is hardly appropriate for the current polycentric setting of governance. The latter casts away a strong sense of some democratic authorization of structures of governance framed according to some idea of the common good.

Chapter 5 discusses approaches that acknowledge the intractable issues related to the translation of foundational constitutionalism at the global level, and that stress that the transformation of the boundaries that were core to modern constitutionalism challenges public autonomy. These approaches argue that the shift in regulatory activity does not allow for the embodiment and enactment of constituent power. They try to retrieve a way in which democratic authorization could at least be triggered, either by a strategy of containment asserting the ongoing significance of constitutionalism and constituent power in the "domestic" context or by a focus on the capacity for dismantling institutional orders (but short of a capability for enacting new ones). From their point of view, a post-state order would be a post-constituent one—one in which democratic agency may survive as an ideal but with few possibilities of being embodied in significant acts of self-rule. In other words, these approaches acknowledge the core part played by constituent power in the modern conceptual apparatus, but they argue that the current patterns of authority do not allow for its translation or recasting. But there is a significant difficulty with these approaches as well: they fall back on a negativistic logic that curtails the promise of the radical notion of agency implied in the notion of constituent power—namely, the notion that institutional orders are for us to (re)build. Hence, their contribution in rethinking democratic authorization is open to question.

Chapter 6 turns to approaches that focus on "narratives of protest" and that relate these narratives with theoretical arguments on democratic authorization. Such narratives play a significant part when discussing constituent power, for three reasons. First, in contention and contestation, people frame their claims as to public authority and public autonomy in some specific ways; such framings inform about how people conceive of the ruling relationship, and about their sense of a (re)location of authority. It is not only the addressees but also the objects of their claims that must be assessed. In the case of the EU, for example, as intergovernmentalism remains a basic characteristic (although not the only one), we can expect claim-making targeting the EU to at least partly implies the government of member states, for the latter are a basic component of the political structure of Europe. But this does not allow to automatically classify these claims as "national", for claims may be directed towards national (state) targets but framed with reference to Europe[22]. Second, the mechanisms and processes by which they interact with each other and with rulers also frame their political identities; they hence impact upon the boundaries of (existing or putative) polities. Third, democratization basically depends on contentious politics (although the latter is not always conducive to democratization).

Approaches discussed in Chapter 6 focus on a transformative ambition and connect it with narratives of agency. In other words, they try to retrieve a constructive side for democratic agency without necessarily building on foundationalism. The broader issue these approaches raise, however, is whether constituent power conceived of as open, reactive, and pre-institutional (outside a constitutional frame) still is *constituent power*. They focus mainly on the case of the EU. Yet, the latter may not require that we depart much from the classical notion of constituent power; therefore, it does not necessarily allow for a generalizable answer to the issue of collective democratic agency in a post- or non-constituent world.

Chapter 7 concludes the book by addressing two aspects that are core to the issue of framing alternate ways of embodying the radical promise conveyed by the notion of constituent power: the standards by which we are to assess whether the new mappings of public authority challenge the sovereign state (the issue of public authority); and the one of democratic authorization in mixed polities. As to the former, I argue that assessing whether we are witnessing a paradigmatical shift requires that we renounce the dualistic conception of the global as composed of states and a society of states, and that we frame the issue in such a way that state power is not equated with public power. As I stress in the chapter's introduction, I do not pretend to address thoroughly the challenge of theorizing public authority in global governance. My more modest aim is to emphasize that we need a more generalizable sense of what is "public" as something "brought by the whole society", a sense that can provide a critical standpoint on specific embodiments of public autonomy. This chapter also stresses that we need to have a more nuanced analysis of the diverse forms of authority in the contemporary world. For if we do not understand and frame public authority appropriately, neither can we expect to be able to frame a conception of collective political agency that can sustain public autonomy for this (our) world.

As I have already said, the notion of constituent power is too much dependent upon statehood for it to have critical purchase on the new patterns of public authority. Recall the conundrum already mentioned earlier: approaches that remain faithful to the radical idea of agency also tend to replicate foundationalism, which is not appropriate in the post- and transnational sphere (if it ever was); and approaches that rightly appreciate the problems raised by attempts to replicate foundationalism fail in offering accounts of agency likely to support meaningful democratic authorization. Yet, as Krisch rightly stresses, constituent power certainly is not the only way to frame public autonomy. And, here, the normative argument that looms throughout the book comes back in: even if we were to conclude that agency and sovereignty are closely connected (epistemologically and ontologically[23]), we nonetheless would have to acknowledge that state sovereignty has actually subjected (or domesticated) public autonomy and democratic authorization through the notion of constituent power. Struggles for civic freedom at diverse levels of those mixed polities (amongst others, by First Nations, transnational social movements, and associations of the global civil society) challenge the very subordination of collective political agency to statehood. People claim the right to have a voice and to participate in building a future in which their dignity, basic needs, and aspirations are recognized. They claim the right to retain some form of democratic authorization as to those regimes by which they are ruled.

Let me clarify that when discussing constituent power, I am not so much concerned with the fact that the invocation of the constituent power of the people in concrete contexts is associated with risks for minorities' rights and political stability. Z. Oklopcic (2014) has discussed the latter issue. He argues that in the arena of democratic struggles, problems arise when the identity of the people is contested, and that constitutional theory has dealt with this problem of antagonistic invocation in two ways: a Schmittian way that makes the homogeneity of the population a condition for the existence of constituent power in a democracy, and a Lockean one relying on docility and exhaustion to guarantee that there won't be too much popular uprisings. From his point of view, in most situations of political upheaval, invoking the concept of constituent power often implies a trade-off between the benefits of participation and inclusion, on the one hand, and the rights of minorities, on the other—a trade-off that benefit the former. He concludes that in the area of national struggles, constitutional theory "should distance itself from the vocabulary of peoplehood and constituent power and instead highlight the hard work of political negotiations and strategizing that is necessary to achieve a common platform between the goals of democratic, social and national emancipation" (Oklopcic 2014, 222).

I do not mean to underestimate the risks on which Oklopcic focuses. But I have chosen, in this book, to rather focus on the political apparatus of Western modernity, and on how it relates to struggles for civic freedom and public autonomy in a different context. Democracy and conditions of democratization are an underlying concern of my work; and I believe there are standards that can be used to assess claims to embody public autonomy (whether as constituent power or as something else). Moreover, I consider the area of national struggles to be a tricky issue because the legitimacy of the claims of minority nations often is obfuscated by invoking stability concerns and individual rights, whereas minority nations' claims do not necessarily challenge these; and stability is not necessarily ensured by the refusal to acknowledge and accommodate such claims. Hence, it is not that I am not aware of the risks emphasized by Oklopcic; nor do I support claims that would let the rights of vulnerable minorities be prey to majorities. In this book, I wish to focus on constituent power as symbolizing collective political agency and as expressing public autonomy, and to capture the prospects for democratic self-rule in a specific context[24].

Let me also stress that when doing so, I think that one should not start with a very specific idea of democracy and then determine how it should be applied to the transnational domain. Of course, we may have standards as to which kinds of social and political practices bring us closer to democracy. For example, we get closer to democracy when categorical inequalities do not translate into political ones and when regimes actually take into account what their citizenry want (and do so without infringing upon the basic rights of individuals, minorities, minority nations, and First Nations). We also need to stress that democracy is a collective endeavour: it is about things we want to achieve together as a body politics of some kind[25]. But from my point of view, starting with a blueprint either leads to overpessimistic conclusions (for example, assuming that we can never meet conditions similar to those that were featured in the national state, and hence that democracy is doomed to fail at any supra- or trans-state level), or to an unduly idealistic tone (for example, assuming the universality of some specific principles). We need to have a close look both at the "dynamics of contention" and at the way public politics[26] is framed, as well as at norm-generating processes. For example, the unveiling of the structure of interests embodied in public law is a basic condition of democratization. As I will explain in Chapter 2, Loughlin argues that oppression is eliminated from the concept of public law because the state is law-governed, because constituent power mediates between democracy and law, and because sovereignty embodies the autonomy of the political. But this structure actually has allowed for the subordination of groups whose legal and normative orders were estranged to (and by) dominant ones. In other words, interests that do not fit into the structure of beliefs that sustain public law, as well as contexts that stage forms of authority that do not correspond to it, are *a priori* excluded. Public law embodies a peculiar view of the common good, framed by specific assumptions. Tully actually seems right to claim that the modern construct of politics is itself conceptually oppressive (see Christodoulidis and Tierney 2008, 6). It may be more inclusive than alternative ones, but that does not mean that it is free from oppression[27].

Let me stress one last thing before turning to Chapter 1. The use of "postnational" may be confusing. In the approaches discussed here, scholars generally use "post*national*" to actually talk of "post*state*". "National" still is widely used to designate the state, even if the nation and the state are two different things, and should be kept distinct (analytically, empirically, and normatively). I do not support any conflation of the state with an encompassing nation; nor am I interested (in the current book) in discussing a "postnational state". I merely have stood by the dominant use, which tend to use "national" to refer to "state" or "statist". This book focuses on constituent power as part of the architecture of the modern state and on how transformations in public authority require that we address in innovative ways the issue of democratic authorization and of its embodiment in a symbolic pole. Challenging constituent power is motivated by a concern with how transformations of some core features of the political challenge our very capacity to embody such democratic authorization[28].

Notes

1 "The concept comes into its own only when the constitution is understood as a juridical instrument deriving its authority from a principle of self-determination: specifically, that the constitution is an expression of the constituent power of the people to make and re-make the institutional arrangements through which they are governed" (Loughlin 2014, 219).

2 Constituent power is "the authorizing force which creates democratic authority in the first place and hence renders democratic rule possible" (Preuss 2011, 82). The act of constitution-making is "an act of 'collective self-attribution' through which [...]

'individuals retrospectively identify themselves as members of a polity in constituent action by exercising the powers granted to them by a constitution'" (Preuss 2011, 82, quoting Lindahl 2007, 19).

3 Tushnet argues that the idea was introduced in constitutional theory in the late 18th century to solve a specific problem in practical politics, namely

> the obvious departures the French Constituent Assembly proposed to make from the authority under which it had been convened. Rather than describing the Assembly as a body acting pursuant to authority delegated to it by the King, Abbé Sieyès described it as a body exercising an originary constituent power on behalf of (or 'for' or 'by') the nation's people as a whole. As such, the Assembly was unconstrained by pre-existing legal rules.
>
> (Tushnet 2015, 645)

Whether one attributes the first formulations of constituent power to debates occurring in the context of the English Revolution or in the context of the French one, though, is less significant for my purpose than the fact that both ascriptions point to the very same meaning.

4 See, for example, the brief overview of the main distinctions between normativism, decisionism, and relationalism in legal theory, below.

5 I use "post-Westphalian" as a shortcut to point to the idea that the current context is significantly different from the one in which the modern state developed and consolidated. I am aware that, as M. Keating (1999) has argued, the state system as we know it is mainly a product of the 19th century and of the Versailles settlement (1919). But whether we agree or not about the "Westphalian fallacy", the current polycentric setting of global governance is significantly different from the structure of authority characteristic of the heyday of the state. See, e.g., Sassen (2006).

6 Let me stress that I use the word "beyond" the state to point to both post- and transnational domains and regimes. I of course do not mean that states are not significant actors anymore; using the word "beyond" only points to the fact that states are embedded in a polycentric setting of governance that challenges sovereignty as the claim to ultimate authority (see particularly Chapters 3 and 7).

7 See Chapter 6.

8 For example, N. Krisch stresses that it is doubtful that foundational constitutionalism (see Chapter 1) is a fitting vision for diverse societies (Krisch 2011, 67).

9 J. Tully has stressed the restricted conception of self-government available in the prevailing language of constitutionalism, itself closely related to the state (Tully 1995, 5).

10 State sovereignty has been built on theses that were actually antithetical to popular sovereignty (Nootens 2013; Nootens 2015; Nootens 2019a).

11 Let me stress that I do not mean to downplay the significance of democratization processes within states (see Nootens 2013). I only mean to stress that constituent power is part to a conceptual apparatus that subordinates popular sovereignty to state sovereignty.

12 Krisch argues that the postnational order is a sphere of fate, not of constitution, and that therefore, it is better understood as post-constituent because of adverse institutional and societal conditions. See Chapter 5. As I will explain, I agree with him that the origins of such an order cannot be ascribed to a constituent power. But I disagree with his proposal to fall back on a *pouvoir irritant* in the postnational order.

13 Once again, this does not mean that I support a conception of democracy restricting it to representative institutions. Constitutionalism "from below" and democratic constitutionalism criticize representative democracy and the imperialism of the current structure of public law, but without falling prey to anti-juridicalism.

14 See Chapter 1.

15 Amongst other things, the debate on constitutionalism in the global context has produced a great number of different constitutionalisms, "ranging from emphasis on human rights and juridical review in international institutions to broader calls for a legalization of postnational politics and a vision of a global order subject to an identifiable constitutional document" (Krisch 2010, 251–2). See also Anderson (2012).

16 According to Loughlin, normativism

> is a peculiarly inadequate expression of constitutional thought. In its positivist variant it either assumes the existence of a sovereign or else a concept of law as a system of norms authorized by some founding norm whose authority is presupposed. In its anti-positivist variant, this type of legal thought focuses on the moral evolution of legality as a social practice but avoids saying anything about the political conditions under which constitutional authority is established [...] In the place of the state normativists substitute an autonomous concept of constitution.
> (Loughlin 2014, 223)

17 This is C. Schmitt's approach, which is not discussed in this book. According to Loughlin, by maintaining unity through identity, Schmitt's attempt can only lead to totalitarianism.

18 As such, constituent power works not only at founding moments but also within the dynamics of constitutional development.

19 For example, are they constitutive or regulative?

20 The book discusses first the issue of the normative resonance of the concept, then the one of its close relationship with sovereign statehood, before turning to the issue of the shift in regulatory activity and to diverse proposals as to constituent power beyond the state. The discussion of these different dimensions of the approaches analyzed here is divided accordingly. For example, Teubner's approach is discussed in Chapters 1 (the notion of constituent power), 2 (the issue of its relationship with sovereign statehood), and 4 (attempts to recast or translate the notion in non-state contexts). Of course, these dimensions are most of the time consistently related; how one conceives of the relationship of constituent power with statehood impacts upon how she addresses the issue of constituent power beyond the state.

21 See also Krisch (2016).

22 Actually, domestication and externalization play an important part in understanding contentious politics in the EU. Claim-making is domesticated when social movements use protest to put pressure on national governments so that the latter negotiate better arrangements at supranational levels (della Porta and Caiani 2009). Claim-making is externalized when national actors' mobilization targets the EU in attempts to put pressure on their own governments (della Porta and Caiani 2009). Intergovernmentalism would interpret domestication as a proof that the state remains the main axis and domain of political claim-making and contention; but domestication may also be interpreted "as evidence of the intrusion of European politics into Europe's national political systems" (Imig and Tarrow 2001, 18).

23 Some may argue that challenging sovereignty implies challenging agency as such, because they belong with the same conceptual world and there is a significant interrelation between these two concepts.

24 Hence, I do not understand my project in this book as one of mere "de-subjectivization", namely, as an attempt to recast constituent power by either replacing the people with a differently conjured collective political subject or treating it as a vocabulary performing a certain function in the formation of constitutional orders (Oklopcic 2014, 204, 224–5).

25 See, e.g., Ober (2008).

26 "Public politics consists of claim making interactions among agents, polity members, challengers, and outside political actors. Contentious politics consists of that (large) subset in which the claims are collective and would, if realized, affect their objects' interests" (McAdam, Tarrow, and Tilly 2001, 12).
27 See also Tully (2007); Tully (2008); Christodoulidis (2007).
28 This has been a major concern of my work for a long time.

References

Anderson, Gavin W. 2012. "Beyond 'Constitutionalism Beyond the State'." *Journal of Law and Society* 39, no. 3: 359–383.

Anderson, Gavin W. 2013. "Societal Constitutionalism, Social Movements, and Constitutionalism From Below." *Indiana Journal of Global Legal Studies* 20, no. 2: 881–906.

Bailey, Saki and Mattei, Ugo. 2013. "Social Movements as Constituent Power: The Italian Struggle for the Commons." *Indiana Journal of Global Legal Studies* 20, no. 2: 965–1013.

Christodoulidis, Emilios. 2007. "Against Substitution: The Constitutional Thinking of Dissensus." In *The Paradox of Constitutionalism. Constituent Power and Constitutional Form*, edited by Martin Loughlin and Neil Walker, 189–208. Oxford: Oxford University Press.

Christodoulidis, Emilios and Tierney, Stephen. 2008. "Public Law and Politics: Rethinking the Debate." In *Public Law and Politics. The Scope and Limits of Constitutionalism*, edited by Emilios Christodoulidis and Stephen Tierney, 1–12. Aldershot: Ashgate.

Colón-Riós, Joel I. 2014. "Five Conceptions of Constituent Power." *Law Quarterly Review* 130: 306–336.

Dyzenhaus, David. 2012. "Constitutionalism in an Old Key: Legality and Constituent Power." *Global Constitutionalism* 1, no. 2: 229–260.

Della Porta, Donatella and Caiani, Manuela. 2009. *Social Movements and Europeanization*. Oxford: Oxford University Press.

Imig, Doug and Tarrow, Sidney. 2001. *Contentious Europeans. Protest and Politics in an Emerging Polity*. Oxford: Rowman and Littlefield Publishers.

Keating, Michael. 1999. "Regions and International Affairs: Motives, Opportunities and Strategies." *Regional and Federal Studies* 9, no. 1: 1–16. https://doi.org/10.1080/13597569908421068

Krisch, Nico. 2010. "Global Administrative Law and the Constitutional Ambition." In *The Twilight of Constitutionalism?* edited by Petra Dobner and Martin Loughlin, 245–266. Oxford: Oxford University Press.

Krisch, Nico. 2011. *Beyond Constitutionalism. The Pluralist Structure of Postnational Law*. Oxford: Oxford University Press.

Krisch, Nico. 2016. "*Pouvoir Constituant* and *Pouvoir Irritant* in the Postnational Order." *International Journal of Constitutional Law* 14, no. 3: 657–679.

Lindahl, Hans. 2007. "Constituent Power and Reflexive Identity: Towards an Ontology of Collective Selfhood." In *The Paradox of Constitutionalism. Constituent Power and Constitutional Form*, edited by Martin Loughlin and Neil Walker, 9–24. Oxford: Oxford University Press.

Loughlin, Martin. 2007. "Constituent Power Subverted: From English Constitutional Argument to British Constitutional Practice." In *The Paradox of Constitutionalism. Constituent Power and Constitutional Form*, edited by Martin Loughlin and Neil Walker, 27–48. Oxford: Oxford University Press.

Loughlin, Martin. 2014. "The Concept of Constituent Power." *European Journal of Political Theory* 13, no. 2: 218–237.

McAdam, Doug, Tarrow, Sidney, and Tilly, Charles. 2001. *Dynamics of Contention*. Cambridge: Cambridge University Press.

Möller, Kolja. 2018. "From Constituent to Destituent Power Beyond the State." *Transnational Legal Theory* 9, no. 1: 32–55.

Nadasdy, Paul. 2017. *Sovereignty's Entailments: First Nation State Formation in the Yukon*. Toronto: University of Toronto Press.

Nootens, Geneviève. 2013. *Popular Sovereignty in the West. Polities, Contention, and Ideas*. London: Routledge.

Nootens, Geneviève. 2015. "Constituent Power and People-as-the-Governed: About the 'Invisible' People of Political and Legal Theory." *Global Constitutionalism* 4, no. 2: 137–156.

Nootens, Geneviève. 2019a. "Légitimation démocratique et souveraineté méta-juridictionnelle de l'État." *ThéoRèmes* 15. https://journals.openedition.org/theoremes/3201.

Nootens, Geneviève. 2019b. "Démocratie et pouvoirs constituants dans les sociétés plurinationales: Quelques problèmes de théorie politique." In *Ré-Imaginer Le Canada: Vers Un État Multinational?* edited by Félix Mathieu and Dave Guénette, 119–140. Québec: Presses de l'Université Laval.

Ober, Josiah. 2008. "The Original Meaning of 'Democracy': Capacity to Do Things, Not Majority Rule." *Constellations* 15, no. 1: 3–9.

Oklopcic, Zoran. 2014. "Three Arenas of Struggle: A Contextual Approach to the Constituent Power of 'The People'." *Global Constitutionalism* 3, no. 2: 200–235.

Preuss, Ulrich K. 2011. "Is There a Constituent Power in the European Union?" In *Le Pouvoir Constituant et l'Europe*, edited by Olivier Cayla and Pasquale Pasquino, 75–92. Paris: Dalloz.

Sassen, Saskia. 2006. *Territory, Authority, Rights. From Medieval to Global Assemblages*. Princeton and Oxford: Princeton University Press.

Shaw, Karena. 2008. *Indigeneity and Political Theory*. London/New York: Routledge.

Teubner, Gunther. 2012. *Constitutional Fragments: Societal Constitutionalism and Globalization*. Oxford: Oxford University Press.

Tully, James. 1995. *Strange Multiplicity: Constitutionalism in an Age of Diversity*. Cambridge: Cambridge University Press.

Tully, James. 2007. "The Imperialism of Modern Constitutional Democracy." In *The Paradox of Constitutionalism. Constituent Power and Constitutional Form*, edited by Martin Loughlin and Neil Walker, 315–338. Oxford: Oxford University Press.

Tully, James. 2008. *Public Philosophy in a New Key, vol. II: Imperialism and Civic Freedom*. Cambridge: Cambridge University Press.

Tushnet, M. 2015. "Peasants With Pitchforks, and Toilers With Twitter: Constitutional Revolutions and the Constituent Power." *International Journal of Constitutional Law* 13, no. 3: 639–654.

Walker, Neil. 2006. "European's Constitutionalism in the State Constitutional Tradition." *Current Legal Problems* 59, no. 1: 1–26.

Walker, Neil. 2008. "Taking Constitutionalism Beyond the State." *Political Studies* 56: 519–543.

Walker, Neil. 2017. "The Return of Constituent Power: A Reply to Mattias Kumm." *International Journal of Constitutional Law* 14, no. 4: 906–913.

1

THE CONCEPT OF CONSTITUENT POWER

The potential impact of the transformation in forms of authority on constituent power as a way of expressing public autonomy first requires assessing the normative significance of the concept and its standing in the edifice of public law as *droit politique*[1]. Since constituent power embodies the idea of the democratic authorization of the basic norms that frame the relationship between rulers and ruled, the concept is summoned, in debates on constitutionalism beyond the state, as a building block of democracy as a meta-value of politics and of a specific idea of legitimation. The first part of this chapter focuses on three dimensions that are particularly significant as to the normative resonance of the concept of constituent power: agency, foundation, and holism. However, although there is a broad consensus on such a normative resonance, there also are approaches that negate or mitigate this specific normative resonance. A fair assessment cannot ignore these. Hence, the second part of this chapter is devoted to the discussion of three such approaches: Teubner's argument for multiple constituent powers who establish themselves through self-referential processes, an argument that ultimately downplays the holistic nature of constituent power's ambition (and, as Lindahl argues, obfuscates the basic political issue of the enforcement of collectively binding decisions[2]); approaches according to which constituent power actually is a reductionist conception of democratic agency because it belongs with a conceptual edifice aiming at institutionalizing laws and constitutions; and D. Dyzenhaus's claim that constituent power actually is anti-liberal because it belongs with theories that deny that law possesses intrinsic normative qualities that make it authoritative. These approaches do not appropriately appreciate the actual meaning of constituent power as a building block of *droit politique*; hence,

DOI: 10.4324/9781003221722-2

neither do they help in providing a fair assessment of the prospects for constituent power in the current context.

Constituent power actually has a specific meaning and function in our political, legal, and constitutional apparatus. Three dimensions are particularly significant. First, constituent power embodies the idea of the people acting together, as equals, to found a polity. It is closely related to the democratic ideal:

> constituent power [...] refers us to a general affirmation of the virtues of self-rule and the standing of democracy as a meta-value of modern politics, one that argues for a popular founding for those political systems that attain a certain threshold of authority and of autonomy. That threshold is reached in these systems that, in terms of their authoritative scope and the quotidian procedures through which such authority is translated into political decisions, are capable of significantly affecting the life-chances of those subject to them and of doing so in a manner that cannot be effectively counter-influenced at the level of any other political system.
>
> (Walker 2007, 256)[3]

Second, the foundation is symbolic, and it is attributed to a people *a posteriori*. It belongs with a structure of justification of legitimate authority related to a foundation attributed to a collective agent (Krisch 2016)[4]. Most of the time, of course, there is no actual foundation by a people. There rather is a claim to authority within an already constituted polity, and such a claim asserts its legitimacy by invoking the people and its constituent power (held to be the source of the constitution) as a symbolic pole. Yet, the idea of a foundation by a people plays a major part in modern constitutionalism. Foundationalism actually has been a core feature of constitutionalism from the 18th century on (Krisch 2011). Third, the concept of constituent power is related to some holistic ambition, namely, the public sphere as offering a comprehensive and authoritative expression of the world, and hence, as being autonomous. Constituent power is a peculiar way of expressing public autonomy, namely, one exercised from the point of view of the whole society, the "public"[5].

These three significant dimensions account for the normative resonance of the concept of constituent power; and they are precisely the ones that are challenged by the current transformations in public authority. I will argue in Chapter 2 that constituent power is intrinsically related to the modern state, and that such dependency requires that we take a step back when assessing the meaning and function of constituent power. Yet, this should not lead us to downplay its normative resonance, nor the ideals it conveys. For doing so would impede us to appropriately tackle the challenges it faces in the current context.

The Normative Point of the Concept of Constituent Power

There is a broad consensus on the normative significance of the concept of constituent power, although there are scholars who have argued either that constituent power does not belong with liberal theories, or that the notion carries with it a public law bias that makes it coercive and leads to downplay direct democracy. Constituent power is most often understood as embodying the idea of the people acting together, as equals, to found a polity—to "constitute" it. Three dimensions are particularly significant, when we try to account for the normative resonance of the concept of constituent power: constituent power as embodying the idea of the people acting together, as equals, to found a polity[6] (to collectively be its authors); the foundation (as symbolic and attributed to a people *a posteriori*) as providing for a specific structure of justification of legitimate authority; and the holistic ambition related to the public sphere as offering a comprehensive and authoritative expression of the world.

Agency

As S. Tierney has stressed, in the idea that the constituent power embodied in the people gives to the government constituted power, the notion of "the people" "takes on a collective persona possessed of a political agency and hence distinguishable from the pre-political or apolitical concept of the 'crowd'. Therefore, it is in the foundation of the sovereign state that the concept of 'the people' as a collective political actor takes life; and it is in this foundation that people and sovereign are bound together by the concept of representation" (Tierney 2008, 17). By making a constitution, the people create themselves as a political agent/subject. This idea is of basic significance. The notion of constituent power implies both that citizens are self-authorizing sources of valid claims and that the addressees are represented as a group. Constituent power embodies the idea of authorization by a people as a collective political agent. It is a concept of representation that converts the multitude into a form of political agency[7]. In other words, constitution-building refers to the construction of the knowing collective subject and the specification of the means and object of the political community:

> On the one hand, the process of elaboration and ongoing adjustment of the scheme of collective action involves the stipulation of a reference point and procedure of collective agency, and so the identification of a collective subject over time. On the other, the substance of the scheme thus elaborated provides the normative guidance and institutional vehicle to articulate and pursue that common commitment as a continuous project of collective action.
>
> (Walker 2016, 335–6)

Constituent power has meant both that the legal order was not to be taken as a natural given, and that the power to change it was located in the people, rather than with kings, nobles, or clergy (Kumm 2016, 701).

Hence, constituent power expresses in constitutional thought the conviction that power is ultimately vested in "the people" (Loughlin 2014). It is a concept of representation that converts the multitude into a form of political agency. More precisely, in the structure of beliefs that constitute the idea of public law, constituent power is the generative aspect of the political power relationship that bounds rulers and ruled within a constitutional order (Loughlin 2003). It generates political power because this is only possible "when 'the people' is differentiated from the existential reality of a mass of particular people (the multitude)" (Loughlin 2014, 228)[8]. Political power is therefore created through a symbolic act in which a multitude of people recognize themselves as forming a unity; it is created through symbolic representation of foundation and constitution, and it is then applied to the action of government. The authority of the constitution hence derives from the construct of the people. That does not mean, though, that political authority lies in the people: the foundations of political authority lie in the state[9]. Constitutional structures are the means by which power is generated. The autonomously conceived public world maintains and enhances its power through the working of *droit positif* (Loughlin 2003).

The particular content of the notion of constituent power—"the historically novel claim for a constitution to derive its legitimacy from the people and the right of the people to make a new one when it saw fit" (Krisch 2016, 672)—explains its discursive importance as a structure of justification (Krisch 2016, 672). Constitution-making allows "for the radical realization of the idea of agency" (Krisch 2011, 49). Constituent power has been a revolutionary concept from the start, because it granted the people the right to make and remake government; such an emphasis on agency provides the legal and political order with a distinctive foundation (Krisch 2016), as I have already stressed in the Introduction. Constituent power, actually, is "a particularly radical element of the modern, foundational strand of constitutional theory and practice" (Krisch 2016, 658).

As it stands, then, constituent power as the embodiment of collective political agency also signifies a virtual equality of citizens implied by the claim of public law to be (at least conceptually) free from oppression, the idea that citizens are to authorize the norms of right conduct, and a specific idea of legitimation. All three elements (virtual equality, authorization, and a specific idea of legitimation) impact upon the normative import of constituent power. First, constituent power expresses a virtual equality of citizens, generated *inter homines* (although it also, at once, founds an actual association divided into rulers and ruled) (Loughlin 2008)[10]. Public law is the language of a mode of rule based on sovereignty, citizenship, democracy, and rights (Loughlin 2008, 57–8); it "claims to be law (*droit*) governed" (Loughlin 2008, 58)[11]. Second, a correct understanding of what a constitution is implies that the norms of right conduct prescribed by it acquire the status of fundamental law *because* they have been authorized by a people, not by some self-evident rationality of their claims (Loughlin 2010, 61). In other words, constituent power embodies the idea that those who are constituted as the subjects of constitutional authority should also be its constituent authors or represented as such. As Walker stresses, it suggests a test of constitutional legitimacy that lies beyond the constitutional text itself (Walker 2007, 248), and hence, is a "direct challenge to the positivist premise that legal constitutional authority is conclusively justified by the fact of its successful reduction to canonical constitutional form" (Walker 2007, 247)[12]. Third, as I said earlier, constituent power also embodies a specific structure of justification, one connecting legitimacy to collective agency in the founding act (Krisch 2016).

Foundation

Indeed, the idea of foundation is core to the modern concept of constituent power. It is true that the limitation of power probably is the most enduring theme of normative visions of constitutions and constitutionalism (Krisch 2011, 40). The theme of the limitation of power became increasingly influential in 17th-century England. But a broader vision arose in the 18th century, with the American and French revolutions. That broader vision came to see the constitution "not only as a limitation of government, but as its very foundation. The main characteristic of the new type of constitution [...] was the comprehensive ambition, the claim to ground the entire system of government and not only to shape it in one way or another" (Krisch 2011, 41). This foundational strand of constitutionalism focuses on calls for new foundations of government. It is "a historically very particular form through which to realize central political values, individual liberty, and collective self-government. It embodies a peculiarly modern trust in the ability of humankind to rationally govern itself, in the power of reason in the design of political institutions, and in the strength of those institutions in realizing a common good" (Krisch 2011, 67). Actually, in the 20th century, there was a far-reaching convergence on the foundational model, born out of the very particular revolutionary projects of the late 18th century (Krisch 2011, 44, 48). Realizing foundational constitutionalism "does not merely imply the creation of a unified set of rules about the exercise of public power, but this set of rules also has to explicate the conditions under which public power can be regarded as an exercise of public and private autonomy" (Krisch 2011, 55). In normatively rich conceptions of constitutions and constitutionalism, a foundational constitution gains centrality as a focus for the self-referential formulation of principles on the side both of democratic processes and rights (Krisch 2011, 52). Foundational constitutionalism was made possible "by the comprehensive ambition of the absolutist state" (Krisch 2011, 54).

Holism

As foundational constitutionalism is "a structure by which a polity can make a comprehensive claim to agency" (Krisch 2010, 252), foundationalism is closely related to holism. More precisely, foundationalism "means adopting a holistic ambition, an ambition to construct a comprehensive, justified political order […]" (Krisch 2010, 253). The idea of foundation embodies the claim to ground the entire system of government and hence allows for the holistic nature of constituent power's ambition. Krisch argues that "[w]ithout regard for this holistic ambition, we cannot account for the communicative strength of this claim in political and social discourses" (Krisch 2016, 673)[13]. This holistic ambition also depends upon the conception of the public sphere as offering an authoritative expression of the world (and hence, as being autonomous). Holism, foundationalism, and agency, hence, are closely related into the structure of justification characteristic of constituent power.

Let me stress that although constituent power is most often ascribed *a posteriori* to the people as a symbolic pole, this ascription was made possible because of statehood. It is statehood that made possible the ascription of constituent power to an "uncontested collective", both because the principle of territoriality offers a neat way to delineate sovereign entities and because of the comprehensive reach of the state—which was made still more powerful with the transition from indirect to direct rule. I will come back on these issues in Chapter 3, as they raise specific challenges for thinking constituent power beyond the state. For now, let me simply mention that even in the state context, foundationalism's comprehensive and holistic ambition raises significant issues—for example, when it comes to dealing with diversity.

I will come back on the nested relationship between these three dimensions, on the one hand, and statehood, on the other, in Chapter 2. For now, let me stress that there is a broad consensus about the normative import of the concept of constituent power, even if scholars emphasize different aspects accounting for such import. In most accounts, the three dimensions are implicitly or explicitly related. In other words, even if there are differences in conceptualizations and interpretations, there nonetheless is a broad agreement on constituent power as a (normative) building block of constitutionalism. However, there also are approaches that depart from that consensus and that either downplay its specific political import or challenge its normative resonance. I now turn to these.

Collective Political Agency? G. Teubner's Societal Constitutionalism

Collective political agency is a core issue, both because it is a building block of the notion of constituent power and because it faces major challenges in the current context of new mappings of public authority (see Chapters 3–6).

While approaches building on a liberal theoretical background (in a broad sense) generally emphasize the unique possibilities for democratic self-rule related to constituent power (and either try to rescue it in some way or lament its fading in the context of a polycentric setting of governance), approaches grounded in systems theory (such as Teubner's) address it in a significantly different way. Teubner argues that functional differentiation is integral to modernity, and that different social orders autonomize and constitutionalize themselves; states do not have a monopoly on constitutionalization processes. It is necessary to ensure both the autonomy and limitations of the different subsystems. But Teubner negates the possibility of a collective actor and effective formal organization in establishing a collective identity; he also downplays its specific political import. Hence, in his approach, the ontological, epistemological, and normative meaning of modern political authorship as conveyed by the notion of constituent power is significantly challenged. Let me stress that in this chapter, I will merely hint briefly at this issue, in order to illustrate departures from the broad consensus on the normative significance of constituent power; Chapter 4 provides a more detailed discussion of the impact of Teubner's conception of constitutionalism and constituent power on agency *per se*.

Let me first briefly recall a few general features of Teubner's societal constitutionalism[14]. The latter emerges from the sociology of law. From this perspective, systems "are first and foremost systems of meanings, phenomenological reductions that allow for the emergence of communicative fields" (Christodoulidis 2013, 633). To understand Teubner's approach to constituent power and agency, it must first be recalled that from the perspective of systems theory, every functional system based on binary coding (e.g., lawful/unlawful in the case of the legal system) is enmeshed with paradoxes of self-reference. Hence, law and politics "are grounded in self-referential communications which revolve around binary codings: lawful/unlawful in the case of the legal system and power-superiority/power-inferiority in the case of the political system" (Möller 2018, 37). The foundational paradox in both systems is that "it is unclear if the establishment of the code was itself lawful or unlawful or can be regarded as an expression of power-superiority or power-inferiority" (Möller 2018, 37)[15]. But social systems invent "mechanisms to conceal their paradoxical origins and to stage themselves as necessary and viable" (Möller 2018, 37). In the case of law, only a strategy of "deparadoxification" has been successful in escaping the paradox; this strategy involves the externalization of the paradox of law towards politics "with the aide of the state constitution. In this way, the law seeks its ultimate legitimation in democratic politics" (Teubner 2016, 31). As to politics, its "internally insoluble paradox" is that of the "binding of necessarily unbound authority" (Teubner 2016, 32, quoting Luhmann). Escaping the paradox was facilitated "when the paradox was externalized towards the law, and this was accomplished, once again, by the state constitution, because the constitution commits sovereignty to the process of law" (Teubner 2016, 32)[16]. Hence, the state constitution is a structural coupling between law and politics; it is characterized by a "reciprocal externalization of the original paradoxes of politics and law" (Teubner 2016, 32). Legal norms stabilize the reflexive effects of the institutions for acquiring and exercising power; and law defuses the paradoxes of political power, since the paradox of self-foundation is externalized to the law.

Constituent power has a direct connection with the foundational paradox, because it is concerned with authorization: "from the perspective of the legal system, the establishment of the code law/unlawful is traced back to a political founding act that is (at least partly) external to the constituted powers of law" (Möller 2018, 37); and "from the perspective of the political system, the establishment of its code (power-superiority/power-inferiority) is relegated to a legal construction which inhibits excesses of political power and relegates its foundation to the legal system" (Möller 2018, 37). This is why (according to such an approach) constituent power "has always oscillated between legalistic approaches, which consider constituent power to be only a concern in the reconstructive reasoning of courts, and being a deeply political issue, which cannot be fully internalized into the legal order" (Möller 2018, 37).

The unique position of state constitutions is due to the totally symmetrical reciprocal externalization of politics towards the law and of law towards politics (Teubner 2016, 32). It does not come from any constitutional monopoly, nor from a hierarchical superiority of the state constitution over subconstitutions, "nor from the state constitutions being the only one to have a legal character" (Teubner 2016, 41). The functions of the constitution (the foundation of an autonomous order and the self-limitation of that order) "cannot be limited to politics" (Teubner 2012, 17). Let me explain briefly why this is so, before returning to the issue of the functions of constitutions. According to Teubner, politics is but one subsystem amongst others. Political constitutions do not exhaust the forms given to the collective potential of society; they "represent exclusively society's specific political potential—its assets, resources of power, and consensus—for the purposes of collective decision-making" (Teubner 2012, 64). Other social systems also externalize their paradoxes of self-reference towards the law (and vice versa); and other sectorial constitutions perform a constitutive function parallel to the one performed by the political constitutions of nation-states, which is to secure the autonomy of their specific medium by making use of constitutive rules to regulate its abstraction "as an autonomous social construct within a globally-constituted function system" (Teubner 2012, 75–6). Constitutionalization is primarily a social process, not a legal one. Its primary aspect "is always to self-constitute a social system" (Teubner 2012, 103). Hence, the theory of the political constitution can be generalized (Teubner 2016, 32). Modern constitutionalism is basically deficient because it has concealed the autonomy of social subareas (Teubner 2012, 5–6).

As I said, the function of constitutions is to secure the autonomy of their specific medium (Teubner 2012, 75–6). A regime's constitution "normalizes both the internal relations of the formal organization [...] and the external relations in their relevant environmental sectors (the interaction with their publics)" (Teubner 2011, 223). More precisely, constitutions have two functions: the foundation of an autonomous order, and the self-limitation of that order. A constitution establishes a distinct legal authority which structures a societal process and is legitimized by it; the primary aspect of constitutionalization, hence, is to self-constitute a social system, with law playing a supportive role[17]. The political constitutions of nation-states have the constitutive function of securing the autonomy of politics acquired in relation to other sources of power; "[t]hey do so by formalizing the medium of political power" (Teubner 2012, 75). State constitutions under liberalism "lay claim to a double function: to constitute political power, and to limit it under the rule of law" (Teubner 2012, 17). In this case, "constitution" means both that the organizational rules for the conduct of politics should be subjected to norms, and that "political power should be autonomous in relation to societal sources of power" (Teubner 2012, 17). As to the former (organizational rules), Teubner argues that

> [i]ndependent political power results from the reflexivity of power processes: in the relationship between *pouvoir constituant* and *pouvoir constitué*, power is applied to power with an independent political collective evolving as part of this process. This is, in the narrow sense, the 'constitution' of political power, which then needs the medium of law to stabilize it, making it relatively independent of power fluctuations and perpetuating the reflexivity of power.
>
> (Teubner 2012, 17)

As to the latter (the autonomy of political power), the creation of boundaries between politics and its societal environs "is implemented via fundamental political rights, with politics imposing self-limitations in regard to the autonomy of the individuals" (Teubner 2012, 17).

Constitutions hence reconstruct collective identity as self-descriptions of a social system, not only in the political system but also in other social systems as well. Collective identity, then, refers to the self-description of a social system, not to a corporate actor or formal organization. Teubner conceives of constituent power as the power of a certain agent to found and shape social institutions (Patberg 2013). It is a phenomenon of social communication; it is a communicative potential, a type of social energy, a power "which, via constitutional norms, is transformed into a *pouvoir constitué*, but which remains as permanent irritant to the constituted power" (Teubner 2012, 62). Any anthropomorphical identification of constituent power with the "people" or the "community" is misleading, because constitutionalization does not form people: it structures communication. However, as power "presents itself in the structural coupling between social systems and the consciousness and corporeality of actual people, it makes sense to connect pouvoir constituant to people" (Teubner 2012, 62–3). It is "*the reciprocal irritations between society and individuals, between communication and consciousness*" that trigger constituent power (Teubner 2012, 63).

Teubner's specific view of the political raises significant issues as to the argumentative thread of this book. I will come back more thoroughly on these in Chapters 2 and 4. For the purposes of the current chapter (that focuses on the three dimensions that account for the normative import of constituent power), let me stress that from the point of view of systems theory, none of the usual options as to what is the "substrate" of constituent power is particularly useful. These usual options are the following: individuals constituting a politically active citizenry; the entire people as a preconstitutional community constituting a polity; pre-political relations taking on genuinely political quality; relations of facts transformed into norms by the use of a border concept; power relations between groups whose compromise on a constitution is then elevated ideologically; and semantic fictions providing a founding myth for imagined communities (Teubner 2012, 62). Rather, the autonomy of social subsystems calls for a multiplication of constituent powers who establish themselves through self-referential processes "by which, *ex nihilo*, they constitute their own autonomy" (Teubner 2012, 65). Constitutionalization does not necessarily equate with the transformation of a group of individuals into a collective actor, and the collective identity of a social system does not necessarily imply any effective formal organization (Teubner 2012, 67). Teubner actually negates the necessity of a collective actor and effective formal organization in establishing a collective identity: economy, science, law, etc. all manage without a collective actor, "and unlike the state, are not represented internally and externally by a formal organization. Their self-foundation does not take place through a formally organized collective, but rather as a communicative self-foundation with no formal organization of the whole system" (Teubner 2012, 67).

Systems theory potentially impacts on our very idea of agency and its normative import. I have stressed that the modern notion of constituent power embodies the idea of a collective political agent; as a symbolic pole, it embodies the capacity for autonomous self-rule by such an agent. Teubner's approach irrevocably challenges these dimensions, by defying the nature and scope of the radical aspect of the modern notion of agency conveyed by the notion of constituent power. For Teubner's emphasis on the constitutionalization of the various subsystems also "downplays the holistic nature of constituent power's ambition" (Krisch 2016, 673); such a move, then, does not allow to account for the claim to achieve self-government, nor to understand "the limitations faced by attempts to transfer the concept into the fragmented and pluralist world of the transnational" (Krisch 2016, 673).

As I said earlier, I will come back on this issue in Chapter 4, when discussing how Teubner recasts constituent power in the transnational order. My aim in this chapter merely is to point briefly to approaches that depart from the broad consensus on the normative and political import of the notion. In Teubner's case, the problem is that the significance and meaning of constituent power are diluted—and hence, that his argument cannot account for the specific normative import of the modern notion of constituent power. He does not directly challenge the normative resonance of constituent power (actually, he rather "multiplies" constituent powers); but he reframes it as self-descriptions representing the potential of the various subsystems, in constitutionalization as a self-referential process by which subsystems constitute their own autonomy[18]. By challenging at once the specifically radical nature of agency conveyed by the modern notion of constituent power, foundationalism, and holism, Teubner substantially dilutes such import—especially when such a move is taken together with the issues raised in Chapter 2 as to the political.

Let me turn now to two approaches that more straightforwardly challenge the normative significance of constituent power: approaches according to which constituent power conveys a public law bias that restricts the possibility of direct democracy; and Dyzenhaus's argument about normative legal theories.

A Public Law Bias? Constituent Power as a Reductionist Conception of Democratic Agency

The basic idea of approaches criticizing constituent power's public law bias is that constituent power belongs with a conceptual edifice aiming at institutionalizing laws and constitutions, whereas democratic protest rather aims at embodying forms of "counter life". In other words, they argue that constituent power is a reductionist conception of democratic agency. For example, C. Volk argues that transnational protest movements do not aim at implementing a new order; nor do they aim at fundamental legal change. The aim of protest is not to institutionalize new laws or constitutions (Volk 2019; see also Niesen 2019b). Translating the practices of transnational protest movements (e.g., direct democracy) into the language of constituent power means missing their core concern, which is precisely to leave behind the juristic grid of understanding (of which public law reductionism is characteristic) (Volk 2019). To qualify as constituent power at the level of theoretical reflection, an actor must articulate an institution-generating and institution-transforming agenda; but transnational protest movements seek to leave behind the traditional grid of understanding and to change cultural codes themselves (Volk 2019, 114). I. Lorey makes a similar argument, stressing that transnational protest movements do not juridically constitute alternative forms of cooperation and coordination that "are to counterbalance the violent [...] character of the classical legal understanding of constituent power, which she locates in its individualizing, homogenizing, representative and coercive effects" (Niesen 2019b, 8). Lorey argues that in state and constitutional theory, constituent power is "always thought from the point of departure of the law and the state; it is the force that lays down the law, connected to the question of what it means in terms of constitutional law, and under the premise of the separation of powers [...]" (Lorey 2019, 122). She builds on A. Negri's work and the assumption of a non-juridically oriented constituent power to argue that the demos "can no longer be enclosed in the constitution and ignored as constituent political power" (Lorey 2019, 125). She argues for "a non-constitutionalist understanding of constituent power" (Lorey 2019, 126). The focus lies "not on an external constitution but on the process of self-constituting, not on a subject of representation but on democratic modes of subjectivation" (Lorey 2019, 126).

Such approaches rightly acknowledge that a focus on institutionalized politics and democracy contributes in de-legitimizing democratic practices that are located "at the gates" (Tarrow 2012) of institutionalized politics. They also rightly point to the fact that constituent power belongs with the paradigm of sovereignty. But they do not allow for a systematic understanding of how claims translate into lasting transformations of the political. Moreover, "[i]n not envisaging any delegation of power at all, Volk's and Lorey's account can afford to ignore the otherwise all decisive flipside of the legalistic understanding of constituent power: the attempted subjection of those who have been entrusted with rule making and coercive power by those who are ruled by them, by means of a legal political constitution" (Niesen 2019b, 9)[19]. Finally, such approaches underestimate the part played by institutions in limiting free-riding, in sustaining an impersonal form of reciprocity, and in socializing individuals so that they comply with norms involving unconditional cooperation—dimensions that have been discussed by A. Føllesdal (2001)[20].

These approaches are therefore different from J. Tully's and J. Colón-Riós's ones. For sure, Tully's democratic constitutionalism challenges the displacement of freedom to representative institutions, criticizes the juridification of the subject that is core to the modern idea of (unformed) constituent power, and argues for a more general idea of popular sovereignty embodied by the condition of consent (see, e.g., Tully 2008a, 114). He criticizes the modern idea of constituent power for understanding the latter "as a capacity or potentiality, prior to taking a concrete form" (Tully 2007, 320)[21]. Constituent powers broadly refer to "the powers of human (individually and collectively) to govern themselves" (Tully 2007, 320). The displacement of freedom to representative institutions limits the "field of possibilities of direct participatory freedom (the exercise of constituent powers) within and against the constitutional forms to which the governed are now subject, directly or indirectly, at the very sites where these unjustly constrain their ability to exercise shared authority over the conditions of their activity" (Tully 2007, 335). Restrictive practices of government and democracy have come to maturity and predominance through the historical process of progressive governmentalization (Tully 2008b, 48–9), a process that includes a juridification of the subject that is core to the paradigm of sovereignty[22]. The problem with the juridical subject is that the forms of knowledge representative of it are a limited form of subjectivity, and should not be taken "as a normative representation of moral and political practices in general" (Tully 2008a, 112). Democracy cannot be reduced to the institutionalized practices of representative government. It is lively, agonistic, and freedom-focused.

Tully's argument builds on a strong contradistinction opposing modern to non-modern constitutional forms. The former constitutional forms are formal; they have attenuated participatory freedom; they build upon a concept of constituent power that exist prior to its actual form[23]; and they are the product of sovereignty in the sense of a ruler that stands in an agonistic relationship with the people (Tully 2007). The latter constitutional forms are customary; they are the exercise of direct participatory freedom; and constituent powers are always already immanent. "Extensive" practices of government and democracy are "the exercise of the abilities of the governed to negotiate the way their conduct is guided" (Tully 2008b, 57 and also 51)[24]. From this point of view, the constitution (the rule of law) and the democratic negotiation of it (popular sovereignty) are equally basic. The project of democratic constitutionalism (as opposed to constitutional democracy) is to expand the field of possibilities of direct participatory freedom by which the members can "negotiate the way and by whom the power to govern their conduct is exercised in the organization" (Tully 2008a, 155). The targets are non-democratic forms of subjection. Struggles to bring institutions and regimes under the participants' shared authority are meant to put an end to the imperialism of modern constitutionalism and its correlates, and to express the equally basic status of the rule of law and popular sovereignty.

Tully's argument assumes that there is a more general idea of popular sovereignty, one that has not been affected by juridification and that does not have a procedural content. Such a more general idea is embodied by the condition of consent. Tully actually contradistinguishes the idea of popular sovereignty as self-rule in accordance with one's customs and ways (see, e.g., Tully 1995, 6), on the one hand, and popular sovereignty as the idea that law is legitimate insofar as it is the product of the people's decision-making, on the other one. Genuinely founding the constitutional association in the sovereignty of the people requires embodying the former condition; it is an enterprise going on along the way, with people always willing "to listen to the voices of doubt and dissent within and reconsider their present arrangement" (Tully 1995, 27). The people are sovereign when they "exercise their powers of self-rule in culturally appropriate ways" and are free "to amend or overthrown the government if it thwarts their powers" (Tully 1995, 192). Therefore, Tully criticizes the limitation of the field of possibilities of direct participatory freedom embodied in the modern notion of constituent power. However, he does not cast aside the rule of law. He rather argues for a democratic constitutionalism that puts popular sovereignty and the rule of law on equal footing. Hence, he must assume that there is some way to rescue the rule of law from the juridification of the subject (Nootens, forthcoming).

In a similar way, Colón-Riós argues that constitutionalism is pervaded by an aspiration to permanency and a focus on representative democracy that actually deprives constituent power of its capacity to reconstitute itself as a polity. He agrees that constituent power is "the source of production of juridical norms" (Colón-Riós 2012, 7), but he defines the people's constituent power "as the possibility of correcting existing injustices through highly participatory episodes of constitutional changes" (Colón-Riós 2012, 7). Hence, "only a conception of constituent power according to which its exercise can be triggered at any moment in the life of a constitutional regime can be made consistent with the basic thrust of the democratic ideal" (Colón-Riós 2012, 8). And only a regime that acknowledges this, and acts upon it, can be considered democratically legitimate (Colón-Riós 2012, 73). Constituent power is "a force that challenges juridical systems from the outside and that, even when institutionalized, might re-emerge at any moment to destabilise it" (Colón-Riós 2014, 336). The idea that a constitution should be placed beyond the scope of popular majorities is at odds with democracy (Colón-Riós 2012, 17). Constituent power is about creating new constitutions without being subject to any form of positive law (Colón-Riós 2012, 102–110). It involves "an unlimited constitution-making faculty, a power that assumes the constitutional regime from the outside and that is authorized to alter it in any way that it considers appropriate. No law, ordinary or fundamental, is outside the scope of constituent power [...]" (Colón-Riós 2012, 111). However, constituent power is subject to an important procedural constraint: "it must be exercised through a process that includes all those who will become subject to the constitutional regime" (Colón-Riós 2012, 111). The exercise of constituent power "should not result in the abolition of—or fail to create—the rights and institutions necessary to facilitate future constituent authorities" (Colón-Riós 2012, 111). There must be some basic institutional guarantees in place (e.g., freedom of expression) and some institutional mechanisms "designed to allow citizens to propose, deliberate, and decide upon fundamental changes to the constitution" (Colón-Riós 2012, 118). Constituent power is a rule-breaking activity, but one that must embody its very objective, namely, the initiation of a new constitutional regime.

Hence, Tully's and Colón-Riós's arguments are different from ones such as Volk's and Lorey's. Although they also acknowledge a bias in public law (e.g., in the case of Tully, a bias that embodies both the denial of interests that do not fit with the structure of public law and the limitation of practices of democratic freedom), they do not challenge the rule of law in itself, nor the significance of institutions and regimes.

Constituent Power as Anti-Liberal? D. Dyzenhaus on Normative Legal Theories and Law's Authority

A different type of critique focuses on the very notion of constituent power as being inconsistent with liberal theories and belonging with theories that deny that law possesses intrinsic normative qualities that make it authoritative. This perspective is the one developed by Dyzenhaus, who has been the "most vocal opponent" of constituent power in constitutional theory (Oklopcic 2014, 225). Dyzenhaus argues that the question of constituent power does not even arise for normative legal theory because that question presupposes that the authority of the legal order has its basis outside the latter. Let me recall that by "normative legal theory", Dyzenhaus means the family of theories including Lon L. Fuller and Ronald Dworkin. He takes this family of theories

> to be committed to showing how legal order and law itself are best understood from the inside, from a participant perspective that argues that legal order has intrinsic qualities that help to sustain an attractive and viable conception of political community. It is [...] those intrinsic qualities that give law its authority and without which there is neither law nor authority. Moreover, while these are specifically legal qualities and a specifically legal kind of authority, the qualities and authority are moral as well as legal, and thus explain why law's claim to authority is justified.
>
> (Dyzenhaus 2012, 233)

He contrasts normative legal theory and "negatively prescriptive political theories" such as Schmitt's. The latter type of theories makes a normative claim about the legal order,

> but one that both comes from a perspective external to the law and denies that law's authority can be founded on the intrinsic qualities of legal order. In particular, they seek to refute the claim of those in the family of normative legal theory that there are intrinsic qualities of legal order that make government under the rule of law tend to serve the values associated with liberal democracy [...] [T]hey are committed to the view that whatever authority a legal order might have must have its basis outside the legal order, for example in a political decision of 'We, the people'.
>
> (Dyzenhaus 2012, 233)

A negatively prescriptive political theory is anti-liberal, since "[i]t equates the allegedly false claim about normativity with liberal ideology, so that the debunking of normativity is in the service of installing an anti-liberal ideology" (Dyzenhaus 2007, 132). Theories belonging with that family are "unable to locate authority in something entirely external for they are drawn to claim that the basis is quasi-legal" (Dyzenhaus 2012, 233). It is this inability that is at the source of the "paradox of authorship", namely, the tension between the idea that "for a people to act as author of the legal forms of constituted power, it must already exist as an author", on the one hand, and the acknowledgement that such an entity is artificial, and hence, must itself be identifiable by legal forms, on the other one (Dyzenhaus 2012, 233–4). Therefore, "negatively prescriptive political theories" are ambivalent "about whether the basis of authority is internal or external to law" (Dyzenhaus 2012, 234). Normative legal theories, on the other hand, "are not subject to this ambivalence since they explain law's authority in general by reference to law's intrinsic qualities, hence the question of constituent power does not arise for them" (Dyzenhaus 2012, 234). Actually, the very idea of legality "is basic to understanding the authority of law in a way that the ideas of a constitution and constituent power are not" (Dyzenhaus 2012, 234). This is a matter internal to law:

> [I]f, in order to understand law, including the role of written constitutions in legal order, we need to understand why a claim to authority is always also a claim to legitimate authority, legal theory has to engage with the question of what justifies the claim as a matter internal to law [...] [W]hat comes into view are principles of legality that condition the exercise of power, indeed, constitute power in such a way that it becomes authoritative.
>
> (Dyzenhaus 2012, 260)

Dyzenhaus also argues that the distinction between constituent and constituted powers within positive law (as in, e.g., D. Grimm) does not solve the problem of fundamental law; it merely displaces it. One way of solving the problem is to see constituent power as somewhat extra-legal; but generally, those who regard the idea of constituent power as of fundamental importance do not see it as entirely extra-legal (Dyzenhaus 2012, 237).

Hence, from Dyzenhaus's perspective, it is the idea of the rule of law that explains the authority of the constitutional order, not constituent power. Constituent power does not belong with liberal theories: it can only arise from the perspective of a theory that denies that law possesses intrinsic normative qualities that make it authoritative. However, Dyzenhaus's perspective departs from the broad consensus on the normative import of constituent power. Although in approaches of liberal democracy there actually often is a tension embedded in the issue of the relationship of constituent power and the rule of law, very few of them solve it by denying so radically the significance of constituent power. This is because there generally is an assumption that democratic iteration and the rule of law also support each other, and that one must take into account norm-generation processes. Therefore, approaches such as Dyzenhaus's are not of much help when one tries to frame the claims to democratic authorization.

Conclusion

This chapter has discussed the normative significance of the concept of constituent power by focusing on three dimensions it embodies and that are key to Western political modernity: agency, foundation, and holism. These dimensions make constituent power a peculiar way of expressing and embodying public autonomy as the claim that authority must have a democratic pedigree. Although there are noticeable differences between scholars tackling the issue of constituent power in current debates about constitutionalism beyond the state, most of them acknowledge the normative resonance of the concept as it is related to these three dimensions. Such acknowledgement leads them either to try to rescue the concept or to lament the disruptions to the modern edifice of public law. Scholars that depart from this consensus can hardly tackle the issue of the tension between constituent power and the rule of law that is inherent to this edifice; or, as in the case of Teubner, they cannot account for the radical promise conveyed by the notion of constituent power.

This does not mean, of course, that the differences between scholars acknowledging the normative resonance of the concept are trivial. As I will explain in Chapters 2 and 3, there are, for example, significant divergences as to the status of constitutions (are they regulative or constitutive?) and to the exact nature of the relationship between rights and constituent power. But more important for my purpose is the recognition that these distinctions most often relate with specific conceptions of sovereign statehood, public law, and constitutionalism. The state actually is a major building block of this conceptual edifice; and the modern concept of constituent power depends upon the state as a sovereign entity embodying the autonomy of the political[25]. Any perceptive and lucid analysis of the challenges faced by democratic self-rule in the current context must acknowledge this nested relationship. Loughlin rightly stresses that it is the political existence of the state that makes possible the existence of "the people". The modern state is a particular way of knowing and being, "in the absence of which the very idea of a constitutional polity is simply unimaginable" (Walker 2010, 295; Loughlin 2003). It is because of this particular "mindset" that constituent power makes sense in constitutionalism as a theory of government. As Loughlin argues, "Once the exercise of imagining the formation of the political unity of a people is abandoned or transcended, then constitutional theory—and with it also the autonomy of the political—is at an end" (Loughlin 2005, 187). Tully has stressed that state sovereignty (as giving rise to "the relative autonomy of the state [...] both from the people and the constitution") is integral to modern constitutionalism, and "structures the constitutional form and the form that constituent powers take within it. That is, the field of 'constitutional form and constituent power' is really a game between the constitutive sovereign and the constituent people *within* and over the constitutional form [...]" (Tully 2007, 322). In other words, constituent power belongs with the conceptual apparatus of a theory of government peculiar to a statist way of knowing, and being into, the world. This is what I am going to turn to in the next chapter. As I hope to show, neither an ongoing reliance on the statist framework nor the relativization of its significance are helpful, when trying to tackle the issue of public autonomy in the context of new mappings of public authority.

Notes

1 The concept of *droit politique* refers to "precepts of political conduct which are needed to ensure the maintenance of the state" (Loughlin 2003, 66); it is required to grasp adequately "the juristic significance of the political concept of sovereignty" (Loughlin 2003, 66). According to Loughlin, the conception of law as *droit politique* has been eroded by the dominance of legal positivism, but its logic was readily understood in the early modern period, for example, in G. Lawson's distinction between real and personal sovereignty (Loughlin 2003, 66–7). In Lawson's distinction, "[t]he focus on real sovereignty, or on constituent power, helps us to understand how the institutionalized separation of powers is not a division but an explication of sovereignty. This helps us to understand how the institutional forms of constitutionalism bolster sovereignty" (Loughlin 2003, 67–8).

2 See Chapter 2.

3 See also Colón-Riós (2012, 102): constituent power "has an important connection with the democratic ideal. In its modern and contemporary formulations, constituent power is attributed to [...] all those who will become subject to the future constitutional regime. Constituent power points toward a democratic constitution-making power, and its popular and collective character makes it incompatible with given or imposed constitutions".

4 It is at once a fiction and a regulative ideal (Krisch 2016).

5 As Krisch explains, it is related to public authority as "the idea of institutions by which a public hopes to assert itself" (Krisch 2012, 985).

6 It hence refers to the virtues of self-rule and the standing of democracy as a meta-value of modern politics (Walker 2007, 256).

7 In the modern reception of the scholastic modelization of being, human power is conceptualized in terms of its ontological productivity, namely, its capacity to bring forth into being. Constituent power is the political manifestation of freedom as autonomy (Lindahl 2015, 165). It is always mediated by representation, though (Lindahl 2015, 165).

8 "Once the representative dimensions of the constituent power are taken seriously, we understand *droit politique* as a set of precepts and maxims enabling the state to maintain itself and to flourish" (Loughlin 2003, 69).

9 The autonomous structure of public power—political power harnessed through the institutionalization of authority and generated "as a product of the relationship between the people and the state" (Loughlin 2003, 70)—depends upon the state, and is the *sine qua non* condition of the existence of constituent power (and, therefore, of equal citizenship). Public law depends upon sovereignty as a representation of the autonomy of the political, which is ultimately an ontological claim. A constitution is valid because it derives from the unified will expressed in the state as the collective representation of the people (Loughlin 2014a, 224); this will is founded not in norms, but in the political existence of the state (Loughlin 2014a, 224). I will come back on this point in Chapter 2.

10 See also Preuss (2007): constituent power must assume the perspective of a hypothetical general will of the people; otherwise, it would lack any constituent character (Preuss 2007, 218). The idea of equality is core to this perspective, since the construction of the nation "presupposes a society of free and equal individuals who constitute themselves as a collective body in the sphere of politics" (Preuss 2007, 214). Individuals "are only free and equal when they rule themselves, i.e. when they are co-authors of the laws to which they are subjects" (Preuss 2007, 214).

11 On Loughlin's claim that the achievement of a system of public law means "that exploitation is eliminated *conceptually* from the world of public law" (Loughlin 2008, 58), see Chapter 2.

12 Constituent power relates to two facets of self-government: authority should possess a democratic pedigree (namely, "those who are 'constituted' as the subjects of constitutional authority should also be its 'constituent' authors") (Walker 2007, 247); and constitutional form should carry a resilient guarantee of democratic fidelity to the goods associated with the constitution (constituent power gives a sense of "democratic collective subjectivity") (Walker 2007, 258).

13 See also, e.g., Kumm, who stresses that for a cognitive frame to be constitutional in the modern sense, it must provide a structure allowing for a holistic construction of public authority and it has to be of foundational significance (Kumm 2009, 323).

14 In this chapter, I emphasize the elements that relate more specifically to constituent power. But in order to do so, I have to recall some claims that are key to Teubner's conception of constitutions and constitutionalization. In Chapter 2, the discussion of Teubner will rather focus on the more general issue of the political.

15 The foundational paradox of law is founded on the binary code legal/illegal, and hence, "gets into a tangle with paradoxes of self-reference when the code is inevitably applied to itself" (Teubner 2016, 31).

16 There is, then, a secret affinity between the communication of power and the normativity of the law, since by transforming themselves into acts of law, acts of power strengthen their efficacy. However,

> politics' bond with the law only become bearable when the law-making machinery in turn guarantees politics a decisive influence on law-making. Only then can the state constitution drive the intricate relation between law and politics so far that a legal secondary codification of politics emerges. The rule of law is extended to cover all political events and thus treat every act of power as an act of law. State constitutions get their unique lustre from this externalization of paradoxes executed in complete symmetry—from politics towards the law and from the law towards politics.
>
> (Teubner 2016, 37)

17 The medial reflexivity of a social system must be supported by law, if we are to speak of constitutions in the strict sense.

18 One must distinguish the operational closure of a social system from its constitutionalization (for which a self-description is enough), because the power processes specific to a system are to be distinguished from other power processes.

19 On anti-juridical conceptions of destituent power, see also Chapter 5.

20 This implies that neither can they propose a sound conception of trust as a condition and correlate of democratic politics.

21 According to him, "[i]f we did not have this concept of a constituent power that exists prior to its actual forms in conjunction with the concept of a disembedded constitutional form, then we would not have the paradoxical relationship between them [...] which is constitutive of the contingent historical ensemble of nomos and demos we call constitutional democracy" (Tully 2007, 320).

22 Following M. Foucault, he argues that there is a juridical ensemble of discursive and non-discursive elements that began to be pieced together in 12th-century Europe and that came to define a major form of the subject, the juridical one. In this system, there is a problematization of the mode of subjection in which two conditions are required if the laws are to be legitimate: they must be universal and impartial, and they must be based on the agreement of the people. Such agreement came to be conceived as a form of procedure, "when the locus of sovereignty shifted from the monarch to the people and confessional pluralism was resolved by granting the right priority over the good [...]" (Tully 2008a, 115).
23 The modern conception of popular sovereignty is dependent upon the modern concept of unformed constituent power (Tully 2007, 320).
24 The two types often occur in the same nexus of dispersed practices of government, and they cannot be understood "without taking into account the agonism between the attempts to govern the participants in a specific way and the responses to that mode of governance" (Tully 2008b, 52).
25 See also Patberg (2016, 37).

References

Christodoulidis, Emilios. 2013. "On the Politics of Societal Constitutionalism." *Indiana Journal of Legal Studies* 20, no. 2: 629–663.

Colón-Riós, Joel I. 2012. *Weak Constitutionalism. Democratic Legitimacy and the Question of Constituent Power*. London and New York: Routledge.

Colón-Riós, Joel I. 2014. "Five Conceptions of Constituent Power." *Law Quarterly Review* 130: 306–336.

Dyzenhaus, David. 2007. "The Politics of the Question of Constituent Power." In *The Paradox of Constitutionalism. Constituent Power and Constitutional Form*, edited by Martin Loughlin and Neil Walker, 129–145. Oxford: Oxford University Press.

Dyzenhaus, David. 2012. "Constitutionalism in an Old Key: Legality and Constituent Power." *Global Constitutionalism* 1, no. 2: 229–260.

Føllesdal, Andreas. 2001. "Union Citizenship: Unpacking the Beast of Burden." *Law and Philosophy* 20, no. 3: 313–343.

Krisch, Nico. 2010. "Global Administrative Law and the Constitutional Ambition." In *The Twilight of Constitutionalism?* edited by Petra Dobner and Martin Loughlin, 245–266. Oxford: Oxford University Press.

Krisch, Nico. 2011. *Beyond Constitutionalism. The Pluralist Structure of Postnational Law*. Oxford: Oxford University Press.

Krisch, Nico. 2012. "Global Governance as Public Authority: An Introduction." *International Journal of Constitutional Law* 10, no. 4: 976–987.

Krisch, Nico. 2016. "*Pouvoir Constituant* and *Pouvoir Irritant* in the Postnational Order." *International Journal of Constitutional Law* 14, no. 3: 657–679.

Kumm, Mattias. 2009. "The Cosmopolitan Turn in Constitutionalism: On the Relationship between Constitutionalism in and beyond the State." In *Ruling the World? Constitutionalism, International Law, and Global Governance*, edited by Jeffrey L. Dunoff and Joel P. Trachtman, 258–324. New York: Cambridge University Press.

Kumm, Mattias. 2016. "Constituent Power, Cosmopolitan Constitutionalism, and Post-Positivist Law." *International Journal of Constitutional Law* 14, no. 3: 697–711.

Lindahl, Hans. 2015. "Possibility, Actuality, Rupture: Constituent Power and the Ontology of Change." *Constellations* 20, no. 2: 163–174.

Lorey, Isabell. 2019. "Constituent Power of the Multitude." *Journal of International Political Theory* 15, no. 1: 119–133.

Loughlin, Martin. 2003. *The Idea of Public Law*. Oxford: Oxford University Press.

Loughlin, Martin. 2005. "Constitutional Theory: A 25th Anniversary Essay." *Oxford Journal of Legal Studies* 25, no. 2: 183–202.

Loughlin, Martin. 2008. "Reflections on *The Idea of Public Law*." In *Public Law and Politics. The Scope and Limits of Constitutionalism*, edited by Emilios Christodoulidis and Stephen Tierney, 47–65. Aldershot: Ashgate.

Loughlin, Martin. 2010. "What Is Constitutionalization?" In *The Twilight of Constitutionalism?* edited by Petra Dobner and Martin Loughlin, 47–69. Oxford: Oxford University Press.

Loughlin, Martin. 2014. "The Concept of Constituent Power." *European Journal of Political Theory* 13, no. 2: 218–237.

Möller, Kolja. 2018. "From Constituent to Destituent Power beyond the State." *Transnational Legal Theory* 9, no. 1: 32–55.

Niesen, Peter. 2019b. "Introduction: Resistance, Disobedience or Constituent Power? Emerging Narratives of Transnational Protest." *Journal of International Political Theory* 15, no. 1: 2–10.

Nootens, Geneviève. Forthcoming. "Popular Sovereignty, Political Contention, and the Boundaries of Democracy." In *Civic Freedom in an Age of Diversity. James Tully's Public Philosophy*, edited by Dimitrios Karmis and Jocelyn Maclure. Montreal: McGill-Queen's University Press.

Oklopcic, Zoran. 2014. "Three Arenas of Struggle: A Contextual Approach to the Constituent Power of 'The People'." *Global Constitutionalism* 3, no. 2: 200–235.

Patberg, Markus. 2013. "Constituent Power beyond the State: An Emerging Debate in International Political Theory." *Millenium: Journal of International Studies* 42, no. 1: 224–238.

Patberg, Markus. 2016. "Against Democratic Intergovernmentalism: The Case for a Theory of Constituent Power in the Global Realm." *International Journal of Constitutional Law* 14, no. 3: 622–638.

Preuss, Ulrich K. 2007. "The Exercise of Constituent Power in Central and Eastern Europe." In *The Paradox of Constitutionalism. Constituent Power and Constitutional Form*, edited by Martin Loughlin and Neil Walker, 211–228. Oxford: Oxford University Press.

Tarrow, Sidney. 2012. *Strangers at the Gates. Movements and States in Contentious Politics*. Cambridge: Cambridge University Press.

Teubner, Gunther. 2011. "Constitutionalizing Polycontexturality." *Social and Legal Studies* 22, no. 2: 210–229.

Teubner, Gunther. 2012. *Constitutional Fragments: Societal Constitutionalism and Globalization*. Oxford: Oxford University Press.

Teubner, Gunther. 2016. "Exogenous Self-Binding. How Social Subsystems Externalise Their Foundational Paradoxes in the Process of Constitutionalisation." In *Sociology of Constitutions. A Paradoxical Perspective*, edited by Alberto Febbrajo and Giancarlo Corsi, 30–48. London and New York: Routledge.

Tierney, Stephen. 2008. "Sovereignty and the *Idea of Public Law*." In *Public Law and Politics. The Scope and Limits of Constitutionalism*, edited by Emilios Christodoulidis and Stephen Tierney, 15–25. Aldershot: Ashgate.

Tully, James. 1995. *Strange Multiplicity: Constitutionalism in an Age of Diversity*. Cambridge: Cambridge University Press.

Tully, James. 2007. "The Imperialism of Modern Constitutional Democracy." In *The Paradox of Constitutionalism. Constituent Power and Constitutional Form*, edited by Martin Loughlin and Neil Walker, 315–338. Oxford: Oxford University Press.

Tully, James. 2008a. "On Law, Democracy and Imperialism." In *Public Law and Politics. The Scope and Limits of Constitutionalism*, edited by Emilios Christodoulidis and Stephen Tierney, 69–101. Aldershot: Ashgate.

Tully, James. 2008b. *Public Philosophy in a New Key, Vol. II: Imperialism and Civic Freedom*. Cambridge: Cambridge University Press.

Volk, Christian. 2019. "Enacting a Parallel World: Political Protest against the Transnational Constellation." *Journal of International Political Theory* 15, no. 1: 100–118.

Walker, Neil. 2007. "Post-Constituent Constitutionalism? The Case of the European Union." In *The Paradox of Constitutionalism. Constituent Power and Constitutional Form*, edited by Martin Loughlin and Neil Walker, 247–267. Oxford: Oxford University Press.

Walker, Neil. 2010. "Beyond the Holistic Constitution?" In *The Twilight of Constitutionalism?* edited by Petra Dobner and Martin Loughlin, 291–308. Oxford: Oxford University Press.

Walker, Neil. 2016. "Constitutional Pluralism Revisited." *European Law Journal* 22, no. 3: 333–355.

2

CONSTITUENT POWER AND THE MODERN STATE

Constituent power is closely related to democratic authorization and the expression of public autonomy. Yet, in the current context, it is significantly challenged because of a shift in regulatory activity (generally acknowledged by the approaches discussed in this book) that raises issues both as to state sovereignty and as to the possibility or desirability of translating the basic notion of constituent power so as to express public autonomy in regimes that combine features of state and non-state polities[1]. This shift in regulatory activity has a significant impact on the dimensions that account for the normative resonance of constituent power because these dimensions depend upon the state as a sovereign entity embodying the autonomy of the political.

As it is the sovereign state that had allowed to presume of (and had shaped) the political unity of the people (and hence, of constituent power), this chapter focuses on state sovereignty as "integral to modern constitutionalism" (Tully 2007, 322). Emphasizing this point allows to acknowledge the relationship of the three dimensions tackled in Chapter 1 (agency, foundation, and holism) with statehood; it also helps in explaining why the perspectives for translating constituent power in different types of polities seem quite limited. If the constitutional "mindset" (including the modern notion of constituent power) depends upon state sovereignty, and if state sovereignty is challenged by the current shift in regulatory activity, then the latter cannot but impact upon the idea and practice of democratic authorization expressed by the concept of constituent power.

In debates about constitutionalism beyond the state, several scholars have actually argued that constitutionalism can be translated to non-state polities. Yet, I hope to show that the framework on which their arguments build is still very much informed by the statist paradigm. The influence of the latter

DOI: 10.4324/9781003221722-3

pervades approaches of post-state constitutionalism. What accounts for the nested relationship between the state and constitutionalism seems to be far more fundamental than a mere historical affinity or analytical connection; therefore, it has a deep impact on attempts to translate or rescue constituent power in mixed polities. We should be particularly concerned with the possibility that the pervasive influence of the statist paradigm leads us to neglect forms of authority and democratic agency that are not easily captured by such a paradigm. The effort in translation may also, then, impair on our ability to develop a new conceptual apparatus that would capture more appropriately challenges to democratic authorization and put forward different ways of embodying the latter. I do not want to deny that there may be specific cases in which the effort in translation may be appropriate and worth it; the EU, for example, may be such a case. But it would be unsound to assume that it can apply to any non-state or mixed polity. Let me stress that this is not to say that democratic authorization makes no sense outside the statist framework; it rather is to say that it would, then, rest on different ways of conceptualizing and institutionalizing self-rule (as well as public power).

At this point, a clarification is needed. I have already stressed that this book is not a book about constitutionalism *per se*. It does not claim to lay out a complete and general conception of constitutionalism, nor to settle the debates about constitutionalism beyond the state. However, constituent power belongs with a specific conceptual world, and is a building block of constitutionalism as a theory of government. Hence, one can hardly tackle the issue of constituent power without also having a closer look at constitutionalism and—especially when analyzing the possibilities for a post-state constituent power—without analyzing debates about constitutionalism beyond the state. However, I am going to focus on aspects related to the pervasiveness of the statist framework and its importance in the work of scholars arguing (or implying) that there is a mere historical affinity or analytical connection between the state and constitutionalism. Whether or not constitutionalism can be considered a pliant resource impacts upon how we can and should conceive of democratic authorization and agency in mixed polities.

More precisely, this chapter discusses three approaches that show that the relationship between statehood and constitutionalism builds on close, intricate, and enduring connections. These approaches exemplify the challenges faced by attempts to translate constituent power in non-state or mixed polities. I will then turn to two scholars (namely, M. Loughlin and J. Tully) acknowledging that state sovereignty is integral to modern constitutionalism. This step is important in my argument: from my point of view, the failure to make explicit the pervasiveness of the statist framework may impair on our ability to propose a fruitful reflection on the issue of democratic authorization beyond the state. This concern is at once practical and normative. It is normative because, as I have explained in the introduction, the current context also is an opportunity to reconsider how struggles for civic freedom have been subordinated to state sovereignty in the political framework of Western modernity[2]. It is practical because there is an urgent need to rethink public autonomy and public authority so as to expand civic freedom. Hence, the reason why Loughlin is right to point to this intrinsic relationship also is the one why we should challenge it (something he does not do[3]). But let us first turn to approaches arguing that states are but one institutional context for constitutionalism.

Non-State Polities and the Constitutional "Mindset"

The argument that states are but one institutional context for constitutionalism generally takes one of two main forms, in debates about constitutionalism beyond the state. Some argue that there is either a mere historical affinity or analytical connection between the state and constitutionalism, and therefore, that it still makes sense to frame public power using constitutionalism, in post-state contexts. Others argue that the statist conception of constitutionalism is misguided. In both cases, though, the statist framework has a pervasive influence, and actually frames the very way the issue of constituent power is tackled. A brief discussion of three different approaches shows that such pervasiveness infuses approaches from different theoretical backgrounds and that it raises specific issues as to democratic authorization in post-state contexts. I am going to discuss Walker's attempt in translating the constitutional mindset, Kumm's argument that the meaningfulness of constitutionalism does not depend upon the state, and Teubner's assumption of societal constitutionalism as a third way (a hybrid constitutionalization that combines state power and external social forces). These arguments have in common a replication of some basic features of statehood, even if they are driven by the claim that the state is but one institutional context for constitutionalism (and hence, that constitutionalism's possibilities are not constrained by the statist framework).

N. Walker and the Meta-political Function of Constitutionalism

Walker argues that constitutionalism has the meta-political function of "shaping the domain of politics broadly conceived" (Walker 2010, 296). This meta-political function is corroborated "both by the etymology of the constitutional idea and by its range of applications prior to the age of the modern state" (Walker 2010, 296). Walker defines constitutionalism as "referring to that species of practical reasoning which, in the name of some defensible locus of common interest, concerns itself with the organization and regulation of those spheres of collective decision-making deemed relevant to the common interest in a manner that is adequately informed by the common interest" (Walker 2010, 296). This sense of common interest possesses an open and reflexive quality; it cannot be equated *a priori* with national/state interest (Walker 2010, 297)[4]. Constitutionalism enables "individuals and groups within a political community to make sense of and to articulate a notion of their common past, to form and pronounce judgments about their common present, and to plan and project various imagined futures" (Walker 2005, 223). The basic structure of the constitutional idea is provided by two key features: the key idea of a constitution as a multifaceted framing mechanism (a cognitive dimension), and the notion that "what it frames is in some sense both already constituted and always under construction" (a motivational dimension) (Walker 2009, 151)[5].

Constitutionalism, then, has its own symbolic power, and "must have some value as a form of knowledge production at the postnational level just as it must have some value as a form of knowledge production at the national level [...]" (Walker 2003b, 35)[6]. In non-state contexts, the constitutional frame of reference may be worth retaining because it is "linked in a powerful and resilient chain of signification to a whole series of *substantive* institutional values" (democracy, accountability, the rule of law, etc.) (Walker 2003b, 33). These institutional values are not held to be dependent on a specific institutional form. Hence, democracy as a principle "cannot be exhausted and limited to its present and typically presupposed institutional representations" (Walker 2009, 170); the idea of democratic authorization does not become redundant if these presupposed representations are not available or adequate anymore.

Constituent power is key to a deeper justification of a constitutional solution: the latter is possible only by focusing on the idea of constituent power as it is connected to self-authorization and democratic iteration (Walker 2009, 170). In post-state entities such as the EU, it is possible to homologue and nurture a sense of a meta-democratically validated transnational political community with a wide-ranging political agenda and a distinct sense of the public good "through a documentary constitutional settlement presented as a self-standing political pact" (Walker 2013, 258). I will come back on this specific issue in Chapter 4. Let me only mention for now that Walker stresses that we don't have an ideal understanding of the supranational conception of constituent power within a postnational configuration characterized by a nonexclusive legal order and a mixed (non-unitary) polity (Walker 2009, 173 and 164–5). In a postnational configuration, states exist alongside a range of emergent post-state sites, so that "the relevant units are no longer exclusive territories with mutually exclusive jurisdictions and citizenries" (Walker 2009, 164)[7]. This implies two particularly relevant points for the purpose of my discussion. First, at least in entities such as the EU, "states authority sources are not sufficient to ground the various forms of postnational regulation" (Walker 2003a, 33). In a postnational context, constitutionalism must address in a different way the problem of the authoritative source and extent of the constitution (Walker 2016, 351); in particular, it cannot feed into a single constituent power[8]. Second, Walker argues for constitutional pluralism as an alternative to a statist approach. The idea of constitutional pluralism allows to capture the sense of indispensability of the structures and values of constitutionalism in the context of the EU, as well as the overlap-in-practice of the jurisdictions of the EU and its member states[9]. The constitution of the EU "is only concerned with transnational institutions and competences" (Walker 2016, 352), and "national jurisdiction over unpooled capacity remains rooted in national acts and systems of constitutional authority" (Walker 2016, 352).

Finally, Walker argues that constitutionalism does not have to be holistic. The constitutional method distinctive to the modern state is holistic: the authority and meaning of the various parts are understood and treated as dependent on the integrity of the whole (Walker 2010, 297–8). Let me recall that Walker distinguishes constitutionalism in the abstract (as a theoretical concept for making sense of and evaluating the social world) and constitutionalism in the concrete (as an object already at use in the social world). Considered as an object concept, state constitutionalism both describes a particular high point of accumulation of various distinct layers of situated constitutional practices (juridical, politico-institutional, popular, and societal) and operates in terms of its own particular formulation of these layers and their relationship with one another (Walker 2010, 298). In the state context, each of the four layers operates holistically: the juridical frame refers to the idea of a self-contained legal order; the politico-institutional frame (the key emerging feature of modernity) refers to a system of institutional specification and differentiation of the sphere of the public and the political; the popular frame refers to the idea of "We, the People" (hence, of democratic self-constitution and authorship); and the societal frame refers to the idea that the constitution "pertains to a particular 'society' self-understood and self-identified as such" (Walker 2010, 299)[10].

However, this holistic framework is not necessarily desirable nor appropriate; it actually tends to be instable; and there are fields in which holism is simply not available[11] (Walker 2010, 303, 305). More precisely, Walker argues that the possibility of a non-holistic constitutionalism should not be dismissed too rapidly, for three reasons. First, the model of holistic state constitutionalism may not be adequate in the face of "the emergence of collective action and coordination problems that simply do not coincide with the political boundaries of the state" (Walker 2010, 304). Second, the more holistic solution is not necessarily the more constitutionally appropriate. Third, there may be value in retaining the language of constitutionalism even when the four frames (juridical, politico-institutional, popular, and societal) do not coincide, because "constitutional language retains a crucial longstop function as a kind of 'place holder' for certain abiding concerns we have. These concerns are, quite simply, that unless we can address the meta-political framing of politics in a manner that remains wedded to ideas of the common interest [...] something of great and irreplaceable value will have been lost from our resources of common living" (Walker 2010, 307). The important thing is that non-holistic constitutionalism can engage in the same meta-political function as state holistic constitutionalism—namely, shaping the domain of politics broadly conceived, "literally 'constituting' the body politics" (Walker 2010, 296).

From Walker's perspective, then, constitutionalism belongs with the deeper legal and political imaginary of the modern age, but this imaginary must be kept distinct from the architecture specific to a state-centred order (Walker 2012, 83; Walker 2013, 262). The issue, as to this chapter, is whether Walker actually succeeds in detaching constitutionalism from statehood. His translation of the constitutional "mindset" builds upon three conditions: that we look at the deeper context in which the constitutional scheme is embedded; that we have "a conception of the constitutionally signifier which is independent but commonly referred to or implied by our familiar constitutional signifiers" (Walker 2003b, 38); and that the common set of references is capable of commanding broad agreement "on a basis of which we may ask pertinent questions as to the appropriate deployment of constitutional reasoning and the appropriate articulation of constitutional design across sites" (Walker 2003b, 38).

His attempt to translate the constitutional idea (and ideal) to mixed polities certainly pays tribute to the normative and symbolic value of constitutionalism. But I am not certain he succeeds in proposing a kind of middle stance between those for whom translation is not an option because constitutionalism is a state-centred idea, on the one hand, and those who understand constitutionalism as a completely mobile set of ideas, on the other. Or rather, and more precisely, he argues for a middle stance—but one that, at the end of the day, remains so close to state constitutionalism that one can doubt it is useful when tackling the issue of democratic self-rule in the transnational domain. Let me explain why this is so.

Walker explicitly acknowledges the dependency of the "familiar constitutional signifiers" (Walker 2003b, 38) on statehood. For example, he stresses that

> [b]oth our diagnosis of the appropriateness of contexts to treatment in constitutional or public law terms and our sense of the relevant standards and values of treatment are heavily influenced by the vast, cumulative datum of established state institutions and practices. Reciprocally, the standing—and our understanding—of existing state institutions and practices as paradigmatically 'constitutional' or 'public' is corroborated by our continuously reinforced sense of what counts as appropriate 'constitutional' or 'public' contexts, values, and standards. What remains to be seen is what, if any, scope there is for either constitutionalism or public law to break out of this confirmatory circle of state-centredness.
>
> (Walker 2013, 244)

It is the meta-political function of constitutionalism that is key to the capacity to break out this circle[12]. Yet, Walker makes sovereignty (which certainly is the most vivid and significant mark of statehood) the basic condition of constitutional polity formation. Sovereignty is the claim to ultimate authority that expresses the mutually constitutive relations between law and politics. It is "the discursive form in which a claim concerning the existence and character of a supreme ordering power for a particular polity is expressed, which supreme ordering power purports to establish and sustain the identity and status of the particular polity *qua* polity and to provide a continuing source and vehicle of ultimate authority for the juridical order of that polity" (Walker 2003a, 6)[13]. Some of his comments on the implications of the "constitutional way of conceptualizing the world" are telling in this respect. Let me stress three of these. First, he argues that "the term *constitution* necessarily implied, and implies, the existence of a discrete and self-contained entity [...] as the object of constitutional reference" (Walker 2009, 150). The idea of the constitution assumes that politics can be located "within certain clearly differentiated containers of social space" (Walker 2009, 151–2); it "sets out [...] to engage in the practices necessary to recognize and shape just such a demarcation and organization of social space" (Walker 2009, 152)—in other words, it provides "a presumptive answer to the question: How to decide how to decide?" (Walker 2009, 152). Second, the requirements for such an object of constitutional reference actually are quite stringent: it requires a degree of societal integration, some "prior propensity to put things in common or basic sense of political community" (Walker 2009, 159). This minimally refers "to a sense of common attachment or common predicament within the putative demos sufficient to manifest itself in three interrelated forms" (Walker 2009, 159): a minimum level of sustained mutual respect and concern ensuring that collective outcomes may be reached and adhered to; trust in participating in dispute resolution, decision-making, and rule following; and a political culture that "can acknowledge and accept difference beyond this core commitment" (Walker 2009, 159). Third, Walker proposes an index of constitutionalization with respect to non-state polities which includes the assertion of sovereignty[14].

But if sovereignty is the basic condition of constitutional polity formation, and if a consistent degree of societal integration is required for an entity to be an object of constitutional reference, then constitutionalism makes sense only for state and state-like entities[15]. Walker could still argue that he has put forward the notion of "late" sovereignty precisely to make sense of a new multi-dimensional order, and that it is possible to imagine ultimate authority (sovereignty) in non-exclusive terms (because of a shift to functionally defined and limited polities) (Walker 2003a). But his definition of sovereignty as well as the way he describes the constitutional way of conceptualizing the world cast doubt on the possibility of translating the constitutional mindset—except maybe for the very specific, and actually *sui generis*, case of the EU. This doubt is reinforced by his claim that a broadly endorsed collective identity (a constitutive unity) is necessary for constituent power. Politics is implicitly framed by the prior resolution of the "who decides who decides" question (Walker 2005, 216). A conception of constituent power cannot float free of actual formative grounds and conditions. Paying attention to the foundations "provides a way of identifying the self-imagined extent and boundaries of the community invoked in the process of ongoing justification" (Walker 2017, 909). The orienting function of emergent collective self-identity can operate only if there is a broadly endorsed collective identity (Walker 2017, 910)[16].

But maybe one should rather turn to approaches that explicitly criticize the statist framework when (re)thinking constitutionalism? As I hope to show next in discussing Kumm's and then Teubner's approaches, it is far from clear they can help to appropriately address the issue either.

M. Kumm and the Cosmopolitan Paradigm

Kumm argues that "[c]onstitutionalism does not require the framework of a state to be meaningful" (Kumm 2009, 263). Constitutionalism is a particular cognitive frame for the construction of legitimate authority (Kumm 2009, 321). It embodies the idea that the exercise of legitimate authority is not unlimited and requires a justification before a higher law "that insists that all posited law must be conceivable by those whom it addresses as the result of a deliberative collective choice of free and equal individuals" (Kumm 2010, 231; see also Kumm 2011, 125). Constitutionalism implies that law must be "reasonably attributed to those whom it addresses", that law is a human artefact (the result of a deliberate choice), and that "the subject matter of that choice concerns the legal and political relationships between persons conceived as free and equal" (Kumm 2010, 213)[17]. For a cognitive frame to be constitutional in the modern sense, it has to fulfill four requirements: it must provide a conceptual structure allowing for a holistic construction of public authority; it must be of foundational significance; its normative point must be the reference to the idea of free and equal persons; and it must be able to integrate debates about how to account for legality, for legitimate procedures, and for substantive constraints and guiding norms for the exercise of public authority (Kumm 2009, 323).

Kumm's critique of the statist paradigm of constitutionalism mainly builds on two main, related claims: the claim that constitutional and public law are underlied by principles that can be translated because they embody universal commitments; and the claim that by giving primacy to "We, the people", democratic statism[18] assigns a contingent role to the content of constitutional norms. The former claim strongly relates claims to constitutional authority to the principles that underlie constitutional and public law. These common principles allow for "a mutually deferential and engaging constitutional practice" that guarantees the "coherence and unity of constitutional practice", even if constitutionalism has a pluralist structure both as to its actors and sources (Kumm 2010, 204). The latter claim serves to establish the contradistinction between the statist and the cosmopolitan paradigms of constitutionalism. In the former paradigm, the authority of the constitution rests on its authorization by the people. Primacy is given "to the idea that We the People as the constituent power can establish just as anything as the supreme law of the land" (Kumm 2010, 210). Hence, in the statist paradigm, the ideas of democracy and human rights, as well as the content of constitutional norms generally speaking, are assigned only a contingent role. The deep structural commitment of democratic statism is not to democracy, but to the political community; it "does not insist on a strong and unqualified connection between genuine democracy and constitutional authority" (Kumm 2010, 211). In other words, Kumm criticizes the idea of "We the People" as a validating source for the constitution as positive law. According to him, the idea of an ultimate constitutional authority linked to one constituent power is misguided (Kumm 2010, 205). This idea is obscure and implausible, because either at the time the constitution entered into force there was no procedure underlying its coming into force that could plausibly be interpreted as the will of the people, or it is not clear why that procedure should have any legitimating force for establishing authority over those it seeks to bind today (Kumm 2010, 208). What makes constitutions rightly regarded as legitimately establishing the supreme law of the land are features "that are largely disconnected from the original circumstances of their ratification" (Kumm 2016, 700)[19].

Therefore, the statist paradigm needs to be replaced by the cosmopolitan one. In the latter paradigm, "The normative presuppositions of constitutionalism are translated directly into a set of basic formal, jurisdictional, procedural, and substantive legal principles that are conceived as underlying existing legal and political practices and in light of which that practice can be reconstructed and assessed" (Kumm 2010, 214). The cosmopolitan paradigm allows for an analysis in which "both national constitutional practice and international law can be meaningfully [...] assessed within the same conceptual framework" (Kumm 2009, 263)[20]. It "repositions national constitutional practice as an integral part of a global practice of law and reconceives public international law in light of constitutional principles. National constitutional law and public international law are conceived as reflecting a common commitment to basic constitutional principles" (Kumm 2009, 271). In other words, they are not separate legal systems: common principles underlie both of them, providing "a coherent framework for addressing conflicting claims of authority in specific contexts" (Kumm 2009, 274). The cosmopolitan paradigm provides a unifying framework for the analysis of the complex structure of doctrines regarding the management of the interface between national and international law. It provides conceptual tools for describing and analyzing the basic structure of the legal world as a whole, "connected to the basic structure of an account of legal and political authority" (Kumm 2009, 266). Within such a framework, a state can plausibly claim legitimate authority only on issues that do not raise questions of justice-sensitive externalities (Kumm 2016, 705)[21]. Constituent power, then, is guided by the idea of a community of free and equal persons governing itself through the medium of law, and as part of an international community[22]. The people associated with statehood and sovereignty, on the one hand, and the international community, on the other one, are mutually complementary constitutive power (Kumm 2016, 704). Hence, states are but one institutional context for constitutionalism—namely, for giving effect to the normative principles underlying constitutional and public law (Kumm 2010, 203). Constitutionalism has to concern itself "with the global legitimacy conditions for the exercise of state sovereignty" (Kumm 2016, 703)[23].

Kumm's approach raises several issues. Once again, I focus here on claims related to the issue of the replication of the statist framework and its consequences upon attempts to rethink public autonomy. From this point of view, significant aspects of Kumm's work seem to actually amount to the translation at the global level of a unifying framework that is indeed quite typical of statehood. One may have already noticed that Kumm explicitly acknowledges that cosmopolitan constitutionalism is a holistic frame (Kumm 2009, 310). This may make it more difficult to tackle specific issues related to a complex scheme of authority such as the one characteristic of the current era. As Walker has argued, Kumm's approach is vulnerable to a charge of utopianism or complacency, because of "the chasm between the cosmopolitan's principles and the actual state of global politics and economics" (Walker 2012, 82). Kumm argues that cosmopolitanism "is actually the best interpretation of much historical and constitutional practice both in and beyond the state" (Walker 2012, 82). However,

> [w]hile he is adept at showing how certain legal sites do demonstrate a sophisticated appreciation of the demands of cosmopolitan public reason, it is notable that these tend to be judicial sites, and tend to be situated in the European stronghold of mature postnational governance. There remains a danger of complacency in this assessment, a failure to explain how public reason can systematically prevail over private interest in contexts where the conditions of public will formation, and the epistemic and authoritative weight associated with such will formation, are often conspicuous by their remoteness or absence.
>
> (Walker 2012, 82)

One may also doubt whether replicating the ambition of rights-constitutionalism to check political power at a larger level (an ambition characteristic of a state-centred perspective and that grounds the normative structure characteristic of constitutionalism) is appropriate to tackle issues of public authority and autonomy in mixed polities. This is precisely why, for example, Walker argues that the possibility of a non-holistic constitutionalism should not be dismissed too rapidly (see above).

Let me also stress that Kumm's discussion of monism and pluralism is somehow paradoxical. As I have explained, he argues that national and international law are underlied by common principles that provide "a coherent framework for addressing conflicting claims of authority in specific contexts" (Kumm 2009, 274). According to him, this does not amount to monism, because monism would imply the primacy of international law, whereas in cosmopolitan constitutionalism, national and international law cannot be conflicting (since they are underlied by common principles)[24]. From his point of view, any conflict between the requirements of the cosmopolitan paradigm and national constitutional rules relating to international law is a mere theoretical possibility, for four reasons: first, the cosmopolitan paradigm provides only background principles; second, "[o]ften enough, national constitutional rules can be reconstructed as plausible interpretations of the requirements of the cosmopolitan paradigm" (Kumm 2009, 278); third, "national constitutional rules relating to international law are often highly indeterminate and incomplete" (Kumm 2009, 278); and fourth, the scope of application of restrictive constitutional rules can be reduced by not applying them in certain types of cases (Kumm 2009, 278). This results in a conception of legality that is not monist because it allows "for legally irresolvable conflict between national and international law" (i.e., it allows for legal pluralism); but is not dualistic either "since the relationship between national and international law is reconceived in light of a common set of principles that play a central role in determining the relative authority of each in case of conflict, ensuring legal coherence" (Kumm 2009, 279). Yet, Kumm also stresses that "[t]he existence of a common unifying conceptual framework of norms makes it possible to describe cosmopolitan constitutionalism as monist, even if the institutional practices it justifies might have a pluralist structure" (Kumm 2009, 279, footnote 34).

According to Kumm, the commitment to a constitutional order depends on whether this order meets some universal criteria of political morality (Walker 2017, 909), rather than on its authorization by a people. Walker has wondered whether from this perspective, constituent power can be retained "in a sufficiently robust sense at the postnational level for it to perform the kind of orienting and legitimating function [Kumm] ascribes to it" (Walker 2017, 908)[25]. He also wonders whether Kumm's particular conception of postnational constituent power "leaves him equipped to identify the right mix to feed into the overall global pool of constitutional authority from such a multi-streamed and multi-level range of constitutional influences" (Walker 2017, 908). This points to a more fundamental problem as to the purposes of this book: Kumm misinterprets the meaning of constituent power as a symbolic pole, and his critique misses the mark both at a conceptual and a sociological level. Hence, when it comes to the issue of the claim to authority relating rulers and ruled in the transnational society, Kumm's focus on the normative significance of the principles underlying constitutionalism and public law ignores the paradoxical but meaningful tension between these principles and democratic authorization. Hence, I hardly see how he can contribute to a thorough reconceptualization of democratic agency. A focus on democratic authorization certainly should not downplay the normative significance of the principles underlying constitutionalism and public law. Still, democracy is about things we want to achieve together as a body politics of some kind[26]. We need to understand how citizens frame their claims as to actual practices of governance, and how, in their interactions with rulers, they contribute to democratize public politics.

G. Teubner's Societal Constitutionalism and the Problematic of Civil Society Institutions

Discussing Teubner's societal constitutionalism is important for the purposes of this book, since it is to be distinguished both from a narrative on the decline of constitutionalism (whose foundations are eroded by processes such as European integration, the emergence of transnational regimes, and the transfer of political power to private actors), on the one hand, and from a "new democratic constitutionalism" juxtaposing a similar story of decline with the demand for a compensatory constitutionalization of world society, on the other. It puts forwards a hybrid constitutionalization that combines state power and external social forces (formal legal norms and civil society's counter power from other contexts), as well as system-internal reflection (Teubner 2012, 84). As P. Dobner (2009) has stressed, Teubner's societal constitutionalism radically departs from the idea of the state as the centre of legal norms and the main container of political power[27]; it takes seriously the blurring of the private/public divide and of the division between domestic and international politics; and it asks how constitutionalism may address the problems of delegitimization, privatization, and globalization[28]. Indeed, as Teubner makes constitutions non-political objects (see Chapter 1) and criticizes both methodological nationalism and modern constitutionalism's neglect of the functional differentiation of society, one could expect a radical break with state constitutionalism. But from my point of view, such a break may be less radical and more problematic than it looks at first sight.

As I explained in Chapter 1, Teubner argues that the functions of a constitution (the foundation and self-limitation of an autonomous order) cannot be limited to politics[29]. Functional differentiation creates a demand for the independent constitutionalization of other social orders (Teubner 2012, 17–8)[30]; and other sectorial constitutions perform a constitutive function parallel to the one performed by the political constitution of the nation-state—namely, securing the autonomy of their specific medium—by making use of constitutive rules (Teubner 2012, 75–6). According to Teubner, modern constitutionalism is basically deficient because it has neglected the functional differentiation of society that is inherent to modernity. The problematic of societal constitutionalism—namely, "the source of the constitutional question in processes of societal differentiation" (Teubner 2011, 212)—"was not caused by globalization, but earlier by the fragmentation of the social whole and the autonomization of fragments during the heyday of the national state" (although globalization has aggravated it) (Teubner 2012, 5–6). Liberal constitutionalism is blind to the constitutionalization of social orders other than politics because of its exclusive orientation towards the individual: such an orientation either degraded social collectives to fictions of the state, or dissolved them into individual social relations (Teubner 2012, 19). Hence, liberal constitutionalism "ignored the problematic of civil society institutions; how is their autonomy to be guaranteed; how are their expansive tendencies to be limited; and how is social integration possible in the face of their centrifugal tendencies" (Teubner 2012, 20).

According to Teubner, in order to avoid the trap of methodological nationalism we need to identify the constitutional subjects that are to "replace nation states to advance the constitutionalization of the global sectors" (Teubner 2012, 60)[31]. We must also abandon the unitary bias of the term "constitution", a bias that "stems from an uncritical transfer of national constitutional concepts to world society" (Teubner 2011, 215)[32]. Actually, "[t]he social conditions which allowed the nation-state to establish a unitary constitution, in principle, do not obtain in the transnational sphere" (Teubner 2011, 216). Teubner's approach clearly opposes holism, and is to be distinguished from both Kumm's and Walker's. He claims that we rather should focus on the fundamental conflicts between the different autonomous fragments of the social whole[33], and try to generalize and respecify the concept of "constitutional subject" tailored to the nation-state "to both its transnational and its civil society equivalents" (Teubner 2012, 60)[34]. Fragmentation is not a shortcoming; it rather is "a factor necessitating the redefinition of the constitutional problems" (Teubner 2011, 216).

Teubner also stresses that we need to challenge the double standard applied to nation-state constitutions and transnational regime constitutions: public lawyers and political scientists tend "to compare an idealized form of the constitutional state with the messy reality of transnational regimes, rather than seeking to compare aspiration with aspiration, and reality with reality" (Teubner 2018, 8). Public lawyers and political scientists apply double standards by treating the problematic relation between the functional logic of social systems and democratic legitimacy "completely differently when it comes to the political system on the one side and to the economy (or other social systems) on the other" (Teubner 2018, 9). Moreover, the assumption of the identity of authors and affected people in nation-states cannot be maintained as to real decisions of real people, because decision-making actually is vested in governing elites that are in competition with each other.

Therefore, the "constitutionally relevant question" (namely, the question of the limits to the expansion of subsystems) is whether global networks, transnational regimes, and the like are capable of bearing constitutions[35]. The answer depends upon the possibility of analogies to the nation-state constituent power, to the self-constitution of a collective, to democratic decision-making, and to the organizational part of a political constitution. Teubner formulates three conditions as to this possibility: the regimes must form typical constitutional structures[36]; the norms of a transnational regime must perform more than merely regulatory of conflict-solving functions; and these norms must develop a sufficiently close connection to their social context. Constitutions outside the state, then, "need to satisfy the requirements of a 'material' concept of constitution, according to which a constitution establishes a distinct legal authority which for its part structures a *societal* process [...] and is legitimized by it" (Teubner 2012, 74)[37].

I will come back in Chapter 4 on how Teubner describes transnational regimes, and how he proposes to translate constituent power to these new settings that express the functional differentiation inherent to modernity. For now, since the purpose of this chapter is to focus on the fact that state sovereignty is integral to modern constitutionalism, let me emphasize Teubner's (non-)stance to statehood. As I have explained, Teubner criticizes methodological nationalism as well as the holism of state constitutions. From this point of view, he stands on solid grounds. Methodological nationalism conveys a deep and problematical bias when it comes to analyzing social issues, including democratic authorization and constituencies. And the holism of state constitutions is inimical to the diversity of constituencies. Yet, Teubner's stance to the legal and the political (and, actually, to statehood) is more paradoxical than it may seem at first sight; and his approach conveys serious shortcomings as to the management of political conflict.

As J. Přibáň has stressed, it seems paradoxical to criticize the political and legal form while using its concept to describe non-political processes (Přibáň 2012). This raises issues as to the meaning of constitutions and constitutionalism. There are threshold requirements for ascribing constitutional meaning (Christodoulidis 2013). These requirements are the following: a social dimension (the subject that the constitution names), a temporal one (the ability of the constitution "to recruit the past in its expectation-binding operation for the future") (Christodoulidis 2013, 645), and a material one ("the threshold of unity that would gather the legal system as a meaningful whole") (Christodoulidis 2013, 645–6). These "are the threshold requirements for ascribing constitutional meaning because we associate with the constitution the constitutive functions of providing unity for the legal system, normatively binding certain key expectations for the future, and naming the subject of popular sovereignty. In this sense, they underpin and subtend any form of constitutional reflexivity" (Christodoulidis 2013, 646). This raises two issues, as to Teubner's work: the one of where to look for the political register within constitutionalization, because the political is not given expression to, except *a posteriori* (which in turn raises the issue of the coupling between the legal and the political); and the question of what gives law its systemic nature (Christodoulidis 2013). Teubner's theory withdraws any primacy of the legal, but the meaning of "constitutional" still points to a function of containment alongside the threshold requirements (Christodoulidis 2013, 646). However, in the transnational sphere, these requirements are unsettled: no constitutional subject can be ascribed as the locus and agent of constituent power, since "the subject is fashioned out of the process itself" (Christodoulidis 2013, 646)[38]; there is no framing function ascribed; and the identity of the system is reconfigured by a slow incremental process as the system goes on (Christodoulidis 2013, 648)[39]. The concepts and rules that Teubner associates with constitutionalization (self-descriptions, generalizations, etc.) "are merely aggregation rules or simply aggregation of rules whose constitutional function comes too late. They are gathering rationalizations that lack the constitutional qualities of being able to perform a framing function or review function, all of which would have required them to *pre-exist* the instance of their application" (Christodoulidis 2013, 649). This makes success in keeping the process in check "a contingent result of the emerging framing rather than its condition" (Christodoulidis 2013, 650). Therefore, the capacity "to draw political distinctions and present political injonctions" is undercut (Christodoulidis 2013, 650). Another reading is possible, on which "the constitution imports a reflexivity that does not immediately yield to the functional imperatives of the economy, and the processes of learning remain fixed to a different normative register" (Christodoulidis 2013, 651). But such a reading requires a normative register. The reflexivity constitutive of societal constitutionalism hence is torn between a functional and a normative dimension, and the clash actually is alleviated via the subsumption of the latter to the former. In other words, what is function re-orients and over-determines what is normative (Christodoulidis 2011, 239; see also Přibáň 2012, 448 ff). At the end of the day, the legal semantics of constitutions merely is a metaphor, since the structural coupling of the legal and other social systems is not guaranteed, and societal constitutions "only provide for help in the systemic self-reference by heteronomous legal definition" (Přibáň 2012, 451).Therefore, "[t]he paradox of the political self-denial and external expansion of the concept of constitution is a hallmark of societal constitutionalism which both completely depoliticizes the concept of constitution and gives it the more prominent political role by relocating it to a higher level of theoretical abstraction and identifying it with both functional differentiation and societal alternatives to institutionalized politics" (Přibáň 2012, 457).

Actually, H. Lindahl raises the issue of whether we can actually "make sense of societal constitutionalism *as constitutionalism* unless it is a mode of *political constitutionalism*" (Lindahl 2011, 230). In other words, "might Teubner's suggestion that we need to move from political to societal constitutionalism be self-defeating because the notion of 'societal constitutionalism' is a particularly subtle manifestation and reinforcement of the presuppositions about politics that have governed state-centred constitutionalism?" (Lindahl 2011, 230). Does it make sense "to vindicate the double gesture of 'generalizing' and 're-specifying' state-centred constitutionalism in terms of an abstractive movement that seeks to capture a purely legal essence of constitutionalism that can then be re-deployed in a non-political setting" (Lindahl 2011, 231)?

Therefore, the issue is to determine what makes the political constitutionalism of the nation-state *political*. Lindahl (2011) argues that Teubner's answer to this question actually is a rather meagre development of the notion of politics implied in political constitutionalism: the centralization of decision-making, a hierarchical structure of norm production, and people-popular sovereignty (in the democratic form). To fully understand the notion of politics built into Teubner's approach, one has to take the notion of politics developed by N. Luhmann's systems theory as the conceptual background of Teubner's discussion (Lindahl 2011)—and hence, to clarify the function of politics in systems theory and how it impinges upon political constitutionalism. The short answer to this question is that in systems theory, the function of politics is "to hold ready the capacity for collectively binding decisions" (Lindahl 2011, 232). Political decisions are binding "to the extent that they operate as authoritative premises for further decisions. Moreover, [...] decisions must be effectively binding" (Lindahl 2011, 232). What is at stake is their enforcement, the capacity to actualize negative sanctions "when a decision fails to bind those to whom it is directed" (Lindahl 2011, 232). In other words, the function of politics "is to decide and enforce decisions despite—and because—of the fact that there is no consensus" (Lindahl 2011, 232). Within societal constitutionalism, we still face the problem of having to take collectively binding decisions; hence, global legal regulation (as any other legal regulation) "depends on a global form of the general function of politics" (Lindahl 2011, 233). Even if Teubner were to concede that societal constitutionalism is political and to rather propose that political power be disaggregated along the lines of the distinct sectoral systems, we could still be facing that problem: we may assist to global political conflicts drawn along sectorial lines, and that would require "the possibility of deploying physical power to enforce decisions" (Lindahl 2011, 235). This presupposes a reference to some representation of a manifold of individuals as a collective, a representation from which individuals can engage in collectively binding decisions and constitutionalize the question of belonging. Hence, "The defense of societal constitutionalism as a form of non-political constitutionalism is only plausible as long as systems theory factors out *le politique* of its account of politics, a move [...] it cannot sustain without leaving unexplained the key concept of a collectively binding decision" (Lindahl 2011, 236).

There is a more troublesome problem with Teubner's approach: his very stance to modernity is problematical. He argues that functional differentiation is inherent to modernity, and hence challenges the political as the representation of an autonomous domain. But functional differentiation builds upon the very structure of public law characteristic of the modern state and of its sovereignty as embodying the autonomy of the political. Without this specific structure (which includes the state/civil society distinction and the public/private boundary), functional differentiation as conceived of by Teubner can hardly be sustained. Merely setting aside the political as but one subarea of a functionally differentiated social world cannot ground a thorough critique of methodological nationalism and liberal constitutionalism; such a critique must build upon an analysis of public power and claims to authority[40]. For it is the claim to authority that is basic to the constitution (in the broad sense of the word) of polities. Moreover, "depoliticizing" constitutionalism may conceal significant inequalities that are built into its very framing; some of these are significant enough to potentially crosscut the subareas of social life and have a cumulative effect that can hardly be contained by the dynamics of generalization and re-specification described by Teubner[41]. Combined with the issues raised in Chapters 1 and 4, such a stance casts a significant doubt on the possibility to embody public autonomy beyond the state starting from such a point of view.

Sovereignty as Integral to Modern Constitutionalism

The approaches discussed up to now in this chapter raise significant issues related to a denial or a relativization of the close, intricate, and enduring connections between statehood and (modern) constitutionalism. From my point of view, the recognition of these connections actually is a basic condition for framing appropriately the issue of collective political agency in complex settings, since the normative resonance of the concept of constituent power builds upon dimensions closely related to statehood. I will now briefly discuss two theoretical perspectives that straightforwardly address these connections. Contrary to the approaches discussed up to now in this chapter, both explicitly acknowledge that state sovereignty is integral to modern constitutionalism. However, they impact differently on the argument about constituent power. For one of them (namely, Loughlin's), non-state polities are not a proper object of constitutionalism; for the other (namely, Tully's), modern constitutionalism (to which state sovereignty is integral) must be distinguished from ancient (and democratic) constitutionalism, so that constitutionalism still is appropriate for non-state polities. They hence have different consequences upon debates about constituent power beyond the state. These consequences are discussed more thoroughly in later chapters. Here I wish to focus upon their argument about sovereignty as integral to (modern) constitutionalism.

M. Loughlin's Epistemic Approach

The significance of Loughlin's approach as to the purposes of this book rests with its focus on the foundation of the sovereign state as the very condition of a concept of the people as a collective political agent. Constituent power, in modern constitutionalism, presupposes the state as the political unity of a people (Loughlin 2014a). Loughlin's approach allows to highlight this feature because it rightly acknowledges that the basic claim is the one to authority, embodied (in the modern structure of public law) by the sovereign state. This is at once an empirical, epistemic, and normative claim[42].

As Walker has stressed, the key insight of Loughlin's epistemic approach is that "the concept of the modern state, understood as a particular type of relationship between territory, ruling authority, and people [...] is a political way of knowing and way of being in the absence of whose emergence the very idea of a constitutional polity is simply unimaginable" (Walker 2010, 295). The domain of the political is a distinct mode of existence whose autonomy is founded on the concept of sovereignty and the existence of the state (Loughlin 2013). Public law depends on sovereignty as an expression of the autonomously conceived public realm; the public sphere can claim autonomy because it can offer an authoritative expression of the world (Loughlin 2008, 59)[43]. In other words, the concept of the state involves a framing/constitutive sense of public law "that is necessarily prior to and a prerequisite of a full, modern articulation of the idea of the 'constitution' and 'public law' [...]" (Walker 2012, 67)[44].

There are two important consequences of this argument, relatively to the purposes of this book. First, the unity of a people depends on the idea that public power (namely, political power harnessed through the institutionalization of authority) acquires autonomy with the establishment of the modern idea of the state (Loughlin 2003, 78). The concept of "the people" as a collective political actor takes life in the foundation of the sovereign state; the state is the collective representation of a people, and it is a unified will (Loughlin 2014a, 232)[45]. Second, modern constitutionalism "forms part of the state-building project" (Loughlin 2005, 198). Modern constitutions are expected both to specify the structure of government and to forge the bonds of the unity of the nation (Loughlin 2010, 52). They are required to serve both instrumental and symbolic purposes:

> In its instrumental role, the constitution gives guidance for the future by establishing the authoritative modes of collective decision making of a nation. In its symbolic function, it provides a point of unity; the

> constitution must operate in such a way as to bolster the established order of things. The instrumental aspect, which expresses the principle of legality, looks primarily to the future, whereas the symbolic aspect, drawing on custom and myth and expressing the principle of legitimacy, primarily makes an appeal to the past.
>
> (Loughlin 2010, 52)[46]

The authority of the constitution derives from the construct of the people. Modern constitutions reflect a more basic change in modern social life: civil society as the paramount force in the public sphere, with a limited role for government[47]. The basic relationships of public law are not constituted by modern constitutions; these relationships evolve from basic circumstances relative to the ways in which governing authority is continually acknowledged (Loughlin 2013, 23). Constitutions are not constitutive; they are regulative. Rights are created within a political world; they do not found it (Loughlin 2013, 23). The status of modern constitutions is conferred only within the frame of positive law. It is the state that makes possible the unity of a people, not the constitution[48].

The consequences of this standpoint as to debates about constitutionalism (and constituent power) beyond the state is that Loughlin actually dismisses any prospect of some comprehensive adaptation of the "state-suffused" register of constitutionalism and public law to a postnational environment (Walker 2012). A post-state world—namely, a world in which sovereignty would have become anachronistic—would mean the end of the political as we know it because it would mean the end of a peculiar way of knowing (and being in) the world in which sovereignty embodies the autonomy of the political. We would then need a completely new model of public authority, because the anachronism of sovereignty would have made public law and constitutionalism at once anachronistic. According to Loughlin, to argue for the constitutionalization of postnational orders is to repackage constitutionalism purely as an expression of liberal-legal constitutionalism, a move in which constitutionalism is presented "as a more or less free-standing set of norms" (Loughlin 2010, 61); it is to make constitutionalism "a meta-theory which establishes the authoritative standards of legitimacy for the exercise of public power wherever it is located" (Loughlin 2010, 61). It is to fuse legality with legitimacy, and to claim that constitutional principles must possess free-standing authority (Loughlin 2013, 24; see also Loughlin 2010).

This stance also explains Loughlin's critique of constitutional pluralism. He argues that the latter's advocates make several mistakes. First, they assert that the foundations of political authority lie in a constitution, whereas these foundations actually lie in the state. Hence, they conflate the concepts of the constitutional regime of a state with the constitution as an institutional normative order. The constitution does not establish the state; it establishes the office of government (Loughlin 2014b, 23). Second, they misunderstand sovereignty. For example, they argue (in the context of the EU) that public authority is now constituted at a multiplicity of sites. But actually, such a standpoint can be maintained only if each site of government can be considered an independent source of authority. And to hold that sovereignty can be divided or pooled is conceptually incoherent: "sovereignty is not a bundle of jurisdictional powers [...] A multiplicity of normative orders without any means of integration means that there is no legal order, and [...] a plurality of constitutional claims undermines the constitutional character of any claim" (Loughlin 2014b, 23). Their basic mistake, actually, "is to assume that a pluralism of values or institutions can also be extended to a pluralism of foundations" (Loughlin 2014b, 29). To make such claims convincing, we would need a robust alternative narrative of political authority. Therefore, in Loughlin's approach, state institutions and practices are the standard by which institutions can be said to be constitutional or public (Walker 2012)[49].

Loughlin actually proposes a brilliant and masterful analysis of the sovereign state as the peculiar way of framing the political in Western modernity. He rightly points to the inherent connection between modern constitutionalism and the modern state. However, his work raises two issues when it comes to discussing constituent power beyond the state. First, as Walker has rightly stressed, it limits our capacity to imagine alternative models. Talking of both Loughlin's and Grimm's work, Walker argues that "[t]heir options, given their dismissal of any plausible prospect of comprehensive adaptation of the state-suffused registers of constitutionalism and public law to a postnational environment, narrow to a defensive consolidation of the reduced remit of a state-centred law, a wishful reminding of that legacy to its Westphalian pomp, or a fatalistic acceptance of the exhaustion of a paradigm" (Walker 2012, 68–9)[50]. Hence, this also challenges the very possibility of collective political agency and democratic authorization in a post- or non-state context; I will come back on this issue in Chapter 3. From my point of view, as I will argue in the upcoming chapters, one can acknowledge the peculiar sociocultural and epistemological framework of the modern state without excluding *a priori* the possibility of collective political agency in a post- or non-state context. Loughlin is right to argue that this will require an alternative narrative of political authority. One must acknowledge, then, that constituent power is but one way of expressing public autonomy (Krisch 2016); the task is to look for alternative narratives and symbols of democratic authorization.

There is another problem as well with Loughlin's work: it erroneously assumes that public law is conceptually free from exploitation. According to him, the achievement of a system of public law "does mean that exploitation is eliminated *conceptually* from the world of public law [...] [T]he establishment of a public discourse that operates on the *principle* of formal political and legal equality and the deliberative procedures of open institutions does at least open up the possibility of achieving a distinctive type of governing arrangement" (Loughlin 2008, 58). From his point of view, exploitation is eliminated from the concept of public law because the state is law-governed, because constituent power mediates between democracy and law, and because sovereignty represents the autonomy of the political (see Nootens 2015). However, it is a particular structure of interests and view of the common good that is embodied in public law. Legal, political, and normative orders that do not fit within this structure—for example, the legal and normative orders of First Nations—are *a priori* excluded. Such exclusion is not merely a historical fact that can be left behind by the recognition of claims to autonomy, for in negotiating with the state and its officials for such a recognition to be achieved, First Nations must often adapt to an ontological frame that cannot render their own ways of framing the polity and self-rule (whether these ways are considered traditional or not)[51].

This is why it is important to turn to a conception that acknowledges the nested relationship of the sovereign state and modern constitutionalism, but that can as well explain why public law actually is not free from oppression. Such a perspective is necessary if we are to capture the struggles for civic freedom characteristic of our age, as well as to emphasize that in dominant views, popular sovereignty has actually been subordinated to state sovereignty.

Constitutionalism, Ancient and Modern

In Tully's approach, constitutionalism and constituent power are rescued by detaching their meaning and import from the statist paradigm that is integral to modern constitutionalism; the latter is conceived of as being distinct from ancient one(s)[52]. Modern (Western) constitutional democracy is characterized by formality and autonomy[53]; by constituent power as a capacity prior to taking on concrete form; by the relative autonomy of the state; by the institutionalization of political, productive and coercive power; by modern techniques of *gouvernementalité*; by a dynamic relationship between constitutional forms and constitutional powers that is "a function of the complex interaction among the *actors* within and against the constitutional formations" (Tully 2007, 325); by world-process discursive formations (meta-narratives of constitutional democratic modernization); and by imperialism. Four major types of interaction between constitutional forms and constituent powers are characteristic of modern constitutional democracy: the juridical containment thesis (when the constitution founds and structures the exercise of constituent powers), the co-originality thesis (when the constitutional form and the constituent powers of democratic self-rule are equally basic), the radical sovereignty thesis (when the people see themselves as a yet unorganized and unrecognized potential agent behind the whole constitutional-constituent formation and bring into being a new type of constitutional formation), and the irresolution thesis (when individuals and groups exercise their constituent power within and against the constitutionalized forms but are "unable to transform the hegemony of the prevailing sovereigns and constitutional forms") (Tully 2007, 326).

I have already explained in Chapter 1 that Tully distinguishes modern constitutionalism from another type of constitutionalism, which he refers to as "embedded", "ancient", "customary", or "democratic". In these non-modern constitutionalisms, laws are "immanent norms within the activities they regulate and which change as subjects interact with them in day-to-day rule following" (Tully 2007, 318). In modern constitutionalism (constitutional democracy), the freedom to criticize, negotiate, and modify the laws has been displaced to representative institutions; but in democratic constitutionalism (as opposed to constitutional democracy), the structures are brought "under the participatory shared authority of those who are subject to them" (Tully 2007, 334). The project of democratic constitutionalism is "to exploit and expand the existing yet severely limited field of direct participatory freedom (the exercise of constituent powers) within and against the constitutional forms to which the governed are now subject, directly or indirectly, at the very sites where these unjustly constrain their ability to exercise shared authority over the conditions of their activities" (Tully 2007, 335).

For the purposes of this chapter, I want to focus on three significant components of Tully's argument. First, recall that from his point of view, constituent power denotes the general idea of the power of humans to govern themselves, individually and collectively (see, e.g., Tully 2007, 320). For example, Indigenous people understand the constituent powers of humans (and non-humans) as "always already immanent in the specific forms of transposable *habitus* they take in the countless normative relationships of interaction (non-formal customary law) humans and non-humans both bear and transform *en passant*" (Tully 2007, 320)[54]. However, from my point of view, these "powers of humans to govern themselves" took a very specific turn with the notion of constituent power. As I have already mentioned, the latter is a very peculiar way of expressing public autonomy, one that belongs with a structure of public law that is itself dependent upon state sovereignty. Acknowledging that modern constitutionalism depends upon the sovereign state requires addressing the very notion of constituent power, since it was born with the juridification of the subject characteristic of modern *gouvernementalité*[55]. I therefore would rather not refer to these general powers of humans to govern themselves as "constituent powers". There is still too much of modern statehood in the expression "constituent power" for it to designate the broad category of the forms of public autonomy.

Second, Tully rightly stresses that the modern constitution is the product of the sovereign state standing "in an agonistic relationship with the people" (Tully 2007, 322). The former is sovereign in the Hobbesian sense, and even when it can plausibly be said to derive its powers from the consent of the governed, "it is still able [...] to exercise sovereignty over them and the constitution that is supposed to limit its power" (Tully 2007, 322; see also Nootens 2013, 2015, 2019). This relates to a significant issue: has popular sovereignty, as expressing the original authority of the people (and the ongoing display of the latter), transformed the very notion of the sovereign rights of the state (Nootens 2019)? In other words, has democratization transformed the structure of the state so that the latter cannot be said to be a Hobbesian state anymore, as it has become a liberal democratic one whose legitimacy builds on individual rights? From my point of view, this is not the case, for it is sovereignty (that embodies the autonomy of the political) that stands as the basic, core concept of public law. Hence, this also requires a nuance as to the claim that the constitution limits the power of the state: the constitution is not constitutive, it is regulative; and it regulates public politics, not the sovereign entity within which the latter goes on. The constitution does not limit the power of the state as a sovereign entity; it frames public politics within states as sovereign entities that are the precondition of the unity of the people, a unity that generates the political power relationship. In other words, when authority is transferred from the prince to the people, the idea of the modern state is not transformed. This is why there remains a basic tension between democratic authorization and state sovereignty (Nootens 2019).

Third, Tully rightly argues that the modern construct of politics is itself oppressive, and that the relationship between modern constitutional forms and constituent powers cannot be understood "unless the imperial and post-imperial supra-state constitutional forms are seen as internally related to the state constitutional forms" (Tully 2007, 319–320). As I have already explained, Loughlin's claim that public law is conceptually free from oppression is disputable, since public law expresses a particular structure of interests and view of the common good—to which some interests and worldviews are inevitably estranged.

Conclusion

I have argued in this chapter that statehood plays a pervasive part in modern constitutionalism. This part is not always explicitly acknowledged. And when it is, it may challenge our very capacity to raise the issue of constituent power beyond the state. Modern constitutionalism is closely dependent upon sovereign statehood. This nested relationship is not only about "our limits of imagination"[56] but also about political modernity itself, as Tully argues. Constitutionalism has taken a very specific meaning with its development as a theory of government in the modern state. Loughlin demonstrates how it belongs with a specific way of being into, and knowing, the world—sovereignty as embodying the autonomy of the political.

Even leading schools of constitutionalism beyond the state share significant, core assumptions with state-based thought (Anderson 2012). Anderson has stressed that both Walker's supranational constitutionalism and Teubner's societal constitutionalism reiterate the divide between the economic and the political; hence, they actually "reinscribe into their own framework the value consensus of liberal capitalism and its effort to remove much of social life from the prospect of democratic supervision" (Anderson 2012, 378; see also Buchanan 2006). Teubner's depoliticized constitutionalism conceal significant inequalities that are built into the very framing of public law (on which functional differentiation is grounded); and it cannot provide a convincing account for collectively binding decision making. Walker makes sovereignty as ultimate authority a precondition of constitutional polity formation.

From my point of view, we need to explicitly acknowledge the dependency of modern constitutionalism upon sovereign statehood. Such explicit acknowledgement allows to scrutinize this relationship critically. Loughlin offers a perceptive analysis of this relationship. However, I do not share some of the conclusions he draws from it, for three reasons. First, acknowledging this relationship also requires acknowledging that public law is not free from oppression. Second, Loughlin continues to analyze the world as it currently is on the basis of the statist paradigm; this, I think, makes him blind to some transformations in public authority significant enough to have a deep impact on sovereignty. Third, his work does not challenge the subjection of popular sovereignty to state sovereignty[57].

The problem of (re)framing constituent power is much more complex than a mere tension between sociological and justificatory/normative approaches, or than the input/output legitimacy. It involves challenging a specific narrative of political authority that builds upon the consolidation of a seizure of power—one that is actually built upon war and preparation for war (see Tilly 1985[58]). From my point of view, the challenge we face is not to retrieve ancient traditions of negotiating freedom. It is to build, frame, and sustain new ones that are appropriate to the context in which we live—a context in which state and non-state polities overlap in a complex setting of public authority that neither monism nor dualism allows to understand appropriately. This is why I am going to turn now to the shift in regulatory activity. This shift significantly challenges both state sovereignty and the three dimensions that account for the normative resonance of the concept of constituent power.

Notes

1 In the theory of International Relations, a "regime" designates a set of "principles, norms, rules and decision-making procedures around which actors' expectations converge in a given area of international relations" (Krasner 1983, quoted by Bradford 2007). Regimes are best seen as institutions involving states and non-state actors "who seek to realize their long-term objectives and structure and stabilize their relations"

(Bradford 2007). In this book, I also use "regime" in a broad sense as well, namely, as "repeated, strong interactions among major political actors including a government" (Tilly 2006, 19).

2 In predominant (statist) views, the "people-as-the-governed" are subsumed under a structure of public law that makes them "invisible" and disempowered (Nootens 2015).

3 This is not Loughlin's main concern, though. For example, as to contemporary developments, Loughlin explains that his main concern has been "to return to the basics and examine the ways in which jurists have characterized the constitution of political authority" (Loughlin 2017, 353–4). I rather am interested in how this close relationship impacts on democratic iteration.

4 From this perspective, constitutionalism provides the normative vocabulary for the mutual articulation of law and politics (Anderson 2012, 364). Only a constitution can provide the symbolic and epistemic basis for a reflection on, or the renewal of, the system of supranational governance through collective authorship. Let me stress, though, that to say that only constitutionalism can provide the symbolic and epistemic basis for such a renewal is not quite the same as saying that we need to use it because we do not have other appropriate resources at our disposal to do so (see, e.g., Walker 2012, 83–4; Walker 2013, 262).

5 All constitutional forms remain posed between description (to determine and record "the nature and character of some discrete object that already possess[es] an innate character") and prescription (to construct that object "as a kind of conventional artefact") (Walker 2009, 152).

6 In order to avoid any confusion, it is important to stress (see the Introduction to this book) that most of the time, when the scholars discussed here talk about the "post-national" order, they mean a "post-state" order. So here, when Walker talks of the national level, he actually is talking of the state (most of the time).

7 The relationship between these different orders of polity is best conceived as "osmotic", namely, "as a generalized process of mutual infiltration" (Walker 2009, 164).

8 This second-order constituent power cannot be of the same nature as the first-order constituent power characteristic of state constitutionalism. I will come back on this point in Chapter 4.

9 In the EU context, constitutional pluralism is defined by three elements: a complex of law embracing "multiple sites [...] each with its own claim to constitutional authority" (Walker 2016, 333); the absence of a dominant understanding that would order the claims to constitutional authority associated with each site within a hierarchy (or reconcile them "by reference to a single meta-authoritative order") (Walker 2016, 333–4); and mutual acknowledgement and accommodation of "the claims of the others as independent sites of constitutional authority" (Walker 2016, 334). The value of the normative contribution of constitutional pluralism remains contentious, though, because its various lines do not focus on the issue of "how we might conceive of an actual 'trans-systemic' order of constitutional authority as a viable prospect" (Walker 2016, 341) and because "the search for a solution that is legal-system transcending yet still *legal* remains deeply elusive" (Walker 2016, 341). In other words, it is not clear how we are to conceive of a trans-systemic order of constitutional authority. The challenge is that the overlapping of heterarchically related constitutional authorities has to become a condition of legitimacy of the combined whole. Let me stress that according to Loughlin, a claim to partial or shared authority does not make sense, because the foundation of political authority lies in the state, not in the constitution; hence, tenants of constitutional pluralism are wrong.

10 The key ingredients of a holistic method of constitutionalism rest in "this combination of structural primacy, institution-transcending substantive rules, insulation of rules of constitutional norm production and maintenance from control by the institutions affected by these norms, and the openness of the same rules to broader forms of public influence and discipline" (Walker 2010, 300).

11 Namely, fields that are characterized by a combination of site-specific self-regulation and diverse external self-regulation, as well as by the absence of an integrated and generic public society (e.g., the field of transnational commercial regulation). Some other forms of post-state regimes, though, "can fit quite well on the 'scale' of constitutionalism considered as a layered set of holistic frames" (Walker 2010, 301) (e.g., the EU and, in a more modest way, the WTO and the UN).

12 Krisch challenges the helpfulness of a conception of constitutionalism expressed at such a degree of generality. At such a level, the principles and values related to constitutionalism may not be helpful in re-specifying collective self-authorization. Building on such a degree of generality to argue that constitutionalism can be taken out of the state context makes the roots of constitutionalism independent of its original context, and the argument becomes circular (Krisch 2011, 36). As Krisch also stresses, Walker's later work acknowledges this problem, but continues to assume that constitutionalism is "open enough for an 'innovative understanding' that makes it applicable to the postnational context" (Krisch 2011, 36). Although Krisch seems to me to be right, I rather want to emphasize that Walker's approach builds on the replication of the core characteristics of statehood. It may make sense in the EU, which is a polity built on states; but it is very difficult to conceive of how it can apply to other forms of post-state regimes.

13 Such a claim is inextricably tied to the paradox of *pouvoir constituant* (the power that enacts law) and *pouvoir constitué* (the law that restrains power) as a "dynamic process of mutual constitution and mutual containment of law and politics" (Walker 2003a, 19). The conceptual key to sovereignty is the double claim of the political requiring a legal frame and the legal requiring the idea of reflexivity of political community and political will (Walker 2006, 67).

14 The other factors are the adoption of a self-conscious constitutional discourse, the development of jurisdictional scope, a claim to interpretive autonomy, the exercise of a residual institutional capacity, the specification of the incidents of citizenship of the polity, and the construction of mechanisms (such as representation) for realizing that citizenship (Walker 2002).

15 According to Anderson, the main theoretical fault line ushered in by globalization is not between state and non-state accounts of constitutionalism, but rather "between those who accept (whether implicitly of otherwise) and work within the politics of knowledge formed within the nation-state era, and those who seek to make these politics of knowledge the key focus of the debate, and even transcend them" (Anderson 2012, 380). Globalization makes a key issue of (1) "the reasoning which has implicitly supported the separation between the economic and the political and state and civil society" (Anderson 2012, 373), and of (2) "the rationale underlying the state-civil society divide that the public sphere enjoys a monopoly on the lawful uses of violence" (Anderson 2012, 373). By reiterating the divide between the economic and the political, Walker's supranational constitutionalism reinscribes in its framework "the value consensus of liberal capitalism and its effort to remove much of social life from the prospect of democratic supervision" (Anderson 2012, 378). I agree with Anderson, but I think it still is worthwhile to discuss the intricate relationship between constitutionalism and statehood, because it allows to stress the pervasiveness of statehood as part of such "politics of knowledge" in discussions about democratic authorization beyond the state.

16 Let me stress that from my point of view, making such unifying traits the precondition of polity formation is to mistake the consequences of state-building for its causes, and hence, to partake in methodological nationalism.

17 A constitution speaks directly in the name of those over whom it claims authority (Kumm 2010, 215). The scope of its authority is the extent to which it fulfils the promise to instantiate constitutional principles (Kumm 2010, 215). These basic ideas give rise to three types of constitutional norms: basic institutions, procedures allowing for appropriate forms of participation and deliberation, and rights.

18 "Democratic statism" conceptually connects the core commitments of modern constitutionalism with the tradition of statehood and sovereignty. It builds upon three basic propositions: that constitutional law establishes the supreme law of a sovereign state; that the authority of the constitution "is based on the idea that it can be fairly attributed to 'We the People' as the constituent power" (Kumm 2010, 204); and that such constituent power "is tied to the existence of a genuine political community that is the prerequisite for meaningful democratic politics" (Kumm 2010, 204).

19 The point of constitutionalism "is to ensure that the claim to legitimate authority [...] is in fact made correctly" (Kumm 2017, 916); it "provides a critical perspective that is internal to the law" (Kumm 2017, 916).

20 By contradistinction, the statist conception of constitutional legitimacy is dualist: a constitution is understood as the supreme law of a sovereign state, but international law is not connected to the establishment of an ultimate authority, nor to coercive powers of state institutions, nor to the self-governing practices of a people. But these assumptions are misguided; national constitutional law has "inappropriately narrowed, morally misconstructed, and falsely aggrandized national constitutionalism by analytically connecting it to a statist paradigm of law" (Kumm 2009, 263).

21 Therefore, the cosmopolitan paradigm allows to take into account the legitimate concerns of outsiders.

22 Hence, Kumm may be said to recast the notion of constituent power by claiming that its application is not restricted to the state domain (see Walker 2017). But see below.

23 See also Walker (2012 and 2017).

24 In a specific context, the presumption in favour of international law could be rebutted if international law violates countervailing principles (namely, the principle of due process, jurisdictional principles of subsidiarity, and the substantive principle of respect for human rights and reasonableness) "in a sufficiently serious way" (Kumm 2009, 277).

25 Walker reads Kumm's work as treating constituent power as a vital building block of a cosmopolitan vision, based on recasting it in normative terms (Walker 2017). From my point of view, though, Kumm very explicitly downplays the normative and political import of the notion by casting away its "sociological credentials".

26 See also Walker (2012). Walker wonders whether Kumm's cosmopolitanism is "not just one more hegemonic move on behalf of a holistic constitutional vision, one that illegitimately downplays democratic pedigree [...]" (Walker 2012, 83).

27 It finds evidence "in an existing legal pluralism, in transnational sectoral regimes like the lex mercatoria, and in the fact that the state is not the only actor on the global scene" (Dobner 2009, 615).

28 But see Anderson (2012): he argues that within the various theories of constitutionalism beyond the state (including societal constitutionalism), understandings of "the constitutional" "remain constant in the pre- and post-globalization literature" (Anderson 2012, 370).

29 Constitutions are non-political objects assisting the self-reference and functional differentiation of social subsystems (Přibáň 2012, 458). The constitution must be disconnected from statehood, as well as decoupled from both institutional politics and the medium of power (Teubner 2012, 60).

30 We can talk of constitutionalization (rather than of mere juridification) once legal norms assume the dual function of founding an autonomous order and of self-limiting it (Teubner 2012, 41). In Teubner's work, constitutionalization designates "the emergence of a recursive, self-referential modality of closure, as a result of the way in which repeated operations crystallize and become entrenched as self-descriptions that in turn acquire a guiding function within the legal system" (Christodoulidis 2011, 238); it is the "incremental, aggregative, fragmentary process of becoming constitutional" (Christodoulidis 2013, 645).

31 Teubner has been arguing at least since 1997 that "the methodological nationalism of modern legal theory is neither capable of conceptualizing the specific of global legal orders nor up to the task of providing adequate normative orientation in the face of the transformed set of conditions confronting contemporary law and politics" (Lindahl 2011, 230).

32 He criticizes the claim that the world society is constitutionalized through the UN (with a basis in the Charter). According to him, such a claim is but a constitutional illusion, grounded in an uncritical transfer of the nation-state's conception of a constitution to global relations. He stresses that such a move "functions as an epistemological obstacle" (Teubner 2011, 218). The UN has gone through a constitutionalization process, but the result is not a world constitution: it is an organizational one. The same is true for the so-called constitutionalization of international law: such a constitutionalization is sectoral; the bodies of norms (*jus cogens*, norms with *ega omnes* effect, and human rights) "are constitutional limitations of international agreements and, as such, function only within international politics in the narrow sense" (Teubner 2011, 219).

33 So that an all-embracing constitutional law would function "simply as a global constitutional conflict of law" (Teubner 2012, 13).

34 I will come back on the issue of generalization and re-specification in Chapter 4.

35 See Chapter 4.

36 And "in particular the familiar superiority of constitutional rules and judicial review of ordinary law" (Teubner 2012, 75).

37 Hence, although societal constitutionalism seems to eschew a public institutional bias, it generalizes a broadly institutional conception of constitutionalism (Anderson 2013, 888).

38 See Chapter 4.

39 According to E. Christodoulidis, constitutional pluralism is not a way out of these problems because a constitution is a point of final normative regress in the system (Christodoulidis 2013, 646).

40 For example, Tully has stressed that a thorough understanding of the nature of modern constitutionalism requires that we take into account the imperial context. Hence, we also need to challenge the relation between power and constitutionalism. From this point of view, societal constitutionalism "does not overcome the 'irreducibly antinomic' nature of constitutional discourse, but rather displaces it to the transnational sphere where the tensions between opposing paradigms of globalization makes it more difficult to avoid than in national settings" (Anderson 2013, 901).

41 See Chapter 4.

42 Loughlin's approach is epistemic because it focuses on the idea of the modern state and the political imaginary associated with it as a comprehensive way of "seeing, understanding and acting in the world", a way which is prior to "a full, modern articulation of the idea of constitution" (Walker 2010, 295).

43 Public law is not a subset of positive law. It relates to the justification, in legal terms, of the very constitution of public authority (Loughlin 2013, 11). It was formed in the modern world "as the jural coding of an autonomously conceived political domain" (Loughlin 2013, 13). Sovereignty is juridical and relates to authority, not to power. See also Mac Amhlaigh, Michelon, and Walker (2013, 3).

44 See also Loughlin (2014b), on the 12 basic propositions of modern public law: (1) sovereignty is the name given to the supreme will of the state, and expresses its condition of legal omnipotence; (2) state and sovereignty are expressions of principles of unity and closure, and signify ultimate authority; (3) sovereignty is not a bundle of jurisdictional powers; (4) the sovereign state is the source of law and "cannot be regarded as being bound by the obligations which that law creates" (Loughlin 2014b, 13); (5) *Kompetenz-kompetenz* is the essential criteria for determining the existence of the sovereign state; (6) "[u]ltimate authority vests in the state, not in its organs of government" (Loughlin 2014b, 13); (7) "[s]overeignty is not impaired by the state entering

into international obligations with other sovereign powers" (Loughlin 2014b, 13); (8) constitutional laws relate to the form of government and the allocation of powers to governmental institutions; (9) constitutional law purports to control the government, not the state; (10) all laws are laws of the state; (11) no law imposes a limitation upon the state itself because the state "is not and cannot be controlled by law, and logically cannot be regarded as the subject of legal rights and duties" (Loughlin 2014b, 14); and (12) the idea of popular sovereignty does not mean that sovereignty remains in the people, it merely indicates that the people is treated as having established the authority of a governmental regime (Loughlin 2014b, 14).

45 Political power is created through the symbolic representation of foundation and constitution, and then applied through the action of government.

46 A constitution "is the arrangement through which rulers and subjects express their beliefs about the authority of government" (Loughlin 2014b, 19). The right by which a governmental agency is able to act "flows ultimately from a set of beliefs held by its subjects about that government's authority to rule" (Loughlin 2014b, 19).

47 Constitutionalism is the promotion of a particular theory of government, namely, a theory of limited and participatory government; it is "a political theory that was developed as part of a liberal philosophy to guide the formation of modern constitutions. Predicating an arrangement of limited government constructed by free, equal, rights-bearing individuals, constitutionalism reflects the concerns of a particular time, place, and social situation" (Loughlin 2010, 61).

48 Compare this assertion with, e.g., Preuss's. Preuss argues that constitutions are constitutive because they create an institutional reality (the collective power of the multitude) that constitutional theory constructs as the source of the constitution. Constitutive norms create institutional facts; they create/corroborate "the interactive normative systems in which those facts have a particular meaning" (Preuss 2010, 41); they "presuppose a plurality of agents who agree that some particular fact 'counts as' an institutional fact" (Preuss 2010, 41). Regulative norms "rather regulate an antecedently existing activity by establishing dictates, prohibitions, permissions, etc." (Preuss 2010, 43).

49 As Walker explains, in Loughlin's work as well as in D. Grimm's, it is

> the putatively democratic or meta-democratic source, whether the cultural substratum of peoplehood [Grimm] or the epistemic framing of publicness [Loughlin], that is fundamental and indispensable in bequeathing legitimacy to the positive forms of constitutional law and public law more generally and so in securing the institutional edifice of an expansive and integrated but self-containing system of government, which systematic achievement is the equally fundamental and indispensable expression of public power.
>
> (Walker 2012, 68)

Grimm's approach is slightly different from Loughlin, since he makes the idea of a constitution dependent "upon certain prior or emergent socio-cultural facts concerning identity, solidarity, and allegiance [...] Since only the modern state has known such a socio-cultural formation, and since even if the modern state is no longer so robust in these terms it still constitutes a standing impediment to the development of similar cultural formation, there can be no real prospect of a full constitutionalism beyond the state" (Walker 2010, 294; see also Walker 2012, 66–7; Grimm 2005; Grimm 2010).

50 I have already stressed the limitations of Walker's own attempt at translating constitutionalism in the trans- or postnational sphere. He nonetheless rightly argues that an attempt such as Loughlin does not even allow to explore this possibility.

51 On this issue, see the excellent books by K. Shaw (2008) and P. Nadasdy (2017).

52 I leave open the issue of whether there is a wider constitutionalism that has a long history (starting with "ancient" constitutions as described by Tully) and will continue to have one after the state. From such a perspective, constitutionalism could make sense without constituent power because the latter has a very specific (modern and state-dependent) meaning, from the 17th–18th centuries on. My focus here is on the fact that in the approaches discussed in the first part of this chapter, some significant features of modern constitutionalism (the one that depends upon the sovereign state) are replicated.

53 Law is disembedded from the activities of those who are subject to it and can structure the field of interaction/recognition compliantly.

54 But see Borrows (2010) on the different sources of Indigenous laws. Tully stresses that saying that some legal orders are customary rather than formal is not to say that the formers do not have a constitution; "any persisting legal order *is* a constitution in the Aristotelian or 'ancient' sense, whether customary or formal" (Tully 2007, 318).

55 See Chapter 1.

56 This idea about "our limits of imagination" and the difficulty to frame new contexts with more appropriate conceptual tools is suggested by Krisch, amongst others. He writes that:

> We tend to fill voids with what we know. When we are thrown into unfamiliar spaces, we try to chart them with the maps we possess, construct them with the tools we already have. Working with analogies, extending and adapting existing concepts, seems usually preferable to the creation of ideas and structures from scratch, not only because of the risks involved in the latter, but also because of our limits of imagination.
>
> (Krisch 2011, 27)

57 As I have mentioned, his enterprise is a different one, focused on the significance of public law as *droit politique*. It is of course valuable on its own right.

58 War and preparation for it were critical processes in the development and consolidation of the modern national state.

References

Anderson, Gavin W. 2012. "Beyond 'Constitutionalism Beyond the State'." *Journal of Law and Society* 39, no. 3: 359–383.

Anderson, Gavin W. 2013. "Societal Constitutionalism, Social Movements, and Constitutionalism from Below." *Indiana Journal of Global Legal Studies* 20, no. 2: 881–906.

Borrows, John. 2010. *Canada's Indigenous Constitution*. Toronto: University of Toronto Press.

Bradford, Anu. 2007. "Regime Theory". Max Planck Encyclopedia of Public International Law. Accessed April 20, 2021. https://ssrn.com/abstract=2770647

Buchanan, Ruth. 2006. "Legitimating Global Trade Governance: Constitutional and Legal Pluralist Approaches." *Northern Ireland Legal Quarterly* 57, no. 4: 654–672.

Christodoulidis, Emilios. 2011. "Of Boundaries and 'Tipping Points': A Response to Gunther Teubner." *Social and Legal Studies* 20, no. 2: 238–243.

Christodoulidis, Emilios. 2013. "On the Politics of Societal Constitutionalism." *Indiana Journal of Legal Studies* 20, no. 2: 629–663.

Dobner, Petra. 2009. "On the Constitutionability of Global Public Policy Networks." *Indiana Journal of Global Legal Studies* 16, no. 2: 605–619.

Grimm, Dieter. 2005. "Integration by Constitution." *International Journal of Constitutional Law* 3, no. 2-3: 193–208.

Grimm, Dieter. 2010. "The Achievement of Constitutionalism and Its Prospects in a Changed World." In *The Twilight of Constitutionalism?* edited by Petra Dobner and Martin Loughlin, 3–22. Oxford: Oxford University Press.

Krasner, Stephen D. 1983. "Structural Causes and Regime Consequences: Regimes as Intervening Variables." In *International Regimes*, edited by Stephen D. Krasner, 1–21. Ithaca: Cornell University Press.

Krisch, Nico. 2011. *Beyond Constitutionalism. The Pluralist Structure of Postnational Law*. Oxford: Oxford University Press.

Krisch, Nico. 2016. "*Pouvoir Constituant* and *Pouvoir Irritant* in the Postnational Order." *International Journal of Constitutional Law* 14, no. 3: 657–679.

Kumm, Mattias. 2009. "The Cosmopolitan Turn in Constitutionalism: On the Relationship between Constitutionalism in and beyond the State." In *Ruling the World? Constitutionalism, International Law, and Global Governance*, edited by Jeffrey L. Dunoff and Joel P. Trachtman, 258–324. New York: Cambridge University Press.

Kumm, Mattias. 2010. "The Best of Times and the Worst of Times: Between Constitutional Triumphalism and Nostalgia." In *The Twilight of Constitutionalism?*, edited by Petra Dobner and Martin Loughlin, 201–219. Oxford: Oxford University Press.

Kumm, Mattias. 2011. "How Does European Union Law Fit into the World of Public Law? *Costa*, *Kadi*, and Three Conceptions of Public Law." In *Political Theory of the European Union*, edited by Jürgen Neyer and Antje Wiener, 111–138. Oxford: Oxford University Press.

Kumm, Mattias. 2016. "Constituent Power, Cosmopolitan Constitutionalism, and Post-Positivist Law." *International Journal of Constitutional Law* 14, no. 3: 697–711.

Kumm, Mattias. 2017. "Constituent Power, Boundaries and Identity: On the Justificatory Depth of Constitutionalism – A Rejoinder to Neil Walker." *International Journal of Constitutional Law* 14, no. 4: 914–924.

Lindahl, Hans. 2011. "Societal Constitutionalism as Political Constitutionalism: Reconsidering the Relation between Politics and Global Legal Orders." *Social and Legal Studies* 20, no. 2: 230–237.

Loughlin, Martin. 2003. *The Idea of Public Law*. Oxford: Oxford University Press.

Loughlin, Martin. 2005. "Constitutional Theory: A 25th Anniversary Essay." *Oxford Journal of Legal Studies* 25, no. 2: 183–202.

Loughlin, Martin. 2008. "Reflections on *The Idea of Public Law*." In *Public Law and Politics. The Scope and Limits of Constitutionalism*, edited by Emilios Christodoulidis and Stephen Tierney, 47–65. Aldershot: Ashgate.

Loughlin, Martin. 2010. "What Is Constitutionalization?" In *The Twilight of Constitutionalism?* edited by Petra Dobner and Martin Loughlin, 47–69. Oxford: Oxford University Press.

Loughlin, Martin. 2013. "The Nature of Public Law." In *After Public Law*, edited by Cormac Mc Amhlaigh, Claudio Michelon, and Neil Walker, 11–24. Oxford: Oxford University Press.

Loughlin, Martin. 2014a. "The Concept of Constituent Power." *European Journal of Political Theory* 13, no. 2: 218–237.

Loughlin, Martin. 2014b. "Constitutional Pluralism: An Oxymoron?" *Global Constitutionalism* 3, no. 1: 9–30.

Loughlin, Martin. 2017. "The Misconceived Search for Global Law." *Transnational Legal Theory* 8, no. 3: 353–359.

Mac Amhlaigh, Cormac, Michelon, Claudio, and Walker, Neil. 2013. "Introduction." In *After Public Law*, edited by Neil Walker, 1–7. Oxford: Oxford University Press.

Nadasdy, Paul. 2017. *Sovereignty's Entailments: First Nation State Formation in the Yukon*. Toronto: University of Toronto Press.

Nootens, Geneviève. 2013. *Popular Sovereignty in the West. Polities, Contention, and Ideas*. London: Routledge.

Nootens, Geneviève. 2015. "Constituent Power and People-as-the-Governed: About the 'Invisible' People of Political and Legal Theory." *Global Constitutionalism* 4, no. 2: 137–156.

Nootens, Geneviève. 2019. "Légitimation démocratique et souveraineté méta-juridictionnelle de l'État." *ThéoRèmes* 15. https://journals.openedition.org/theoremes/3201

Preuss, Ulrich K. 2010. "Disconnecting Constitutions from Statehood." In *The Twilight of Constitutionalism?*, edited by Petra Dobner and Martin Loughlin, 23–46. Oxford: Oxford University Press.

Přibáň, Jiří. 2012. "Constitutionalism as Fear of the Political? A Comparative Analysis of Teubner's *Constitutional Fragments* and Thornhill's *A Sociology of Constitutions*." *Journal of Law and Society* 39, no. 3: 441–471.

Shaw, Karena. 2008. *Indigeneity and Political Theory*. London/New York: Routledge.

Teubner, Gunther. 2011. "Constitutionalizing Polycontexturality." *Social and Legal Studies* 22, no. 2: 210–229.

Teubner, Gunther. 2012. *Constitutional Fragments: Societal Constitutionalism and Globalization*. Oxford: Oxford University Press.

Teubner, Gunther. 2018. "*Quod omnes tangit*: Transnational Constitutions Without Democracy?" *Journal of Law and Society* 45, special issue 1: S5–S29.

Tilly, Charles. 1985. "War Making and State Making as Organized Crime." In *Bringing the State Back In*, edited by Peter B. Evans, Dietrich Rueschemeyer, and Theda Skocpol, 169–187. Cambridge: Cambridge University Press.

Tilly, Charles. 2006. *Regimes and Repertoires*. Chicago and London: University of Chicago Press.

Tully, James. 2007. "The Imperialism of Modern Constitutional Democracy." In *The Paradox of Constitutionalism. Constituent Power and Constitutional Form*, edited by Martin Loughlin and Neil Walker, 315–338. Oxford: Oxford University Press.

Walker, Neil. 2002. "The Idea of Constitutional Pluralism." *Modern Law Review* 65, no. 3: 317–359.

Walker, Neil. 2003a. "Late Sovereignty in the European Union." In *Sovereignty in Transition*, edited by Neil Walker, 3–32. Oxford: Hart Publishing.

Walker, Neil. 2003b. "Postnational Constitutionalism and the Problem of Translation." In *European Constitutionalism Beyond the State*, edited by Joseph H.H. Weiler and Marlene Wind, 27–54. Cambridge: Cambridge University Press.

Walker, Neil. 2005. "Europe's Constitutional Momentum and the Search for Political Legitimacy." *International Journal of Constitutional Law* 3, no. 2-3: 211–238.

Walker, Neil. 2006. "European's Constitutionalism in the State Constitutional Tradition." *Current Legal Problems* 59, no. 1: 1–26.

Walker, Neil. 2009. "Reframing EU Constitutionalism." In *Ruling the World? Constitutionalism, International Law, and Global Governance*, edited by Jeffrey L. Dunoff and Joel P. Trachtman, 149–176. New York: Cambridge University Press.

Walker, Neil. 2010. "Beyond the Holistic Constitution?" In *The Twilight of Constitutionalism?*, edited by Petra Dobner and Martin Loughlin, 291–308. Oxford: Oxford University Press.

Walker, Neil. 2012. "Postnational Constitutionalism and Postnational Public Law: A Tale of Two Neologisms." *Transnational Legal Theory* 3, no. 1: 61–85.
Walker, Neil. 2013. "The Post-national Horizon of Constitutionalism and Public Law: Paradigm Extension or Paradigm Exhaustion?" In *After Public Law*, edited by Cormac Mac Amhlaigh, Claudio Michelon, and Neil Walker, 241–263. Oxford: Oxford University Press.
Walker, Neil. 2016. "Constitutional Pluralism Revisited." *European Law Journal* 22, no. 3: 333–355.
Walker, Neil. 2017. "The Return of Constituent Power: A Reply to Mattias Kumm." *International Journal of Constitutional Law* 14, no. 4: 906–913.

3

A RECONFIGURATION OF PUBLIC AUTHORITY?

If states are not merely one institutional context amongst others for constitutionalism—in other words, if statehood and constitutionalism are intertwined in a nested relationship—then the issue of how transformations in public authority impact upon the form and functions of states is a basic one, when discussing constituent power beyond the state. The issue is whether transformations in public authority call for a reconceptualization of collective political agency. My focus here, then, is less on the inherently agonistic relationship between state sovereignty and popular sovereignty and its normative impact than on how struggles for civic freedom can be framed and sustained in a "post-Westphalian" context—one in which state and non-state polities coexist and overlap.

As Anderson stresses, one central issue of the debates about globalization "concerns the extent to which political power any longer resides exclusively, or primarily, in the governmental institutions of the nation-state" (Anderson 2005, 3). A particularly important point is the one of the impact of the combination of different types of regimes (e.g., territorial and functional) upon territorial sovereignty as the core feature of the modern state and its specific way of embodying public power. Although the approaches discussed in this book broadly agree that there is a shift in regulatory activity, they disagree as to its consequences upon the major feature of statehood, namely, sovereignty. Most of these approaches acknowledge that governmental decision-making is occurring beyond the structures of the nation-state to an increasing extent, and that national legal orders are permeated by international and transnational legal norms (Loughlin 2010). This undermines the claims of modern constitutions to be comprehensive in their reach (Loughlin 2010, 62). Krisch (2010) focuses on the polycentric setting of governance. Walker (2010) discusses

DOI: 10.4324/9781003221722-4

the various challenges to the effective political capacity of the state and the dissemination of legal concepts of publicness. Thornhill (2013b) argues that the legal system is increasingly differentiated. Teubner (2012) focuses on the tension between the self-foundation of autonomous global subsystems and their political-legal constitutionalization. Grimm (2010) stresses the shrinking of the constitution to a partial order.

However, there is no consensus on the significance and meaning of the impact of such transformations on the political itself (nor on public law). Actually, "[f]or some, globalization, and its accompanying reconfiguration of political power, amounts to nothing less than the demise of the paradigm of modernity, making untenable the idea of the nation state as the main organizational principle of society" (Anderson 2005, 3). But for others, there has not been a paradigmatical shift yet. Hence, some understand the shift in regulatory activity as eroding the identity between state power and public power (see, e.g., Grimm 2010 and Krisch 2010), whereas others argue that it has not made sovereignty anachronistic (see, e.g., Loughlin 2010; Loughlin 2017).

This chapter is intended to bridge the discussion on constituent power and its nested relationship with state sovereignty, on the one hand, with the discussion of different arguments as to constituent power beyond the state, on the other one. The specifics of how each of the approaches discussed in Chapters 4–6 understand these transformations will be discussed in these chapters, in order to contextualize how scholars tackle the issue of constituent power in this context. Chapter 7 will then wrap up the discussion by focusing on the issues of public autonomy and democratic authorization in mixed polities. The purpose of the current chapter rather is to illustrate that one may acknowledge the current shift in regulatory activity without interpreting this as being also a shift in public authority that challenges the very structure of public law. There are different ways to make such a claim. I discuss two different options here: Loughlin's argument that sovereignty has not been made anachronistic; and Thornhill's argument that there is no necessary relationship between the political system in which legitimacy is produced by law itself, on the one hand, and statehood, on the other one. According to the first argument, there has not been any fundamental change of paradigm yet because the legal concept of sovereignty is concerned with authority, and there is no conclusive evidence, up to now, that it has been displaced. The second argument also holds that there has been no significant change up to now, but in this case, the argument rests upon the claim that there is no original homology between statehood and society's politicality and that therefore, public law "preserves its defining function in reflexively demarcating an autonomous political domain in society" (Thornhill 2013b, 48).

Both of these arguments involve some significant problems, from my point of view. Loughlin's tackles the issue from a dualistic perspective that conflicts with assessments of how public power is undergoing significant transformations that impact upon public authority itself. He underestimates how states themselves have contributed to settle institutions endowed with autonomous status. Such institutions perform specific functions, for sure; but these are nonetheless basic ones that reshape the public/private boundary. As to Thornhill's argument, it disregards the basic fact of the political, namely, that authority also depends upon a seizure of power (a pre-constitutional polity formation); as Loughlin rightly stresses, constitutions and rights are created *within* a political world. As I will stress in Chapter 7, the state participates in a specific representation of what is public. It hence must not be equated with it; but neither can its significance from such a view be downplayed. Thornhill also assumes that we can simply dispense with a representation of popular will formation; hence, he evades the issue of democratic authorization.

After having discussed both these approaches, I will then turn to the related issue of the impact of current transformations in authority on the three dimensions that account for the normative resonance of the concept of constituent power. This allows to frame the issue of constituent power beyond the state in the following (though preliminary) way: how can collective political agency as an expression of public autonomy be conceptualized in a potentially different context, one in which the modern hope of comprehensively and purposively ordering a delimited polity seems to have to be given up?

Is Sovereignty Anachronistic? M. Loughlin and the Political Reality of the State as the "Institution of Institutions"

Loughlin acknowledges that governmental decision-making is occurring beyond the structures of the nation-state to an increasing extent, and that national legal orders are permeated by international and transnational norms. He agrees that this undermines the claims of modern constitutions to be comprehensive in their reach (Loughlin 2010, 62). But from his point of view, these institutions are "mainly regulatory agencies that possess an economic-technical rationale" (Loughlin 2017, 358). Therefore, the situation leads to a political crisis, not to a jurisprudential one. In other words, there may be a crisis of representation of political authority, since the complex network of governmental institutions "undermines the notion of the political as the domain in which collective unity is maintained" (Loughlin 2017, 358). This "generates a political crisis born of the difficulty of sustaining the idea of 'the people' as a symbolic representation of collective will formation" (Loughlin 2010, 62). But this has not made sovereignty anachronistic. Practices of government may change, but as long as sovereignty as the expression of the autonomously conceived public realm is not itself challenged, it is groundless to talk of a paradigmatical shift[1]. If we were to agree on such a shift, we would have to redefine the whole conceptual apparatus of public law.

Sovereignty is juristic. It should not be conflated with the ability of a nation-state fully to control its material conditions and destiny (Loughlin 2014b, 10). The legal concept of sovereignty is concerned with authority, namely, the right of a government to be obeyed (Loughlin 2014b, 12). In a conceptual sense, such authority "is unrelated to the power it is able to exercise" (Loughlin 2014b, 12); it "derives not from its power but from its constitution" (Loughlin 2014b, 12). Sovereignty "is absolute, perpetual, and illimitable, whereas government is conditional, provisional, and limitable. Sovereignty is conceptual, government is empirical; sovereignty is juridical, government is sociological. Sovereignty cannot be divided, but government not only can but—for power-generating reasons—must be divided" (Loughlin 2013, 22). Sovereignty "is an expression of [the] autonomously conceived public realm, and it cannot be overcome without jettisoning the entire modern practice of public law" (Loughlin 2013, 21)[2].

The basic issue, then, is whether globalization displaces the political reality of the state as the "institution of institutions". According to Loughlin, evidence as to this empirical question is up to now inconclusive. From his point of view, pluralists actually are concerned with contemporary limitations on power and confuse them with questions of authority (Loughlin 2014b, 12). For example, analyzing Walker's investigation of the implications of contemporary developments for the concept of law, he argues that such an exercise is misconceived for three reasons: empirical developments in law as a regulatory practice do not necessarily resound at the level of the concept[3]; it is not appropriate to convert a series of empirical issues (e.g., whether globalization has displaced the political reality that in the modern world most institutions have derived their existence or mode of operation from the state's action or acquiescence) into conceptual claims; and the basic issue actually is how the social bonds of a collective groups can be maintained[4] (Loughlin 2017, 359).

So, Loughlin argues that the crisis of representation and the issue of how to maintain a common world have not jettisoned sovereignty, which is basically about authority (the right of a government to be obeyed). If I understand him correctly, the issue of whether globalization has displaced the political reality of the state as the "institution of institutions" turns upon determining whether these new regimes are institutions endowed with an autonomous status and have aims of a general nature (rather than performing limited and particular functions) (see Loughlin 2017, 357). But the issue is not merely one of the limitations of power (although for some versions of rights-based constitutionalism this is what is at stake). One may argue that national (i.e., state) capabilities have been deeply transformed (including from the inside) and actually contribute to disassembling the territory/authority/rights assemblage characteristic of the national state (Sassen 2006). In her work on the disassemblage of the national, S. Sassen has demonstrated how some state capabilities are transformed and contribute to build a rather different political order. Such transformations are difficult to capture with a perspective such as Loughlin's because the latter conveys a dualistic perspective opposing statehood to the institutions of globalization. Hence, it cannot help us to understand how states themselves have contributed to establish and legitimate institutions endowed with an autonomous status. As I will explain in Chapter 7, a core issue is the one of the standards we shall use to account for such transformations and to assess them. On the one hand, we need a criterion for delineating what is public that does not automatically (implicitly or explicitly) equate it with statehood. On the other one, we also need to be able to critically assess whether sovereignty as a legal concept is significantly challenged. The latter issue is particularly tricky because of the entanglement of forms of authority, of the blurring of boundaries (private/public, inside/outside), of the transformations in models of authority, and of the formation of new types of territorialities[5].

A Free-Standing Political Domain? C. Thornhill and Rights as the Functionally Dominant Element of the Public-Legal Order

There is another way to argue that there has been no paradigmatical shift: it is to argue that we have misunderstood the actual nature of the relationship between statehood and society's politicality. Thornhill's basic claim is that rights are the functionally dominant element of the public-legal order (they have been right from the start, according to him) and that public law's defining function is preserved in the formation of an autonomous inter- or transnational arena (Thornhill 2013b, 48–9)[6]. I will focus here on three dimensions of his argument: rights as an inner-coding for power; the functional nexus between law and the political that is at the genesis of public law; and the globally autonomous position of the legal system[7].

According to Thornhill, it is the principle of rights-based legitimacy that allowed the emergent political system to presuppose its constituent power as a constant and pre-defined element of its own inner structure, because of the assumption that power drawn from rights-holders was automatically legitimate. The exercise of constituent power always has been dependent upon an inner juridical reference to rights (Thornhill 2012, 385): constituent power is pre-constituted by rights because it is vest in a group of persons as rights holders (Thornhill 2012, 383). The claim that state institutions are authorized through constituent power is "a device for the projective simplification and the extended inclusionary reproduction of society's political function" (Thornhill 2012, 384). This function actually is allowed by the principle of rights-based legitimacy: the abiding functional legacy of classical constitutionalism is the fact that "the political system distilled constituent power internalistically, in rights" (Thornhill 2013b, 594). Rights are an inner-coding for power, and the perennial defining feature of constitutionalism is that rights produce reserves of power for modern society (Thornhill 2012, 376). They are "prerequisites for the abstraction of political power as a positively reproducible societal phenomenon [...]" (Thornhill 2013b, 55)[8]. From Thornhill's perspective, then, "[l]egitimacy was always produced by law itself: it was produced, primarily, by the surrogation of constituent power by rights" (Thornhill 2012, 399).

Therefore, rights should not be understood as checks on power, but rather as "the foundation for the constructive formation of the state as a repository of society's political power: as the center of an autonomous political domain" (Thornhill 2013b, 41)[9]. Constitutions and constitutional rights are

> reflexively internal articulations of law and power that are generated—sociologically—from *within power*, and [...] create an adequately abstracted medium for the societal circulation of power. The structural coupling of law and power in a constitution, thus, might be seen as an element of power's own internal differentiation, displacement and transmission within a certain socio-historical conjuncture, responding to and expressing power's specific resources of societal adaptivity.
>
> (Thornhill 2011, 247)[10]

In other words, rights are the functionally dominant element of the public-legal order. Modern politics has always been coded as rights; this becomes acutely visible in contemporary transnational public law (Thornhill 2013b, 55). The increasing differentiation of the legal system only makes more explicit the function that rights have always been playing in political modernity.

Thornhill argues that there is no necessary relationship between the political system in which legitimacy is produced by law itself (and in which constituent power is surrogated by rights), on the one hand, and statehood, on the other one. There is no original homology between society's politicality and statehood. According to him, "the 'comprehensive structural coupling between politics and law' (allegedly) observable 'in the constitutions of nation-states' is nothing more than a fiction—it semantically duplicates a societal condition which never factually existed" (Thornhill 2011, 245)[11]. The classical idea of the state "cannot be used as a standard against which levels or processes of *constitutional fragmentation* in contemporary society might be reliably identified or measured" (Thornhill 2011, 245)[12]. The formation of the political is tied to the positivization of law, and it is this functional nexus (law/the political) that is at the remote genesis of public law. Public law, basically, has an "original abstractive function [...] in facilitating the iterable transmission of power" (Thornhill 2013b, 47); these functions of inclusion and abstraction performed by public law "are both preserved and intensified" in the formation of an autonomous inter- or transnational arena (Thornhill 2013b, 48).

The internal reference to rights allows for two significant moves. First, it allows law to dispense "with its original reliance on founding structures such as representation of popular will formation" (Thornhill 2013b, 53). As I said earlier, from Thornhill's perspective, constituent power is pre-constituted by rights because it is vested in a group of persons as rights holders (Thornhill 2012, 383). Rights are the decisive source of inclusionary cohesion. Constituent power is a projection through which the political system "could imagine itself as externally authorized while in fact excluding external agents (the people) as originating sources of law" (Thornhill 2013a, 587). The externality of constituent power is a projective fiction that allows the political system to reproduce its power autonomously (internally). But rights are the dominant force in the generation of democratic power[13]. Perceptions of a decline of constituent power in contemporary constitutionalism, hence, "suffers from excessive literalism"—an interpretation that originates in a literalistic misconstruction of classical constitutionalism (Thornhill 2012, 376). Second, the internal reference to rights also allows public law to consolidate a *free-standing* political domain in the transnational society: public law retains its original abstractive function (namely, to facilitate the iterable transmission of power); and it "relies to an increased degree on the quality of rights as institutions internally promoting the inclusionary abstraction of power" (Thornhill 2013b, 43)[14].

The third significant dimension to be stressed is that according to Thornhill, the legal system is increasingly differentiated because of the increasing consolidation of international law. The legal system has acquired a globally autonomous position. There has been a rising importance of international law, especially in the field of international human rights laws. Some selected international human rights norms began to acquire standing as universal *jus cogens*, and international human rights law "gradually began to assume direct effect within national societies" (Thornhill 2016, 414). A transnational constitutional order was placed, in part, above the legal structures of national states, so that "domestic constitutions lost their classical position as defining points in a national hierarchy of public-legal norms, and the position of national constitutional norms was relativized by international legal norms which at the least rivalled their authority" (Thornhill 2016, 415). After 1945,

> the claim that national public law could extract legitimacy from a founding, pre-legal act lost plausibility. [...] [I]n fact, national public law increasingly derived its validity, not from the implied originating act of a national people, but rather from a generalized construction of the persons who were subject to it, which was originally produced and promulgated in international law. At this time, the law began, quite generally, to explain its authority by accounting for itself [...] as applied to persons endowed with certain characteristics and certain entitlements, which

> were constitutionally protected under international law: that is, by claiming that it was essentially proportioned to its addressees as individual rights holders. For this reason, the rise of international human rights law led to a process in which the law internalized the basic constituent power of its own authority.
>
> (Thornhill 2016, 415–6)

The generation of legitimacy for public law became an act performed within the law. This transformation has a twofold consequence as to the role of legal procedures in the production of political legitimacy and the construction of constitutional norms. First, there is a growing differentiation of the legal system as a subsystem of global society (Thornhill 2016, 416). Second, there is a powerful impulse towards self-constitutionalization in the international legal order (Thornhill 2016, 416). Rights supplant constituent power because they act as the final point of normative regress. Constituent power must be understood as an inner-juridical function: it is exercised inner-legally "as the secondary enactment of a normative context that has already been enacted" (Thornhill 2016, 441). Constituent power has been absorbed into rights, and hence, "should be erased from the contemporary political imagination" (Thornhill 2016, 426). The site of global democracy is transferred from politics to law. The co-originality of rights and democracy is preserved, though, because as constituent power becomes normatively independent of "the people", "secondary powers of constitutional norm formation can be accorded to many persons" (Thornhill 2016, 427)[15]. An alternative process of systemic inclusion is occurring through the integration of citizens as judicially constructed holders of rights (Thornhill 2018, 115). Constituent power is now only explicable "as part of an emergent, global constitution in which analogues to classical modes of political agency cannot simply be presupposed" (Thornhill 2016, 413).

Therefore, both Loughlin and Thornhill challenge the idea of a paradigmatical shift related to public authority. They both do so on the ground of arguments related to public law. From Loughlin's point of view, there is no paradigmatical shift because the juridical concept of sovereignty as ultimate authority (*Kompetenz-kompetenz*) (which is basic to public law) has not (yet) been jettisoned. From Thornhill's, there is no paradigmatical shift because public law preserves its defining function (the one of reflexively demarcating an autonomous political domain in society); classical readings of constitutionalism actually have misunderstood the actual nature of the relationship between statehood and society's politicality.

My aim here is not to propose a thorough comparison of Loughlin's and Thornhill's work. I merely wish to emphasize contradistinctions that are significant for the purposes of this chapter (that focuses on the issue of the possible impact of the shift in regulatory activity on sovereignty as core to statehood), as well as for the dimensions that account for the normative resonance of constituent power (dimensions that are themselves dependent upon statehood). From this point of view, I am particularly interested in the issues of the political domain itself and of constituent power. One will already have understood that the state plays a very different part in Loughlin's and Thornhill's arguments, even if Thornhill agrees with Loughlin that public law has preserved its defining function. In Loughlin's work, public law, sovereign statehood, and constitutionalism are closely related—actually, they depend upon each other. Public law relates to the justification, in legal terms, of the very constitution of public authority; it is "the jural coding of an autonomously conceived political domain" (Loughlin 2013, 13)[16]. It depends upon sovereignty as an expression of the autonomously conceived public realm. Therefore, the concept of the state is (in a sense) prior to it. Modern constitutionalism is part of the state-building project. As Mac Amhlaigh, Michelon, and Walker explain, from such a perspective,

> those who claim to see in the contemporary departure of governmental authority to private and supra-state sites either the demise or the rebirth of public law fail to appreciate the resilience or the significance of its deeper foundations. Some reduce public law to its positive state-centred manifestations, and so see only destabilization and loss, while others engage in an unanchored normativism which hypothesizes a new post-national legal world without attending to the need for a corresponding reimagining and re-embedding of the political domain similar to that which brought forth the juridical model of the modern state.
>
> (Mac Amhlaigh, Michelon, and Walker 2013, 3–4)

The state grounds an epistemic framing of publicness that is fundamental "in bequeathing legitimacy to the positive forms of constitutional law and public law more generally" (Walker 2012, 68)[17].

Thornhill rather focuses on rights' function as an inner-coding for power that sustains a free-standing political domain. As I said, from his point of view the coupling between law and politics in the constitutions of nation-states actually is a fiction. The basic process is the positivization of law; the political is tied to the latter. A correct understanding of public law focuses on the latter "as a system of inclusion which abstracts a strict political arena in society, enabling the political system to adapt through the use of rights to varying and often deeply contingent demands for differentiated political inclusivity in modern societies" (Thornhill 2013b, 47)[18]. Approaches that argue that there is a decline in the status of public law fail on three grounds, according to him: they adopt "a static and rather sociologically under-reflected definition of public law" (Thornhill 2013b, 46); they fail "to reflect on the emergence of the political as an adaptative sociological process" and "tend to retain a highly agency-centred or even anthropological account of political formation" (Thornhill 2013b, 46); and they do not show enough sensitivity "to the formative and inclusionary role of rights qua political code" (Thornhill 2013b, 47). The perennial defining feature of constitutionalism is that rights produce reserves of power for modern society (Thornhill 2012, 376); rights "consolidate the primary function of public law in tracing and preserving a distinct political arena in society" (Thornhill 2013b, 55).

Therefore, there also are significant differences between the two approaches (Loughlin's and Thornhill's) as to constituent power. Thornhill argues that law can dispense with constituent power, and that the internal reference to rights allows public law to consolidate a free-standing political domain in the transnational society. The site of global democracy is transferred from politics to law. Constitutions are functional preconditions for the positive abstraction of political power (Přibáň 2012, 461). Let me stress that contrary to Krisch, I do not understand Thornhill's approach as trying to recast the notion of constituent power by adapting it "to the realm of the feasible" in the new transnational reality (Krisch 2016, 671). Thornhill actually reinterprets the notion of constituent power from a functionalist perspective, subjecting it to the function of rights; this move does not apply only to the transnational domain, but also to the development of states. Hence, it is less an attempt at adapting the concept to the realm of the feasible than a reinterpretation of what it actually has meant.

In Loughlin's work, legal authority is generated by the symbolic act through which a multitude recognize themselves as forming a unity; constituent power (the unified will that is founded in the political existence of the state) expresses the generative aspect of the political power relationship (Loughlin 2014a, 218, 231)[19]. The norms of right conduct prescribed by constitutions acquire the status of fundamental law because they have been authorized by a people, not by some self-evident rationality of their claims. Constitutionalism is not a free-standing set of norms (Loughlin 2010, 610). It is constituent power that mediates the tension between democracy and law, because the constitution's validity derives from the unified will of the people (a will that depends upon the political existence of the state). Constituent power, though, is not the actual power of a multitude. It converts the latter in a form of political agency by reconstituting the people in a particular way (Loughlin 2014a; Loughlin and Walker 2007, 3). It is this symbolic act that creates political power.

As I have already explained, one issue with Loughlin's analysis is that as it makes collective political agency dependent upon the state, it can hardly propose a frame for thinking constituent power beyond the state. And as he equates state power with autonomous public power, he underestimates the significance of the current transformations in public authority. His approach makes it difficult to properly assess the actual nature and impact of these transformations. There are significant problems as well with Thornhill's approach. I wish to stress three of them that are important as to the purposes of this book. First, one could argue that the argument about constituent power being surrogated by rights actually builds upon a certain reading of the experience of the EU, and that it is then applied *a posteriori* to state-building. But the experience of the EU is very peculiar; the EU is a *sui generis* case, and its specific conditions can hardly be generalized or translated to other transnational regimes. Moreover, one may wonder whether Thornhill's analysis is not actually an attempt to read the causes of a social phenomenon out of its consequences; if it is the case, then it is risky, for one may be misled to mistake the latter for the former. The second problem relates with the function of rights. As I have explained, from his perspective the formation of an independent political domain is "to a large degree the outcome of the distillation of law as a medium of exchange and temporal and geographical inclusion" (Thornhill 2013b, 28). As he also acknowledges at some point, though, the original formative dimensions of public law "only became enduringly structured as a result of their coupling with laws of state providing for relatively uniform and internally defined rights" (Thornhill 2013b, 40). However, this dimension is much more important than what he allows for. Authority basically depends upon a seizure of power—some pre-constitutional polity formation. As Loughlin rightly stresses, constitutions and rights are created within a political world; this is why they relate people to power-holders along specific principles. It is public politics that has been constitutionalized and democratized from the 17th century on, in Western states; this has not significantly transformed the very notion of the sovereign rights of the state. A perspective such as Thornhill cannot account for this basic fact of the political. Therefore, neither can it explain how subjects and objects of law are to relate in the transnational domain, because in order to do so, he would have to ground his argument on an analysis of the patterns of authority specific to the latter domain.

Third, surrogating constituent power opens the issue of the symbolic pole of collective political agency and democratic authorization. This dimension is absent from Thornhill's functionalist perspective. I discuss this issue in Chapter 4.

An Impact on the Normative Resonance of the Concept of Constituent Power?

As they negate that there has been any paradigmatical shift, the two approaches discussed up to now in this chapter make it difficult to assess the impact of the shift in regulatory activity on the dimensions that account for the normative resonance of the concept of constituent power. Hence, they also make it more difficult to analyze the prospects for constituent power beyond the state. Let me recall that these three dimensions (foundation, democratic agency, and the holistic nature of the ambition of constituent power) are closely related and that they depend upon the political as the representation of an autonomous domain. Foundational constitutionalism is "a structure by which a polity can make a comprehensive claim to agency" (Krisch 2010, 252), and it embodies the ambition to construct a comprehensive political order[20]. This structure of public power endowed with a comprehensive reach is embodied by the state. Let me explain briefly how the shift in regulatory activity impacts upon the three dimensions that account for the normative resonance of the concept of constituent power.

The Issue of Foundation

As I explained in Chapter 1, the foundational model has been a core feature of constitutionalism from the 18th century on. It embodies the claim to ground the entire system of government; it was made possible by the comprehensive ambition of the absolutist state (Krisch 2011). Foundational constitutionalism rests upon a structure of public power (which reach is comprehensive) as well as upon an uncontested collective. The part played by the foundational tradition in modern constitutionalism is so important that "if we want to tap into constitutionalism's legitimate potential for the postnational sphere we need to connect with the foundational tradition [...]" (Krisch 2011, 53)[21]. Foundational constitutionalism is an appealing vision because "it is a structure by which a polity can make a comprehensive claim to agency and wrestle its affairs back from the forces of chance, history, and power. And it is a structure in which central pillars of modern political thought—the rule of law, individual rights, and collective self-government—are brought together" (Krisch 2010, 252)[22]. The tendency to refer to foundational constitutionalism "is visible in the many approaches that seek to give the current, largely unstructured, historically accidental, and power-driven order of global governance a rational, justifiable shape in which the powers of institutions and their relationships with one another are clearly delimited" (Krisch 2010, 253). However, this amounts to a holistic ambition "to construct a comprehensive, justified political order", and it raises serious problems, many of which would require "a transformation of the societal basis on which the global order rests" (Krisch 2010, 253). In other words, "foundational constitutionalism would pose high, perhaps radical demands, on the existing structures and institutions of postnational governance, and would go further than most proposals of postnational constitutionalism today" (Krisch 2010, 253).

The greatest challenge to the globalization of constitutionalism is the divided character of the global polity (Krisch 2011, 59). In the postnational sphere, there is no structure of public power with a comprehensive reach.

Reordering the polycentric setting of global governance "so as to redeem foundational aspirations may not involve a world state with a centralized government, but it would, at the very least, require rules to define the relationships between the different forms of existing public power, and it would have to extend to other forms of power public institutions are unable to tame at present" (Krisch 2011, 54–5). But there is also a challenge related to the absence of an uncontested collective: the unified set of rules characteristic of foundational constitutionalism "has to explicate the conditions under which public power can be regarded as an exercise of public and private autonomy. One of the main challenges behind this task if to clarify what self-government through a constitution could mean in a space such as the postnational in which there is no uncontested collective that could express its will in constitutional terms" (Krisch 2011, 55). The gap with reality may be too big to be bridged. Krisch concludes that

> [m]ost approaches to postnational constitutionalism are too thin to redeem the full promise of the domestic constitutionalist tradition and therefore cannot provide the continuity they seek. They emphasize processes of legalization and limitation of postnational governance but thereby hark back to a particular tradition of power-limiting constitutionalism which in the domestic context has been marginalized by the more demanding and comprehensive strand of foundational constitutionalism. Yet realizing the latter vision in the postnational sphere would [...] require massive social and institutional change.
>
> (Krisch 2011, 67)[23]

Therefore, the assumption that the postnational ought to be structured in a way that continues on the constitutionalist path is misguided (Krisch 2011, 67). Moreover, as Krisch stresses, there is another problem as well with foundational constitutionalism: it is even doubtful it is a fitting vision for diverse societies (Krisch 2011, 67). Hence, even if we were to conclude that foundational constitutionalism is workable for polities that do not have a comprehensive ambition akin to the one of the (absolutist) state, the argument that it is inimical to diversity would still have to be addressed[24].

As I will explain in the following chapters, the foundational issue is significant in how some scholars (e.g., N. Walker) tackle the issue of post-state constituent power. But for others (e.g., N. Krisch and K. Möller), the challenges raised by the transnational sphere as to democratic agency require that we focus on contestation rather than on foundation. Yet, the latter move also is problematic, for a focus on contestation actually challenges the authorship dimension of democratic agency—and hence, the extent to which such agency can be framed as grounding the political order[25].

The Issue of Democratic Agency

Constituent power is a symbolic, *a posteriori* reconstruction of a people as the source of a constitution. Although it is usually exercised only in exceptional circumstances, it is at once conceptual, practical, and normative, since it endows the people with the capacity to challenge a constitutional order and to contribute to its reconstruction. As it is closely related to a comprehensive and holistic ambition, constituent power as symbolizing democratic agency is significantly challenged by the fragmented and polycentric structure of contemporary global governance as well as by the assumed absence of an uncontested collective. But democratic agency nonetheless is a very powerful and significant piece of Western political modernity. It is core to the conditions of self-rule embodied in the idea of constituent power. People are conceived of as autonomous agents, and peoples are seen as the appropriate entities of self-government. Translating such a vision to other contexts—ones in which there is no uncontested collectives and a combination of territorial and non-territorial regimes—may be very difficult, if not impossible. Yet, as I will explain latter on, renouncing agency basically means forfeiting our capacity to challenge governing relationships and to (re)build institutions.

Thinking about constituent power beyond the state also raises an issue pertaining to a broader debate within social science, the one of agency and structure. I of course cannot propose a thorough analysis of it here. But I nonetheless have to touch upon it briefly, because some of the approaches discussed in this book build on sociological functionalism. These approaches focus on the functions of specific elements of social structures. Thornhill for example aims at explaining the primary elements of classical constitutional theory and practice "from a position that is functionally internal to the systemic structure of modern society" (Thornhill 2014, 358). He tackles norms such as constituent power and subjective rights

> as *internal adaptative self-constructions* of society's different systems—especially the legal/political system. These norms [...] evolved [...] as formulae *within* the legal and political exchanges of society. As such, they originally enabled the political system to adapt to, and to abstract itself in relation to, changing societal structures, and autonomously to perform its functions (that is, to produce political power, and to distribute power through acts of legislation) in the context of increasingly differentiated societies.
>
> (Thornhill 2014, 358)

These norms are, hence, reflexively attached to changing systemic functions in society. From this point of view, the emergent global constitutional order can be interpreted "as part of deeper patterns of societal adaptation, in the context of embedded processes of systemic formation" (Thornhill 2014, 359)[26]. Thornhill's perspective is interested in the social construction of power, but it tackles it through the functions played by different elements of a system rather than, e.g., as resulting from mechanisms and processes through which agents interact[27]. Although Thornhill acknowledges that constitutional normativity reflects continuous social processes (Thornhill 2014, 357), his approach nonetheless is vulnerable to the more general critique of systemic accounts[28]. Such accounts may still incorporate a "thin" version of agency as being core to constituent power; in other words, one may build on such a framework and yet acknowledges that constituent power embodies a view of agency peculiar to the functionally differentiated modern society. But then, as we have seen, constituent power actually is surrogated by rights. Moreover, there is no thorough analysis of the significant issue of actors' constitution, nor on how interactions are constitutive of social meanings. Teubner, for one, negates the necessity of a collective actor and effective formal organization in establishing a collective identity. He acknowledges that constitutionalization requires a constitutional subject; but it is far from clear who or what this subject is, or how its agency is to be articulated and unfolded. Hence, approaches such as Thornhill's and Teubner's are quite different from those that understand the current order as a post-constituent one and that retreat back on destituent power or contestation because foundational constitutionalism is not appropriate for the current context. The latter approaches argue that in such a context, we also have to renounce constituent power and a comprehensive claim to regulate both public and private autonomy[29]. The former approaches, up to a point, renounce agency as such.

The Issue of the Holistic Nature of the Ambition of Constituent Power

As I explained in Chapter 1, the concept of constituent power also is related to a holistic ambition, the one of the public sphere as offering an authoritative expression of the world and as being autonomous. This assumption is dependent upon statehood, because the latter allowed to ascribe constituent power to an "uncontested" collective. The postnational order challenges the holistic ambition of constituent power because it stages a "multiplication of publics" (Krisch 2016). This multiplication of publics makes it difficult—if possible or desirable at all—to conceive of a comprehensive political order[30]. As I will explain in Chapter 7, new mappings of public authority challenge the sovereign state as embodying the autonomy of the political (namely, sovereignty as the expression of a public realm conceived as autonomous). Constituent power expressed the idea of a comprehensive founding through self-government as a way of expressing public autonomy; it presupposes the state as the political unity of a people. These requirements are met only in some subdomains of the postnational order. On the one hand, state and non-state forms of public power combine in mixed polities; there are transformations in models of authority. On the other one, "emergent territorialities" (Sassen 2006) make it difficult to account for (fluctuating) constituencies. But for sure, in mixed polities, the latter cannot claim to be holistic nor comprehensive—at least not in the sense that was assumed when public power was framed by statehood.

Conclusion

To some scholars, the current context elicits some sense of a loss because the growing incongruency between public power and state power endangers democratic self-determination by a collective agent. To others, the notion of constituent power can nonetheless be rescued and recast, so as to continue to embody democratic self-rule. However, not just anything can count as constituent power. Up to now, I have tried to clarify the most significant dimensions of the notion, and their close relationship with statehood. This is a major issue when trying to specify the conditions of democratic agency in a different context, one in which the sovereign state as embodying the autonomy of the political is significantly challenged. The shift in regulatory activity is substantial enough to challenge state sovereignty; and hence, it also raises the issue of constituent power in mixed polities. This issue can be stated in the following way: how can collective political agency as an expression of public autonomy take shape in a significantly different context, one in which the modern hope of comprehensively and purposively ordering a delimited polity seems to have to be given up?

Let me stress that there is no reason (at least *a priori*) to think that agency as such must be forsaken. Challenging a specific conception of agency does not mean renouncing agency itself. I take the idea that we (as agents, as citizens or would-be citizens, and as ruled) can make and remake institutions framing what is public to be core to democratic authorization. I agree with Walker that the latter does not become redundant because typically presupposed institutional representations are not available anymore, or because they have become inadequate. However, as I have stressed in the Introduction, we should not start with a blueprint of democracy and try to translate it into the postnational domain, for this often leads to either overoptimistic, overpessimistic, or unworkable conclusions. Amongst other things, it often involves replicating (implicitly or explicitly) features characteristic of statehood that do not account for the specific conditions of the current context. Such a replication actually jeopardizes democratic authorization. The basic issue is the one of public politics in polycentric settings of governance, and of its democratization.

Notes

1 "Contemporary governing networks are complex, but that does not mean that public law has lost its symbolic power—nor that the modern discourse of law is a façade masking the realities of power networks" (Loughlin 2013, 22). Public law is concerned with the establishment and regulation of governing authority. Let me stress that at times Loughlin acknowledges that the political crisis may have an impact on public law because the latter actually is the medium through which a common world is maintained.

2 From the perspective of public law,

> law should not be conceived as a bridle on an otherwise unrestrained exercise of power; law (as droit politique) is itself a power-generating phenomenon. Like freedom, power is generated by the operation of droit politique. Political power is a special type of power created by the drawing together of 'the people' in an institutional frame. This type of symbolic power is founded on the 'consent' of the people, is rooted in trust, and is generated through the imposition of controls and checks on those who hold positions of authority.
>
> (Loughlin 2013, 21)

3 Law's identity as an institution persists "even as its membership and normative structures change through time" (Loughlin 2017, 357).

4 This is the issue of creating and sustaining "a common world" (Loughlin 2017, 359); it is a problem of political imagination.

5 For example, Sassen stresses that one should be careful not to draw a simplistic opposition between the territorial and the functional. See Chapter 7.

6 Thornhill's approach is "informed by Luhmann's theory of functional differentiation and his description of constitutions as the overarching form of European political modernity resulting from a pluralist functional structure of modern society" (Přibáň 2012, 459). Constitutions are functional preconditions for the positive abstraction of political power. Teubner's *Constitutional Fragments* and Thornhill's *A Sociology of Constitutions* share the sociological functionalist perspective. They both "highlight the necessity of decoupling normative political and legal theory from the sociology of law and politics, and the need to embrace the sociological perspective in order to comprehend the complexity of current constitutional, political, and legal problems at national and transnational global levels" (Přibáň 2012, 465).

7 See also Krisch (2016) and Möller (2018).

8 They allow power "to account for itself as authorized by a public constituent power which it internalizes within itself, and from which it projects its normative authority and performs acts of stable inclusion [...]" (Thornhill 2013b, 55).

9 He disagrees with the liberal conception of rights "as elements of the political system countervailing the abstraction of the political domain, or withdrawing certain societal practices from the authority of public law" (Thornhill 2013b, 46). Rights rather are institutions that internally promote the inclusionary abstraction of power; they "direct and extend new structures of public law and reconfigure societally articulated processes of political inclusion" (Thornhill 2013b, 47).

10 The coding of power in relation to rights was "the most essential moment in the construction of power *as specifically and irreductibly political*" (Thornhill 2013b, 41). It raises the iterability and inclusionary force of political power; it endows society with capacities for pre-emptive adaption to future demands for comprehensive political inclusion; and it "produces political power as a highly abstracted and differentiated societal commodity, whose social universality is limited to collectively resonant but also quite circumscribed and deeply contingent processes of inclusion [...] The public-legal coding of power through rights is the code of modern political power" (Thornhill 2013b, 41). See also Přibáň (2012).

11 Hence, it is not surprising that it has no counterpart at the level of world society.
12 Let me stress here the difference between Thornhill's and Teubner's interpretation of rights. According to the former, rights create an abstracted medium for the circulation of power; according to the latter, rights limit power. Thornhill argues that Teubner's view is a semantically over-literal and historically simplified view of statehood and does not attempt to conceptually disarticulate power from the state.
13 From this perspective, constituent power "is primarily a resource for augmenting the power of the system through enhanced legitimation" (Krisch 2016, 672).
14 The growth of public law forms beyond the state is "a way in which an ever more versatile menu of rights become vital to—even constitutive to—the practice of selectively inclusive forms of transnational politics" (Mac Amhlaigh, Michelon, and Walker 2013, 4).
15 Let me stress that Thornhill also argues that global constitutional law as a normative apparatus does not originate outside the power of national states; actually, most states "came fully to operate as states—that is, as systems of *categorically public legal inclusion*—by virtue of the fact that they integrated international law into their domestic legal order in order to palliate problems that had historically impeded their effective public abstraction and differentiation" (Thornhill 2018, 107).
16 See Chapter 2, note 43.
17 See Chapter 2, note 49.
18 The first constructions of public law were articulated responses to the structural requirement for consolidating the political as a distinct functional realm (Thornhill 2013b). Early public law evolved as an instrument for cementing and giving order to juridical power, representation, and rights; in other words, public law is the theoretical corpus that facilitated the first inclusionary abstraction of political power.
19 Constituent power has to do with the question of how legal authority is generated within the political domain (Loughlin 2014a, 224).
20 Such an order builds upon a specific structure of justification.
21 Walker, for example, precisely argues for the applicability to post-state entities of a version of constitutionalism bearing a family resemblance to state-based foundational constitutionalism. See Chapter 4.
22 "Constituent power is inextricably linked to the foundational dimension of constitution-making: a political community conceives itself as supreme power (or is retrospectively constructed in that vein) and establishes a mode of collective self-government in the medium of a higher-ranking legal order" (Möller 2018, 33).
23 I would argue, though, that even when conceived in the more limited sense of a check on political rule, constitutionalism as a theory of government developed (from the 16th century on) through attempts to frame the relationships between rulers and their subjects as holders of rights within consolidating states. Let us think for example of the first secular constitutional theory, namely, the one elaborated by the Huguenots in their struggle with the French monarchy (see, e.g., Skinner 1978; Nootens 2013).
24 See the examples discussed in the Introduction, as well as Tully (1995). The assumption of an uncontested collective (embodied by the state) is key to modern constitutionalism, but it does not withstand scrutiny. Let us think for example of First Nations and minority nations.
25 See Chapter 5.
26 Let me recall that Thornhill's functionalist method is based to some degree on Luhmann's systems theory. According to Thornhill, this standpoint allows "to renounce the construction of constitutional norms as simply materialized principles" and "to penetrate the reflexive adaptive meanings contained beneath the literal surface of constitutional concepts" (Thornhill 2014, 359). This allows for a broad sociological analysis "of the correlation between constitutional norms, changes in societal structure, and evolving social demands for political power and law" (Thornhill 2014, 359). However, contrary to Luhmann, Thornhill claims to observe the legal and political systems of

modern society "as essentially homologous", and to observe the legal norms "as real norms" rather than "hyper-fictitious projections of inner-systemic communications" (Thornhill 2014, 358–9).

27 For example, in early modern Europe, the dependency of rulers on military entrepreneurs and capital-holders had the effect of empowering a logic of balancing. The early timing of trade expansion and a relative preservation of medieval "constitutionalism" weakened the logic of domination. In ancient China, in contradistinction, nascent constitutional rights were ultimately rolled back because there, coercion-wielding rulers pursued self-strengthening reforms that tip the balancing logic to their advantage (Hui 2001). Framing the analysis in such a way embodies a relational perspective that emphasizes social relationships and specific processes/mechanisms rather than the systemic function of peculiar elements of societal structures.

28 See, e.g., Tilly (2008).

29 Walker's approach does not face this issue because he argues for translating a version of constitutionalism that bears a "family-resemblance" to state-based foundational constitutionalism (although with a second-order constituent power). See Chapter 4.

30 "[T]he holistic concomitants of constituent power [...] may be a dubious starting point for a revival on the transnational level. At first sight, it could seem more promising to address the normative challenges of the transnational sphere through rights-based accounts or simply the role of law which are more apt to be fully internalised in a coherent legal system without appealing to *the* nation or *the* people" (Möller 2018, 33).

References

Anderson, Gavin W. 2005. *Constitutional Rights After Globalization*. Oxford and Portland: Hart Publishing.

Grimm, Dieter. 2010. "The Achievement of Constitutionalism and Its Prospects in a Changed World." In *The Twilight of Constitutionalism?* edited by Petra Dobner and Martin Loughlin, 3–22. Oxford: Oxford University Press.

Hui, Victoria Tin-Bor. 2001. "The Emergence and Demise of Nascent Constitutional Rights: Comparing Ancient China and Early Modern Europe." *Journal of Political Philosophy* 9, no. 4: 373–403.

Krisch, Nico. 2010. "Global Administrative Law and the Constitutional Ambition." In *The Twilight of Constitutionalism?* edited by Petra Dobner and Martin Loughlin, 245–266. Oxford: Oxford University Press.

Krisch, Nico. 2011. *Beyond Constitutionalism. The Pluralist Structure of Postnational Law*. Oxford: Oxford University Press.

Krisch, Nico. 2016. "*Pouvoir Constituant* and *Pouvoir Irritant* in the Postnational Order." *International Journal of Constitutional Law* 14, no. 3: 657–679.

Loughlin, Martin. 2010. "What Is Constitutionalization?" In *The Twilight of Constitutionalism?* edited by Petra Dobner and Martin Loughlin, 47–69. Oxford: Oxford University Press.

Loughlin, Martin. 2013. "The Nature of Public Law." In *After Public Law*, edited by Cormac Mc Amhlaigh, Claudio Michelon, and Neil Walker, 11–24. Oxford: Oxford University Press.

Loughlin, Martin. 2014a. "The Concept of Constituent Power." *European Journal of Political Theory* 13, no. 2: 218–237.

Loughlin, Martin. 2014b. "Constitutional Pluralism: An Oxymoron?" *Global Constitutionalism* 3, no. 1: 9–30.

Loughlin, Martin. 2017. "The Misconceived Search for Global Law." *Transnational Legal Theory* 8, no. 3: 353–359.

Loughlin, Martin and Walker, Neil. 2007. "Introduction." In *The Paradox of Constitutionalism. Constituent Power and Constitutional Form*, edited by Martin Loughlin and Neil Walker, 1–8. Oxford: Oxford University Press.

Mac Amhlaigh, Cormac, Michelon, Claudio, and Walker, Neil. 2013. "Introduction." In *After Public Law*, edited by Cormac Mac Amhlaigh, Claudio Michelon, and Neil Walker, 1–7. Oxford: Oxford University Press.

Möller, Kolja. 2018. "From Constituent to Destituent Power Beyond the State." *Transnational Legal Theory* 9, no. 1: 32–55.

Nootens, Geneviève. 2013. *Popular Sovereignty in the West. Polities, Contention, and Ideas*. London: Routledge.

Přibáň, Jiří. 2012. "Constitutionalism as Fear of the Political? A Comparative Analysis of Teubner's *Constitutional Fragments* and Thornhill's *A Sociology of Constitutions*." *Journal of Law and Society* 39, no. 3: 441–471.

Sassen, Saskia. 2006. *Territory, Authority, Rights. From Medieval to Global Assemblages*. Princeton and Oxford: Princeton University Press.

Skinner, Quentin. 1978. *The Foundations of Modern Political Thought*, vol. I and II. Cambridge: Cambridge University Press.

Teubner, Gunther. 2012. *Constitutional Fragments: Societal Constitutionalism and Globalization*. Oxford: Oxford University Press.

Thornhill, Chris. 2011. "Constitutional Law From the Perspective of Power: A Response to Gunther Teubner." *Social and Legal Studies* 20, no. 2: 244–247.

Thornhill, Chris. 2012. "Contemporary Constitutionalism and the Dialectic of Constituent Power." *Global Constitutionalism* 1, no. 3: 369–404.

Thornhill, Chris. 2013a. "A Sociology of Constituent Power." *Indiana Journal of Global Legal Studies* 20, no. 2: 551–603.

Thornhill, Chris. 2013b. "Public Law and the Emergence of the Political." In *After Public Law*, edited by Cormac MacAmhlaigh, Claudio Michelon, and Neil Walker, 25–55. Oxford: Oxford University Press.

Thornhill, Chris. 2014. "Rights and Constituent Power in the Global Constitution." *International Journal of Law in Context* 10, no. 3: 357–396.

Thornhill, Chris. 2016. "The Global Legal System and the Procedural Construction of Constituent Power." *Global Constitutionalism* 5, no. 3: 405–442.

Thornhill, Chris. 2018. "The Sociological Origins of Global Constitutional Law." In *Sociology of Constitutions. A Paradoxical Perspective*, edited by Alberto Febbrajo and Giancarlo Corsi, 99–124. London and New York: Routledge.

Tilly, Charles. 2008. *Explaining Social Processes*. Boulder and London: Paradigm Publishers.

Tully, James. 1995. *Strange Multiplicity: Constitutionalism in an Age of Diversity*. Cambridge: Cambridge University Press.

Walker, Neil. 2010. "Beyond the Holistic Constitution?" In *The Twilight of Constitutionalism?* edited by Petra Dobner and Martin Loughlin, 291–308. Oxford: Oxford University Press.

Walker, Neil. 2012. "Postnational Constitutionalism and Postnational Public Law: A Tale of Two Neologisms." *Transnational Legal Theory* 3, no. 1: 61–85.

4

TRANSLATING CONSTITUENT POWER ON A SUPRANATIONAL OR GLOBAL SCALE

The modern notion of constituent power relates to a specific way of conceiving of legitimation and democratic authorization. It embodies the idea of authorization by a people. It implies both that citizens are self-authorizing sources of valid claims and that the addressees are represented as a group (they are not a mere "multitude"). It refers to "the standing of democracy as a meta-value of modern politics" (Walker 2007, 256). In other words, constituent power is a specific way of expressing public autonomy. The interest in the role of constituent power in the transnational (global) domain is driven by discomfort with the democratic deficits and technocratic bias of transnational constitutionalism (Möller 2018, 33). There is both a tendency to a procedural usurpation of constituent power by already constituted power (courts, executives) and a constitutionalization of hegemonic projects on substantive grounds (most importantly, institutions and regulations of the transnational economy that are biased towards free trade and a liberal notion of private property) (Möller 2018, 34)[1]. In such a context, evocating a foundational power could reinsert "the necessary irritation of hegemonic projects" (Möller 2018, 34). If shifts in regulatory activity significantly transform public power but there is no way to trace the latter back to some collective political agency expressing public autonomy, then there is (at least from the point of view of democratic theory) some sense of a loss[2].

As I have explained, constituent power as a way of expressing public autonomy depends upon state sovereignty as embodying the autonomy of the political. Therefore, a major issue when balancing the democratic ideal conveyed by the modern notion of constituent power with the circumstances of the global polity is how much of it can and should be retained or translated. Constituent power is not a trivial issue that can merely be set aside: to raise

DOI: 10.4324/9781003221722-5

the issue of constituent power is to raise the issue of political authority, of its narrative(s) and conceptual framework, of public autonomy, and of collective political agency; it is to try to retrieve a symbolic pole to which the generation of political power can be attributed in a manner consistent with democratic authorization.

Chapters 4–6 are devoted to discussing approaches that tackle this issue. These approaches do so in different ways and by starting from different analyses of both modern constitutionalism and the impact of the current shift in regulatory activity. As I explained in the Introduction, I am going to focus on three broad types of perspectives on the issue of constituent power as a way of expressing public autonomy in the current setting: approaches for which constituent power can be, or needs to be, contextualized or translated in the postnational domain, and for which such a contextualization/translation does not present seemingly insurmountable analytical or normative challenges (Chapter 4); approaches that challenge the very possibility of collective authorship in a post-state context and rather propose either to fall back on reinforcing domestic constitutionalism or on the notion of destituent power (or *pouvoir irritant*) (Chapter 5); and finally, approaches that focus on narratives of protest in order to relate the latter to some sense of political agency very akin to constituent power[3] (Chapter 6).

The current chapter focuses on approaches for which the translation of the notion of constituent power into the postnational domain does not present seemingly insurmountable challenges. I hope to show that although they try to retrieve some sense of collective political agency that would abide by the ideals of modernity in complex settings, they nonetheless either stand by the basics of state constitutionalism or fail to propose a narrative of collective political agency. In the first case, it is doubtful they can actually contribute to recast constituent power in the polycentric setting of contemporary mixed polities. In the second case, the problem rather is that if we are to rescue, somehow, the idea of public autonomy and democratic authorization, then we need an alternative narrative of collective political agency.

Three such claims will be discussed here: Walker's claim that a postnational constituent power is possible through a documentary settlement presented as a self-standing political pact; Preuss's claim that sovereignty is a "pliable" resource and that constitutions also apply to political formations that do not incorporate territorially defined multitudes; and Teubner's claim that constitutionalism is a social process that is not specific to politics and that the constitutional question can be projected onto the world society. I hope to show that although they try to retrieve a sense of how constituencies can self-organize in complex settings, they either fail to reconceptualize a notion of collective political agency correlative to the transformation of public authority, or claim to retrieve some notion of constituent power but based on a depolitization of constitutions and a mitigation of the prospects for agency. The first two approaches (Walker's and Preuss's) still uphold the basics of state constitutionalism; the third (Teubner's) claims to recast constituent power but does so by depoliticizing constitutions and downplaying the significance of democratic collective agency (basically falling back on dissent, actually), hence raising significant challenges for democratic authorization.

A Self-Standing Political Pact: N. Walker's Post-State Foundational Constitutionalism

Walker argues for the applicability to post-state entities of a version of constitutionalism bearing a family resemblance with state-based foundational constitutionalism. According to him, "it is possible, through a documentary constitutional settlement presented as a self-standing political pact, to homologate or nurture a sense of a meta-democratically validated transnational political community with a wide-ranging political agenda and a distinct sense of the public good" (Walker 2013, 258; see also Walker 2012, 78). This possibility turns upon the meta-political function of constitutionalism[4]. Postnational constitutionalism actually starts "from the premise that it is both desirable and possible to adapt a historically state-concentrated discourse of legal authority to the increasingly dense post-state regulatory environment" (Walker 2012, 63)[5].

Walker acknowledges that the argument for a postnational constituent power remains vulnerable to a number of failures and charges, amongst which a failure of initiative (as in the EU case), a failure to reinforce the socio-political contours of the presupposed political community, and the charge that a popularly endorsed constitutional initiative is inappropriate to most contexts of transnational regulation. But he nonetheless claims that "extant notions of constitutionalism and public law remain vital, and so must be treated as at least minimally pliant resources in the short-term in the unavoidable matter of reflecting upon and responding incrementally to discrete shifts in our juris-generative circumstances" (Walker 2013, 262).

As I said, he argues that postnational constituent power is possible through a documentary constitutional settlement presented as a self-standing political pact. This is consistent with foundational constitutionalism and with the fact that in the modern political apparatus, constituent power is attributed *a posteriori* to a people as a symbolic pole. He also acknowledges, though, that the issue of the authoritative source and extent of a constitution must be addressed differently in the supranational context. It is important to stress that most of Walker's argument about postnational constituent power is developed in his discussion of EU's constitutionalization. But as he allows for the constitutionalization of different types of regimes in the postnational domain, one can assume that the discussion of postnational constituent power is not intended to be limited to the European context, even if the latter is a *sui generis* case. In the case of the EU, the "double sovereign" of European citizens and of the already constituted peoples of the member states cannot feed into a single constituent power. A new kind of constitutional dualism is needed, based on an explicit recognition that the constitution of Europe and its constituent authority "is only concerned with transnational institutions and competences" (Walker 2016, 352)[6]. We need to refocus on the idea of constituent power under the self-authorizing frame[7]. Such a move allows to find something in the constitutional idea that would stand "both as a critical diagnosis and as a means of transcendence of the present predicament" (Walker 2009, 170). The idea of constituent power under the self-authorizing frame connects with the idea of democratic iteration—namely, "the sense in which democracy as a principle cannot be exhausted and limited to its present, and typically presupposed, institutional representations" (Walker 2009, 170). The democratic principle remains relevant even if its present institutional forms are inadequate; actually, it "becomes all the more relevant just because these institutional forms are no longer adequate" (Walker 2009, 171).

Core to Walker's argument as to the EU is the ascertainment that

> the range of autonomous authority available to the European Union is now so great that the case in democratic principle for a purely path-dependent, state-delegated and internationalist conception of democratic pedigree and form in the European Union is arguably no longer sufficient, and the need for a new and direct democratic grant of supranational authority alongside the continuing spheres of (undelegated) national democratic authority has become more profound.
>
> (Walker 2009, 171)

From a more general perspective (not only, then, in the case of the EU), Walker stresses the various challenges to the effective political capacity of the state. The emergence "of collective action and coordination problems that simply do not coincide with the political boundaries of the state" (Walker 2010, 304) means that transnational regulatory development contains something new, "whether in the form of hybrid structures such as the EU or WTO or through the more radical forms of societal constitutionalism" (Walker 2010, 304)—namely, non-holistic constitutional forms characterized by site-specific self-regulation combined with diverse external regulation (Walker 2010, 302). In such a context, legal concepts of publicness disseminate: they come to be applied to non-state contexts "through an iterative and progressive process of conscious adaptation, or tacit affirmation of resemblance, to the statist heritage" (Walker 2012, 73)[8]. What is lacking, though, is a "common 'we' perspective, and point of commitment from which to address all questions of common interest" (Walker 2010, 307).

The need for "a new and direct democratic grant of supranational authority" (Walker 2009, 171) faces conceptual, symbolic, and political difficulties.

Conceptual difficulties stem from the fact that we do not have an ideal understanding of the supranational concept of constituent power within a more relational postnational configuration—namely, a non-exclusive legal order and a mixed (non-unitary) polity (Walker 2009, 164–5). In such a polity (and here we head back to the discussion of the EU case in Walker's work), states exist alongside a range of emergent post-state sites, so that the relevant units are no longer exclusive territories with mutually exclusive jurisdictions and citizenries. Hence, the second-order people "can never be just like the otherwise political unencumbered and unmediated 'people' of our first-order state imaginary; the second-order people necessarily describes a compound structure" (Walker 2009, 172; see also Walker 2007, 265). The resilience of the original national constituent powers must be acknowledged. Moreover,

> [u]nlike other pluralist group-based understandings of the ingredients of constituent power at the state level, where the groups in question tend to belong to the same category of conceptual order (e.g., community of affinity, language, or territory), this is not true of states and people(s). How we forge a meaningful sense of constituent power out of such a hybrid of incommensurables—one that does not collapse into its component parts and/or presumptively favour one component over the other—remains a key puzzle.
>
> (Walker 2009, 173)

The need for a new type of democratic grant of authority also faces symbolic and political difficulties. Symbolic ones relate to the fact that constitutionalism is a contested currency, and that therefore, its symbolic capital "is itself a precarious and contingent achievement of social construction manifesting implicit agreement that written constitutions can frame political community in [...] various ways [...]" (Walker 2009, 173). Political difficulties stem from the fact that states will not willingly divest themselves of authority (Walker 2009, 173).

Therefore, the EU faces a mix of epistemic and motivational problems. On the one hand, it does not have "a basic grammar for the new language of political authority it must speak" (Walker 2005, 221). On the other one, it lacks the basis for nurturing the sense of common engagement necessary to legitimize the polity and mobilizing its citizens politically (Walker 2005, 221). These problems are mutually reinforcing and make constitutional momentum elusive. Yet, there is a need to constitutionalize the supranational order, because "only a constitution or its functional equivalent can provide the symbolic and epistemic basis for renewal and reflection upon the system of supranational governance through a process of collective authorship" (Walker 2016, 351). As I explained earlier, Walker argues that the particularity of the constitutional way of conceptualizing the world lies in its framing logic: it sets the framework "within which and in accordance with which we engage in collective forms of practical reasoning we call 'politics'" (Walker 2009, 152). He seems to imply that a written constitution allows to avoid resolving the polity question *ab initio* (see, e.g., Walker 2005, 219–20).

As I said earlier, in Walker's postnational constitutionalism, the double sovereign of the citizens of the EU, on the one hand, and of the peoples of the member states, on the other one, cannot feed into a single constituent power. There is a first-order constituent power specific to each member state (the national constituent powers) and a second-order constituent power that cannot meet the requirements of the first-order one but still embodies the collective authorship of a Constitutional Treaty seen as a step to the constitutionalization of the EU as a specific type of polity. The latter is a "thin" constituent power – a constituent power "light"[9].

The basic problem is that as Walker tends to broaden the idea of democratic iteration to account for the fact that authority can't anymore be conceived of as being path-dependent upon a delegation of their powers by states, he actually replicates foundational constitutionalism. He does so quite explicitly. Yet, foundational constitutionalism may not be appropriate in the global, polycentric context. Of course, Walker's most significant pieces on constituent power deal with the case of the EU. As I have already said, the latter is a *sui generis* polity and its context is quite different from the global one of transnational regimes and networks[10]. However, when discussing constitutionalism, Walker intends his work to apply to non-state polities broadly speaking. For example, he also sees the WTO and the UN as capable of fitting "quite well on the 'scale' of constitutionalism considered as a layered set of holistic frames" (Walker 2010, 301)[11]. Yet, his discussion of constitutionalism very much stands by the basics of statehood constitutionalism. The most notable feature of the latter is sovereignty, which Walker holds to be the necessary condition of constitutional polity formation[12]. As to constituent power more specifically, then, the problem is that because he replicates the basic conditions of state constitutionalism, democratic agency in non-state polities can only be a kind of constituent power "light", a by-product of some first-order constituent power that would have been delegated somehow (most probably, indirectly through member states). The conditions for a "thick" constituent power cannot be met in non-state polities because these conditions (at least, as Walker conceives of them) depend upon the state.

This is quite obvious when one takes a close look at Walker's argument about the EU lacking a settle sense of its subjects as well as of the domain of the political community. Practically, the issue of the new type of democratic grant of authority (in supra-national contexts) relates to problems of collective action "arising when the interdependence and reciprocal externalities of state decisions reach a certain pitch of intensity" (Walker 2005, 218–9). In the specific case of the EU, the Union is both the product and a reinforcing cause of external pressures on states. But there nonetheless still is a deep controversy over the idea of a postnational constituent power. According to Walker, the EU actually covers much of the ground that the material constitution of an existing constitutional polity would cover[13], but it lacks a settled sense of its subjects and of their ties to the political community, as well as of the domain of the latter. The issue of the political identity of the subjects and of the proper domain of the polity has not been resolved definitively (Walker 2005, 220). There is no "strong unifying traits or sources of 'we feeling' such as common language or the traditions and affective symbols of a developed civil society to which the claim to form a political community could appeal" (Walker 2005, 220). There is no mobilizing dynamic related to "some obvious and catalytic event [...] to help forge that sense of political community" (Walker 2005, 220). The Union does not claim territorial exclusivity; actually, it seeks autonomy without territorial exclusivity, "namely, an independent claim to authority over a territory that is co-extensive with the territories of the original (state) political communities and over populations that continue to understand themselves also as members of these original political communities" (Walker 2005, 220–21). It also lacks "the critical standard and background presumption supplied by the idea of a potentially unlimited and so self-limiting domain as a general template for its proper sphere of action" (Walker 2005, 221). In other words, the EU is not a state[14]. And this is why it can only expect to rely on a second-order constituent power[15]. The analysis of Walker's argument, then, shows that the replication of foundational constitutionalism and the argument for a pluralism "light" (see Chapter 2) does not allow to frame a conception of collective political agency that can sustain a thick conception of democratic authorization in a polycentric setting[16].

A Post-State Constituent Power: U. Preuss and Freedom *Inter Socios* as the Basic Fact of Society

There are very similar problems (but for different reasons) with U. Preuss's approach. I will briefly summarize these problems here. Whereas Walker argues for a post-state foundational constitutionalism in which a second-order people describes a compound structure and overlaps with the first-order peoples of member states, Preuss argues more directly for a post-state constituent power. He focuses on the idea that we have entered a phase of sovereignty in which self-rule is reconceptualized "as the capacity of a collective to interact with other communities and share with them control of their life conditions on a global scale, irrespective of territorial boundaries" (Preuss 2010, 39). The advent of the constitution already had signaled that the establishment of a regime of collective self-rule by constituting "We, the people" can be disconnected from the territory, and that hence, the sovereign power of the state did not exist "prior to and independently of the society" (Preuss 2010, 33).

Freedom *inter socios* is the basic fact of society, and hence of sovereignty and constitutionalism; it actually is this quality of embodying the power of the polity as a distinct collective entity that defines sovereignty[17]. The idea of the constitution is not intrinsically bound to the concept of the territorially bounded state, since actually, it "disconnected the idea of sovereignty from the control over a territory and connected it with the idea of collective self-rule of a multitude" (Preuss 2010, 37). The creation of constitutions "was identical with the creation of the constituent power of the people" (Preuss 2010, 37)[18]. Constitutions' essential promise is "to establish systems of collective action based on principles of equal participation, accountability, and rule of law" (Preuss 2010, 46). This definition applies to political formations that do not incorporate territorially defined multitudes. Polities, actually, are entities which provide for the common security and welfare of a group—a function which is no longer the monopoly of states. Hence,

> a modern-day definition of a constitution as the fundamental source of authority must include both states and new political formations not based upon territoriality [...] [W]henever a multitude whose members are demarcated against the outside world establish a regime through which they pursue the goals of common defense and/or common welfare and establish rules about the formation of a common will which are able to generate obligations and responsibilities for the individual members, this multitude has constituted itself as a distinct entity shaped by a constitution.
>
> (Preuss 2010, 43)

These essential promises of the constitution are lacking in some spheres, and this justifies including institutionalized schemes of horizontal and non-coercive social coordination in the concept of a constitution (Preuss 2010, 43). The idea of constitutionalism

> remains a viable concept for modes of social organization which are not intrinsically based on the use of the coercive means of the state [...] Constitutions can create schemes of cooperation across physical, social, and cultural boundaries because they do not presuppose shared values or shared understandings of social practices. They may produce a common cognitive and normative horizon in that they create institutional facts which generate new possibilities of action among aliens [...].
>
> (Preuss 2010, 46)

Therefore, constituent power is possible at a non-state level—for example as a supranational European power, since it denotes "the capacity of the members of a group to constitute themselves as a polity and to create authority in the first place" (Preuss 2011, 86). The constitution is "the outcome of a constitutive act which enables a group to form and sustain a polity, it is the embodiment of a self-constitution which includes elements of self-binding. Prior to the constitution there is no (collective) Self which could have given instructions to the constituted Self" (Preuss 2011, 86)[19].

As in the case of Walker, Preuss's discussion of constituent power mostly focuses on the EU. According to him, an EU constituent power is conceivable, provided we abandon "the statist alternative that the EU is either the polity of a unitary people or it is no polity at all" (Preuss 2011, 89). The EU is a *sui generis* polity: "the contracting states have constituted themselves as Member States of a Union which itself, being endowed with an autonomous legal order and legal personality, embodies the political will of the peoples to connect their political fate to each other" (Preuss 2011, 91). There are four consequences as to constituent power. First, the EU has a distinct constituent power of its own, one that is different from the single constituent powers of the Member States (Preuss 2011, 91). It is not a second-order constituent power. Second, the peoples of the Member States have agreed to a distinct political identity of their Union (Preuss 2011, 91). Third, the hypothetical *Kompetenz-kompetenz* of the EU "would not include the authorization to transform the union of states into a federal state and to downgrade the Member States to mere constituent states without international legal subjectivity" (Preuss 2011, 91)[20]. Fourth, "the existence of the combined constituent power of the Member States does not eliminate their particular national constituent powers" (Preuss 2011, 91). As the EU is a *sui generis* polity, its constituent power is *sui generis* as well: "First, it is brought to bear through the conclusion of a multilateral status contract between already constituted entities. Secondly, it effects the status passage of independent states into Member States of a polity without homogenizing and unifying them into one body" (Preuss 2011, 92). It is the very act of constitution-making that creates the source of authority, "which in the case of Europe would entail a polity in which the democratic and the federal element form a modern version of the ancient ideal of a mixed constitution" (Preuss 2011, 84). If the European constituent power is understood in the traditional sense of collective self-creation (as it did in Sieyès and Schmitt), then that would imply conceptualizing the constitution of a unitary state, and discarding "the idea of a polity consisting of a union of distinct nations organized in independent states" (Preuss 2011, 84).

There are two problems with Preuss's argument, as to the reconceptualization of collective political agency. At first sight, he may seem to avoid the issue raised by Walker's reliance on sovereign statehood as the model of constitutional polity formation. He argues that sovereignty rather relates to the collective will of a multitude (independently of territorial delineation and shared values) and that constituent power simply is the *a posteriori* recognition by the members of a group that they have created themselves as such in order to act collectively. This does not depend, then, upon the state. He frees both the idea of the constitution and the notion of constituent power from statehood for the purpose of propelling the constitutional question to mixed polities. The notion of constituent power stands on its own, as an (even more) symbolic pole related to the capacity for collective action in contexts in which the boundaries of the polity have yet to be determined. Preuss stresses the idea of a union of states; he opposes the one of homogeneization and unification of the latter into one body. But by doing so, his argument conveys a shortcoming that in a way is the reverse of the one conveyed by Walker's claims: Preuss incorrectly downplays the significance of sovereign statehood for the conceptualization of the notion of constituent power. He mistakes the relationship between them for a contingent one—whereas, as I have argued, it actually is a closely intertwined one, that requires that we challenge the very notion of constituent power[21].

The second problem I wish to stress is that he seems to imply that the transnational is made of horizontal and non-coercive schemes of social coordination. But this is either naïve or simplistic. Non-state polities sometimes also are vertical and coercive; let us think of the WTO, for example. One must allow for complex patterns in which state and non-state (hierarchical, heterarchical, or horizontal) polities share in the enactment of public authority, if one is to tackle accurately and appropriately the issue of democratic authorization in the current context. Patterns of authority may rely on coercion, even when the latter take a form different from the "command" model[22]. This justifies taking a closer look at a wholly different approach, the one of Teubner.

Non-Political Constituent Power: G. Teubner and the Principle of Self-Contestation in Transnational Regimes

In order to understand Teubner's approach to constituent power, it is useful to recall that he focuses on the tension between the self-foundation of autonomous global subsystems and their political-legal constitutionalization. As functional differentiation now encompasses the whole world, constitutions are to counter autonomous social spheres. This role is played not only by the traditional political constitutions, but also by "emerging civil constitutions" (Anderson 2012, 366). The nation-state "can no longer be regarded as the only possible constitutional subject" (Teubner 2012, 73): institutions in the private sectors are being constitutionalized as well (Teubner 2012, 73). But there is no transnational counterpart to the nation-state constitution as the structural link between law and politics within which the externalization of the legal paradoxes towards the political system can take place. Hence, law diverts its paradox to other social systems rather than externalizing it to politics, so that the question of its legitimation "is no longer answered with the 'legislator's will', but more probably with the inner rationality of the social subsystems involved" (Teubner 2016, 33)[23]. The constitutions of subsystems are enlisted for externalizing paradoxes. Law-making processes are actually replaced by "social norm production that is transformed into applicable law" (Teubner 2016, 34).

In a context in which there is no centralized political system, and in which constituencies are fluctuating, global constitutionalism aims both at breaking down "the close structural couplings between the function systems and nation-state politics and law" (Teubner 2012, 76) and at enabling function-specific communications to become globally interconnected. Transnational regimes are both highly specialized and overdetermined. Hence, their constitutional norms and principles are solipsistic and imperialistic, because they "only establish their operative rules for the single functional sector of world society to which they are connected" (Teubner 2018, 22)[24]; and they tend to rely on one main idea (Teubner 2018, 23). The regimes are interacting with their subjects via a variety of regulatory devices. Limitative norms are required because the Washington consensus has unleashed a destructive dynamic in which the systems try to maximize their partial rationality, following "an inexorable growth imperative" (Teubner 2012, 79). The issue is that because of the one-sided function orientation of social sectors, particular rationalities (subrationalities) collide with one another as well as with a comprehensive rationality; and function-maximization collides with its own self-reproduction. This requires that subsystems engage in a process of self-critical reflection and in self-restraint (Teubner 2012, 82). A social system can limit its own possibilities through relying upon its own resources, but these self-limitations arise "only under immense external pressure, as the result of fierce constitutional battles" (Teubner 2012, 86). The task, then, is to generate "a sufficiently large degree of external pressure [...] on the subsystems to push them into self-limitations on their options" (Teubner 2012, 84). These counter-structures are generated when the system-specific medium turns against itself; in other words, they are generated by medial self-limitation (money by money, law by law, etc.) (Teubner 2012, 88)[25].

Societal constitutionalism actually reacts to the issue of how "to increase external pressure in order to stem the negative externalities of autonomous subsystems by means of their internal self-limitation" (Teubner 2012, 41). Constitutionalism can counter the expansionist tendencies of subsystems when they endanger individual or institutional autonomy. The constitutional question (namely, the question of the limits to the expansion of subsystems) can therefore be projected onto the world society (see, e.g., Teubner 2011, 211). Transnational constitutionalism is to perform constitutional functions via both constitutive and limitative rules (Teubner 2012, 102). Although constitutional structures "have long existed in the transnational sphere" (Teubner 2011, 213), up to now the new global constitutional orders have established mainly constitutive rules "which have normatively supported the freeing-up of various rationalities at the global level" (Teubner 2012, 10). Counter-movements are appearing, though, "which formulate limitative rules in order to counteract self-destructive tendencies and to limit damage to their social, human, and natural environments" (Teubner 2012, 10). Limitative constitutional norms are usually sought when tipping-points are reached—namely, when the destructive energies created by the one-sided function orientation of a social sector bring about collisions (either between sub-rationalities, between a social sector and the comprehensive rationality of the world society, or of function-maximization with its own self-reproduction). The challenge for a global constitutionalism, therefore, is "how can sufficient external pressure be brought to bear on the subsystems so that the self-limitation of their possible courses of action becomes effective?" (Teubner 2011, 225)[26]. Let me stress that when he talks about norms of "a constitutional quality", Teubner has in mind some notion of "superior norms", ones "that define where the decision making power should be located, how violations should be handled, and how third parties should be included" (Teubner 2011, 221, quoting Dilling et al. 2008)—in other words, mechanisms of self-restraint that are to reduce intrusions on other actors and other domains (Teubner 2011, 221)[27].

What about constituent power, then? Let me first recall that from Teubner's perspective, constituent power is a communicative potential, a type of social energy, a power "which, via constitutional norms, is transformed into a *pouvoir constitué*, but which remains as permanent irritant to the constituted power" (Teubner 2012, 62)[28]. Constitutions reconstruct collective identity as self-descriptions of social systems. As globalization features "a series of heterogenous processes of constitutionalization" (Teubner 2016, 34), the quality of constituent power "necessarily also changes" (Teubner 2016, 35). Three features stand out of Teubner's work, as to constituent power. First, Teubner frames the issue as being the one of determining which constitutional subjects will replace nation-states "to advance the constitutionalization of the global sectors" (Teubner 2012, 44). In other words, we need to determine whether global networks, transnational regimes, and the like are capable of bearing constitutions. The answer to that question depends on whether "such non-state institutions exhibit sustainable analogies to the nation-state pouvoir constituant; to the self-constitution of a collective; to democratic decision-making; and to the organizational part of a political constitution in the strict sense" (Teubner 2012, 8). Teubner argues that there actually are invocations of constituent power that emerge in small pocket of transnational governance. What we need to do is to "generalize and respecify" the concept of constitutional subject tailored to the nation-state "both to its transnational and civil society equivalents" (Teubner 2012, 60). But what does that mean, exactly? As to generalization, Teubner argues that the principle of political representation "needs to be generalized and replaced by the principle of self-contestation of transnational regimes" (Teubner 2018, 14). To generalize from political constitutionalism means "identifying a formal and abstract legal structure that defines constitutions as such" (Lindahl 2011, 231). Re-specification means that self-contestation "needs to be established with wide variations that reflect the extreme epistemic diversity among issue-specific transnational regimes" (Teubner 2018, 14). Generalization brings us away from the context of the nation-state, while re-specification means being sensitive to the self-reproduction of different fields and spelling out the principles in ways appropriate to the receiving fields (Christodoulidis 2011, 240)[29].

The second feature that stands out is that, as I have already said, in transnational regimes political representation is replaced by self-contestation. These regimes must be responsive to external irritations and must institutionalize internal dissent (Teubner 2018, 14). Transnational regimes actually require "a great variety of modes of self-contestation" (Teubner 2018, 26), because they use mediums of communication of very different kinds. This builds upon a recontextualization of the QOT (*quod omnes tangit*) principle that reframes the latter as "self-contestation in diverse context-adequate forms" (Teubner 2018, 14–5)[30]. Such a recontextualization implies four basic aspects. First, in issue-specific regimes, there is no one well-defined collective; there rather are extremely fluctuating constituencies. Regimes' driving machine for democratic self-contestation is the inherent tension between members, rule addressees, and affected outsiders (Teubner 2018, 17). Hence, "[i]t is only when outsiders' protest, stakeholders' interest articulation, and internal organized dissent are working together in concert that an externally induced self-contestation becomes feasible" (Teubner 2018, 22)[31]. Second, as transnational regimes exclusively follow the rationality criteria for their sector (which makes them highly specialized) (Teubner 2018, 22), self-contestation risks being paralyzed by the narrow tunnel vision. The solution to this is "a well-ordered system of various spheres of ethical life. The result would be an institutionalized mutual contestation between the different spheres" (Teubner 2018, 23–4). That could work either by "internalizing conflict orientations into the decisions of the conflicting regimes themselves or externalizing them to inter-regime negotiations" (Teubner 2018, 24). In the former case, the conflicts are shifted to the constitutions of the regimes because the norms of a regime are reconstructed before the forum of their own constitution; in the latter case, they are shifted to adversarial negotiations between regimes[32]. Third, procedures of contestation must be developed in opposition to diverse sources of authority. In public regimes, self-contestation attacks the medium of political power, but "in other regimes resistance needs to be developed to other mediums of communication—against money, knowledge, law, digital calculation—because transnational regimes use them in their own particular spheres of action through a series of unique communication processes" (Teubner 2018, 26). It is counter-expertise that becomes the relevant counter-power (Teubner 2018, 27)[33]. Fourth, transnational public ordering can increase its legitimacy only if it realizes the horizontal protection of constitutional rights:

> the negotiation of antagonistic interests within contracting has a certain self-contesting potential which allows for the articulation of dissent. But this is possible only under two conditions of ideal contracting: that there are no power asymmetries between the contracting parties and that the contract does not develop negative externalities for third parties. The traditional legitimation of rules via contractual justice comes to an end when problems of power asymmetries or negative externalities arise. This is the situation when private power begins to endanger the freedom of other private parties which in its turn requires the interference of horizontal effects of constitutional rights as the legitimation basis for the transnational law production.
>
> (Teubner 2018, 28)

The "horizontal effect" of fundamental rights is not purely a problem of political power within society. The real task is "the limitation by means of rights of all expansionist tendencies of social subsystems, including those which do not function through the medium of power" (Teubner 2011, 215). Fundamental rights must be effective against social communicative media themselves, rather than against individual or social actors[34].

The third feature that stands out from Teubner's work as to constituent power for the purposes of this chapter is that Teubner's recontextualization of the QOT principle focuses on dissent. According to Teubner, the identity of the authors of the law and affected people is not the timeless hardcore of democracy—and actually, it "can no longer be maintained for real decisions of real peoples but only for the hypothetical situation of the ideal discourse among hypothetical participants" (Teubner 2018, 11)[35]. The democratic nation-state has been both the apex and the end of the symbiosis between identitarian consensus building and the enlargement of internal dissent (Teubner 2018, 11). The identitarian consensus can still be realized, but only at the local level (Teubner 2018, 12). As transnational institutions "are weak candidates for identitarian consensus building", they should rather focus on the dissensus element (Teubner 2018, 13). The democratization of transnational institutions should not be looked as a guarantee of the identity between rulers and ruled, but "it can be realized as a guarantee for forceful organized dissent, which challenges the decisions of power holders effectively [...]" (Teubner 2018, 13). A theory of "organized dissent" does not strive for the rightness of political decisions; it rather concentrates "on a 'right to contingency', which opens alternative world constructions. At the center of democratic communication lies not the naïve hope for the one best solution, but the confrontation with alternative world views" (Teubner 2018, 13). Hence, "Transnational regime democracy requires that efficient decision procedures create the space for the possibility of dissent as a precondition of an independent selectivity distributed within the society" (Teubner 2018, 13)[36].

Therefore, Teubner certainly aims at challenging the way foundational constitutionalism, holism, and agency relate in the statist paradigm. His attempt at recasting constituent power is quite different from the ones by Walker and Preuss. However, his work also raises significant issues. As I have already explained in Chapter 2, Teubner's stance to statehood is more complex than it may seem at first sight, and his approach conveys significant shortcomings as to the management of political conflict. These shortcomings impact upon the capacity to recast a notion of political agency that can ground democratic authorization. More precisely, I wish to stress two such issues: the issue of a collective actor and the one of the exact function of constituent power. As to the former, Teubner argues for a conception of agency that actually downplays the role of actors themselves. He casts aside collective political agency. As to the latter, one can argue both that Teubner replicates the logic of subordination of the "people-as-the-governed" in the diverse subsystems and that he makes self-critical reflection and self-restraint dependent upon medial self-limitation rather than upon a constitutional subject.

Teubner explicitly tackles the issue of individual human agency in a paper on the rights of non-humans (Teubner 2006). In that paper, he recalls that Luhmann's work carries a change concerning the identity of collective actors: it is not a group of people, but a series of messages (Teubner 2006, 500), and "[u]nder the double condition that a chain of communication communicates about itself, that is, creates a self-description, and that communicative events are attributed to this self-description as actions, the social reality of a collective actor is emerging with decision-making structures of its own and binding effects on the social system" (Teubner 2006, 500–1). Rather than asking what kind of ontological properties an entity has to possess in order to be an actor, Luhmann argues that under certain conditions, the environing social system[37] "constructs this entity via the semantic artefact of an 'actor'" (Teubner 2006, 501). Actually, "it is the surrounding social system—and not the entity itself—that constitutes identity, capacity for action and communication, rights, and duties" (Teubner 2006, 501). Individual and collective actors "are created by social attribution. Their social reality lies in the socially binding self-description of an organized social system as a cyclical linkage of identity and action attribution" (Teubner 2006, 501)[38].

Therefore, grounds of "self-foundation" are not to be ascribed to an agent, but to "social communication flows" (Přibáň 2012, 450). Let me also recall that Teubner contradistinguishes functional subsystems from formal organizations; from his point of view, the collective identity of a social system does not necessarily imply a formal organization. Self-description is enough for constitutionalization; hence, the latter does not necessarily mean the transformation of a group of individuals into a collective actor (Teubner 2012, 67)[39].

The important thing for the purposes of this chapter (and book) is that Teubner stresses that what makes an entity an actor is "the attribution of communicative events to [such] entity as 'its' acts and the attribution of rights to [such entity]" (Teubner 2006, 498). But by focusing on systemic attribution of (collective) identity, Teubner's account actually downplays the significance of actors' relationships in the framing of political identities[40]. Přibáň has rightly stressed that the focus on the interface of individual consciousness and social communication "does not indicate any constitution of the people as a collective with political identity or intersubjective communication power" (Přibáň 2012, 448)[41]. But if this is the case, what does democratic authorization really mean, in fragmented constitutional settings?

This leads us to the second (and related) issue, the one of the exact function of constituent power. Let me recall that Teubner conceives of constituent power as a self-description representing the potential of a subsystem. It is a self-referential process by which a subsystem constitutes its own autonomy. This applies not only to politics but also to other subsystems. Hence, constituent powers are multiplied. He also acknowledges the self-foundation of autonomous global subsystems (just as, one may add, the state was in a way "self-founding"). Constitutions of subsystems are to perform the same function as the nation-state's constitution, namely, to counter autonomous social systems via constitutive and regulative rules. The main difference is that there is no transnational counterpart to the nation-state's constitution as to the structural link between law and politics, so that law diverts its paradox to other social systems. Hence, the question of legitimation is answered with the inner rationality of each system involved.

But this way of framing the issue of transnational constitutionalism raises two problems as to public autonomy. First, Teubner (rightly) makes the self-foundation of subsystems the basic fact of authority. But by multiplying constituent powers, he basically replicates the subjection of constituent power to established structures of authority—not only within the state, this time, but within each subsystem. Let me recall that I have argued that the notion of constituent power actually subordinates the "people-as-the-governed" to state sovereignty. Teubner merely replicates this logic in the diverse subsystems characteristic of functional differentiation. Therefore, he does not contribute to the resolution of the issue of democratic authorization. Of course, Teubner stresses that subsystems must engage into a process of self-critical reflection and in self-restraint. He argues that they can limit their possibilities by relying on their own resources, but that this requires immense external pressures. The issue, then, is: who is to generate such pressure? Actually, the answer for Teubner is more an issue of "what" than of "who": counter-structures, he explains, are generated by medial self-limitation (money by money, las by law, etc.). No constitutional subject can be ascribed as the locus and agent of constituent power; at the end of the day, "the subject is fashioned out of the process itself" (Christodoulidis 2013, 646).

At this stage, then, we are still looking for the exact function (and subject) of constituent power. And this raises broader issues. If we have to rely on self-systems internalizing limitative rules generated by external pressure, how is transnational constitutionalism to counter the expansionist tendencies of subsystems by performing constitutional functions, exactly? As I have explained, three notions are basic to such a process: generalization, re-specification, and contextualization. Constituent power is understood as expressing itself in self-contestation and organized dissent. These, in turn, raise two basic issues that are left unresolved by Teubner: how can fundamental rights be effective, when they basically depend either on the internalization of conflict orientations or on adversarial negotiations? And how can dissensus ensure the jurisgenerative capacity needed for the expression of public autonomy? Teubner makes the democratization of transnational institutions a guarantee for forceful organized dissent; but he does not convincingly explain how such a democratization is to proceed.

At some point, Teubner acknowledges that self-limitation and self-constitutionalization are achieved through societal mobilization (e.g., of consumer groups, eco-activists, etc.), and that this is what supports "reflexive learning pressures". However, he also assumes that social subsystems need to take account of their public responsibility, so that one may infer that the internal differentiation of social spheres "does not consist of the internal autopoietic operations and functions of social subsystems and therefore needs to be reformulated as the specific operation of the politics of civil protest and dissent reflected and internalized by other social systems" (Přibáň 2012, 454). But countervailing powers have a clear and restricted task: hybrid constitutionalization and constituent power as social energy are not meant to revoke the regime, "because this would undermine the evolutionary course of functional differentiation" (Möller 2018, 45).

To summarize, Teubner refocuses constituent power on self-contestation, organized dissent, and a "right to contingency". However, I will argue in Chapter 5 that constituent power cannot be equated with dissent. A focus on dissent does not settle the issue of the constructive and jurisgenerative dimension of constituent power as a way of expressing public autonomy. Moreover, as the concept of the constitution is depoliticized, the issue of binding rules also is set aside, in Teubner's work. Hence, it seems that challenging foundational constitutionalism and holism starting from the perspective of societal constitutionalism implies downplaying the perspective of a common good and its framing by a collective political agent in democratic ways.

Conclusion

In this chapter, I have focused on approaches that argue for the possibility to somehow recast the notion of constituent power in order to move it to the transnational or global sphere. The conundrum that is raised by the discussion is the following: approaches that translate or recast some version of foundational constitutionalism can sustain the assumption that collective political agency is core to democratic authorization; but those who challenge foundational constitutionalism (here, from the perspective of societal constitutionalism) fare less well as to this critical component of the notion of constituent power. The former can be criticized for standing by foundationalism, which is hardly appropriate in a polycentric setting with peculiar forms of authority. The latter can be criticized for casting away collective political agency, which embodies the belief that we as humans can (re)design institutions according to some conception of a common good[42].

Is there a way out of this conundrum? In other words, is there a way to frame a conception of collective political agency appropriate to this new context, a context that cannot be properly captured by foundational constitutionalism? Or shall we give up the enterprise of redefining collective political agency beyond constituent power? There may actually not be sustainable analogues to constituent power in the transnational domain[43]. But does this warrant to cast aside any notion of some collective political agency? In the next chapter, I turn to approaches that challenge the very possibility of constituent power in a post-state context. Such approaches acknowledge the intractable challenges related to the translation of foundational constitutionalism at the global level. They rightly stress that the transformation of the boundaries that were core to modern constitutionalism challenges public autonomy. And they look for "triggers" for constitutional or public law changes. But they also lament the loss of a peculiar way of expressing public autonomy, and retreat either on containment or contestation.

Notes

1 For example, Niesen (2017b, 222) argues that reverting to a notion of constituent power in global constitutionalism is "necessary, plausible and useful" because of the problem of constituent usurpation (namely, when international treaties or supra-state constitutions risk affecting domestic constitutions without being authorized by constituent power).

2 This sense of a loss is unequivocal in Krisch's work on *pouvoir irritant*. He argues that ascribing the origins of the postnational order to a constituent power would stretch the notion too far, and that the idea can survive on a normative plan but in a negativistic logic of contestation (Krisch 2016). No new constitutional order can be built out of such a logic.

3 The third type of approaches differ from the first one by focusing on how people frame their claims and by trying to relate these framings to theoretical options. Approaches of the first type rather translate some version of constitutionalism in the postnational domain.

4 See Chapter 2.
5 He contradistinguishes postnational constitutionalism from postnational public law. The former focuses on the constitutive (input) side of state-like law; the latter stresses the output side. According to him, this is a "stubborn fault-line" in the debate over the future of constitutionalism and public law. But postnational constitutionalism and postnational public law share a substantive common ground, namely, the same combination of endorsement of the statist legacy and post-state aspirational horizon. They also display "the same basic range of *forms* of reference" (Walker 2012, 63–4).
6 It is this problem of the authoritative source and extent of the constitution that is at the core of the debate between pluralism and federalism (Walker 2016, 351). Walker stresses that the federalist tradition depends upon a statist approach (Walker 2016); "the supposed superiority of the federal vision as a means to characterize and to shape the dual power system of the EU depends to a significant extent upon just these statist or 'state-like' tendencies that the Euro-federalists are at pain to deny" (Walker 2016, 345). From his point of view, as the question of the EU sovereignty remains unresolved, "the status of any central constitutional claim must be considered to be that of a partial or relative authority, dispositive of matters only from the perspective of the European people acting together supranationally and only for these matters in which they are acting together supranationally" (Walker 2016, 346, footnote 46).
7 Let me recall that he points to five frames accounting for the various layers of constitutional practices: the juridical, political-institutional, authorizing, social integration, and discursive frames (see, e.g., Walker 2009). The idea of a specialized political system (the political-institutional frame) "does not necessarily imply [...] a type of authorization that claims either a democratic founding or a continuing democratic warrant" (Walker 2009, 157). But as the specialized system of political rule introduces the idea of a sphere of authority that constructs itself and provides for its own (secular) justification, constitutionalism (at least in the state tradition) "tends to be a precarious achievement unless and until joined by a claim of collective self-authorization" (Walker 2009, 158).
8 "Even for those most skeptical of transnational legal publicness, therefore, the propensity for non-robust strains of legal publicness to pass from state to transnational must be recognized as an inevitable feature of the evolution of law's discursive register in an age of the development of new transnational circuits of economic and cultural power" (Walker 2012, 73).
9 This conception is therefore different from, e.g., J. Habermas's one, in which constituent power is vested in citizens in their simultaneous roles of citizens of states and citizens of the EU (namely, in individuals as members of two demoi). See Habermas, (2017); Patberg (2017a and 2017b); Niesen (2017a and 2017b). Habermas's *pouvoir constituant mixte* implies the concept of a non-state federation, with an emphasis on the values of the persistence of the constitutional orders of the member states (Patberg 2017b). I do not discuss Habermas's nor J. Cohen's arguments, in this book, because they already have been thoroughly analyzed (amongst others, by Krisch, Patberg, and Niesen).
10 The EU has reached a higher degree of integration than most transnational regimes and networks.
11 See Chapter 2.
12 See Chapter 2.
13 Namely, extensive decision-making jurisdiction over first-order issues, sophisticated second-order institutional complex for deliberating on and resolving first-order differences, as well as self-assertion of the principles of supremacy and direct effect (Walker 2005, 219).
14 His stance actually is sometimes paradoxical. He acknowledges that the difficulty of imagining the EU as a legitimate political and legal construction other than by invoking the structures and values of constitutionalism (Walker 2016, 334) is hard to reconcile with the EU non-state form.

15 Walker's constitutional pluralism merely captures the overlap-in-practice of the jurisdictions of the EU and its member states.

16 One should also stress that citizens of the EU are not impacted only by decisions taken by European institutions of member states, but also by decisions taken in some transnational or global regimes. And it can also be argued that the path-dependent, state-delegated democratic authorization is thinner in the broader transnational domain than in the EU.

17 The processes of collective self-organization and the arrogation of sovereign power are mutually constitutive of each other. The purpose of unifying the multitude into one body is to create their capacity to act collectively, and even if sovereignty means absolute power, the latter is now a defining element of the corporate unity of the people and means "the multitude's capacity of self-rule" (Preuss 2010, 35). Sovereignty merely embodies the power of a polity as a distinct collective entity, whether the latter is territorially defined or not.

18 Let me recall that according to Preuss, constitutions are constitutive, rather than regulative (see Chapter 2). It is the constituent power of the people that transforms the multitude into a people, not the control over the coherence and continuity of the territory. From then on, the territory was not anymore essential to the existence of the polity, from his point of view.

19 The idea of constituent power is that "in an act of collective retroactive attribution the people who live under the constitution legitimize the constitution by invoking their unconstituted will to constitute themselves as a polity, i.e. to live under a common constitution" (Preuss 2011, 86).

20 The objective of the EU is a union rather than a traditional federal state in which statehood would be associated with sovereignty as unitary, indivisible, and supreme. The idea of a union "clearly excludes the idea of a federal state with one people and one constituent power" (Preuss 2011, 88). Members both retain their distinct national identities and develop an autonomous sphere of governance.

21 His argument that the EU should be conceptualized as a union, though, is important in opening paths providing alternatives to statehood.

22 As Krisch stresses, this does not mean that these forms of authority are weak. See Chapter 5.

23 Let me recall that he argues that in the externalization of the legal paradoxes towards the political system of the nation-state, law-making was ascribed coherently to the political-parliamentary process. This was achieved through fictions: the fiction of the comprehensive hierarchy of legal norms, the fiction of the state's reception of social norms, and/or the fiction of the relegation of the latter into the purely factual domain (Teubner 2016, 32). See Chapter 1.

24 National constitutions, in contradistinction, were conceived as holistic orders in which regulations (even the ones of highly specialist regulations) "are embedded in a dense fabric of national norms arising from the most varied area of life. This produces internal conflicts between the divergent norms, principles, and policies that claim validity and are resolved within the broad normative context" (Teubner 2018, 22).

25 The criterion guiding the transfer of the limitative function from politics to other subsystems is the one of societal compatibility: social systems "must align their independent constitutions and their constraints to their communicative media [...]" (Teubner 2012, 88). Krisch explains that a conflict-of-law model can also be seen "as an inspiration to manage conflicts between different legal sub-orders not through overarching rules but through reliance on the capacity of these sub-orders to define adequate rules for mutual engagement. As in traditional conflict-of-laws, certain issues could then be subject to more than one set of rules, and the different legal subsystems would seek to define for themselves when to claim authority or to cede it to another level" (Krisch 2011, 76).

26 This requires "hybrid" regulation: "the exercise of state power, the enforcement of legal rules, the strong influence of social countervailing power from other spheres—media, public discussion, spontaneous protest, intellectuals, social movements, NGOs, trade unions—must apply such massive external pressure to the functional systems that their self-limitations become truly effective" (Teubner 2011, 225). As I said earlier, this can only work within the logic specific to a subsystem, though: external interventions must be "translated into self-limiting impulses and transformed into a regime constitution" (Teubner 2011, 225). It is of particular urgency "to limit the societal dynamics freed up by the constitutive rules. The task, then, is to identify the real structures of the existing global constitutionalism, to criticize its shortcomings and to formulate realistic proposals for limitative rules" (Teubner 2011, 214).

27 Primary candidates are international organizations such as the WTO.

28 See Chapter 1.

29 The uses of the dialectic of generalization and respecification "mainly regards the use of fundamental rights. To explain the dynamics of the emergence of fundamental rights for the 'world society', Teubner asks what elements might be generalized from the tradition of nation-state constitutionalism that might be respecified in the global context of advanced functional differentiation" (Christodoulidis 2013, 640). Such contextualization is one way to understand how the constitutional function might be uploaded from the national to the global level. The other way is to look "at what functional equivalents (to the national constitution) uphold functional differentiation and the autonomy of social systems at the global level, crucially in respect of both their separateness and their connectedness, the latter in terms of mutual cognitive adaptability and coevolution" (Christodoulidis 2013, 640).

30 *Quod omnes tangit, ab omnibus contestari debet.*

31 Outsiders are what Krisch refers to as *pouvoir irritant*. According to Teubner, "[t]heir decisive role is regime contestation but not regime foundation" (Teubner 2018, 18). If their protest is to have real effects, it needs to be supported by counter-rights and firmly institutionalized transparency. The courts must protect such resistance.

32 The normative issue is whether counter-institutions "can increase the chances for opening the regimes to marginalized discourses" (Teubner 2018, 25).

33 Procedures of self-contestation must build on "the constitutional principle of 'epistemic subsidiarity'" (Teubner 2018, 27). The relation between science and politics is highly context-dependent, and epistemic legitimacy is not based only on scientific input but also "on the values, interests, and preferences of local and national communities" (Teubner 2018, 27).

34 However, as Christodoulidis (2013) stresses, Teubner's thesis of mutual cognitive adaptability between systems (and hence, of a balance between the constitutive and the limitative) is challenged by the structural asymmetry between the economy and the political-legal complex, at the global level.

35 Representation by governing elites and competition among such elites have replaced participation by everybody.

36 Teubner also argues that one cannot assume that public international governance can in principle claims a higher degree of legitimacy than private governance because there does not seem to be any correlation between the type of governance arrangements and the degree of acceptability of governance.

37 Namely, "a closed and autonomous ensemble of recursive communications which encounters the entity" (Teubner 2006, 501).

38 For example, a state becomes a collective actor because the international system of war and peace constructs its actors and forces entities to take this form if they are to participate in international politics.

39 See Chapter 1. According to Teubner, Luhmann does not go far enough, though, because he limits collectives to social systems between human individuals.

40 By contradistinction, a relational approach such as the one argued for by D. McAdam, S. Tarrow, and C. Tilly (in the field of political sociology) treats "social interaction, social ties, communication, and conversation not merely as expressions of structure, rationality, consciousness, or culture but as active sites of creation and change" (McAdam, Tarrow, and Tilly 2001, 22). From this point of view, actors are "socially embedded and constituted beings who interact incessantly with other such beings and undergo modifications of their boundaries and attributes as they interact. Actions consist [...] of interactions among such sites. Identities do not inhere in fixed attributes of such sites, but in connections between those sites and the interactions in which they are involved" (McAdam, Tarrow, and Tilly 2001, 56). A relational perspective does not cast aside collective political agency; it rather focuses on mechanisms and processes through which agents identify (and are identified) as (political) actors.
41 See also Blokker 2012.
42 Actually, it casts away the basic political question of how to enforce collective decision-making, as I explained in Chapter 2.
43 More precisely, there may be some cases (e.g., the EU) in which is it not unrealistic to argue that we can translate part of our political apparatus, structures, and institutions. But generalizing from this particular case is not necessarily warranted.

References

Anderson, Gavin W. 2012. "Beyond 'Constitutionalism Beyond the State'." *Journal of Law and Society* 39, no. 3: 359–383.

Blokker, Paul. 2012. "Constitutions and Democracy in Postnational Times: A Political-Sociological Approach." *Irish Journal of Sociology* 20, no. 2: 68–90.

Christodoulidis, Emilios. 2011. "Of Boundaries and 'Tipping Points': A Response to Gunther Teubner." *Social and Legal Studies* 20, no. 2: 238–243.

Christodoulidis, Emilios. 2013. "On the Politics of Societal Constitutionalism." *Indiana Journal of Legal Studies* 20, no. 2: 629–663.

Habermas, Jürgen. 2017. "Citizen and State Equality in a Supranational Political Community: Degressive Proportionality and the *Pouvoir Constituant Mixte*." *Journal of Common Market Studies* 55, no. 2: 171–182.

Krisch, Nico. 2011. *Beyond Constitutionalism. The Pluralist Structure of Postnational Law*. Oxford: Oxford University Press.

Krisch, Nico. 2016. "*Pouvoir Constituant* and *Pouvoir Irritant* in the Postnational Order." *International Journal of Constitutional Law* 14, no. 3: 657–679.

Lindahl, Hans. 2011. "Societal Constitutionalism as Political Constitutionalism: Reconsidering the Relation between Politics and Global Legal Orders." *Social and Legal Studies* 20, no. 2: 230–237.

McAdam, Doug, Tarrow, Sidney, and Tilly, Charles. 2001. *Dynamics of Contention*. Cambridge: Cambridge University Press.

Möller, Kolja. 2018. "From Constituent to Destituent Power Beyond the State." *Transnational Legal Theory* 9, no. 1: 32–55.

Niesen, Peter. 2017a. "The 'Mixed' Constituent Legitimacy of the European Federation." *Journal of Common Market Studies* 55, no. 1: 183–192.

Niesen, Peter. 2017b. "Constituent Power in Global Constitutionalism." In *Handbook on Global Constitutionalism*, edited by Anthony F. Lang Jr and Antje Wiener, 222–233. Cheltenham: Edward Elgar.

Patberg, Markus. 2017a. "A Systematic Justification for the EU's *Pouvoir Constituant Mixte*: Principles of Constitutional Politics in Supranational Polities." *European Law Journal* 23: 441–453.

Patberg, Markus. 2017b. "Introduction: The EU's *Pouvoir Constituant Mixte*—Exploring the Systematic Potential of an Innovative Category." *Journal of Common Market Studies* 55, no. 2: 165–170.

Preuss, Ulrich K. 2010. "Disconnecting Constitutions from Statehood." In *The Twilight of Constitutionalism?* edited by Petra Dobner and Martin Loughlin, 23–46. Oxford: Oxford University Press.

Preuss, Ulrich K. 2011. "Is There a Constituent Power in the European Union?" In *Le pouvoir constituant et l'Europe*, edited by Olivier Cayla and Pasquale Pasquino, 75–92. Paris: Dalloz.

Přibáň, Jiří. 2012. "Constitutionalism as Fear of the Political? A Comparative Analysis of Teubner's *Constitutional Fragments* and Thornhill's *A Sociology of Constitutions*." *Journal of Law and Society* 39, no. 3: 441–471.

Teubner, Gunther. 2006. "Rights of Non-Humans? Electronic Agents and Animals as New Actors in Politics and Law." *Journal of Law and Society* 33: 497–521.

Teubner, Gunther. 2011. "Constitutionalizing Polycontexturality." *Social and Legal Studies* 22, no. 2: 210–229.

Teubner, Gunther. 2012. *Constitutional Fragments: Societal Constitutionalism and Globalization*. Oxford: Oxford University Press.

Teubner, Gunther. 2016. "Exogenous Self-Binding. How Social Subsystems Externalise Their Foundational Paradoxes in the Process of Constitutionalisation." In *Sociology of Constitutions. A Paradoxical Perspective*, edited by Alberto Febbrajo and Giancarlo Corsi, 30–48. London and New York: Routledge.

Teubner, Gunther. 2018. "*Quod Omnes Tangit*: Transnational Constitutions Without Democracy?" *Journal of Law and Society* 45, special issue 1: S5–S29.

Walker, Neil. 2005. "Europe's Constitutional Momentum and the Search for Political Legitimacy." *International Journal of Constitutional Law* 3, no. 2-3: 211–238.

Walker, Neil. 2007. "Post-Constituent Constitutionalism? The Case of the European Union." In *The Paradox of Constitutionalism. Constituent Power and Constitutional Form*, edited by Martin Loughlin and Neil Walker, 247–267. Oxford: Oxford University Press.

Walker, Neil. 2009. "Reframing EU Constitutionalism." In *Ruling the World? Constitutionalism, International Law, and Global Governance*, edited by Jeffrey L. Dunoff and Joel P. Trachtman, 149–176. New York: Cambridge University Press.

Walker, Neil. 2010. "Beyond the Holistic Constitution?" In *The Twilight of Constitutionalism?* edited by Petra Dobner and Martin Loughlin, 291–308. Oxford: Oxford University Press.

Walker, Neil. 2012. "Postnational Constitutionalism and Postnational Public Law: A Tale of Two Neologisms." *Transnational Legal Theory* 3, no. 1: 61–85.

Walker, Neil. 2013. "The Post-National Horizon of Constitutionalism and Public Law: Paradigm Extension or Paradigm Exhaustion?" In *After Public Law*, edited by Cormac Mac Amhlaigh, Claudio Michelon, and Neil Walker, 241–263. Oxford: Oxford University Press.

Walker, Neil. 2016. "Constitutional Pluralism Revisited." *European Law Journal* 22, no. 3: 333–355.

5

A POST-CONSTITUENT ORDER?

Some approaches acknowledge the normative significance of constituent power in the modern conceptual apparatus but rather than recasting or translating it for the post- or transnational domain, they argue that the shift in regulatory activity that characterizes the polycentric context does not anymore allow for its embodiment and enactment. These approaches try to retrieve a way in which democratic authorization could at least be triggered through containment or contestation. But they negate the possibility for collective authorship to be embodied in a notion akin to constituent power in mixed, non- or post-state polities. They either try to assert the ongoing significance of constituent power and constitutionalism at the state level (containment) or to endow contestation with a democratic orientation that would retain the capacity for dismantling institutional orders but without the capacity for enacting new ones (destituent power and *pouvoir irritant*). In other words, they acknowledge that a post-state order would also be a post-constituent one, and they restrict democratic agency to a limited role, either within states as part of this global order or as a trigger for contesting transnational regimes.

Such approaches are different from ones that challenge constituent power as a significant normative category. Contrary to the latter, they acknowledge its core role in the modern conceptual apparatus, as well as its close relationship with democratic authorization and public autonomy. And contrary to the approaches discussed in the previous chapter they do not regard the current context as allowing for the translation or recasting of constituent power. From their point of view, the polycentric setting of governance and the shift in regulatory activity challenge the very possibility of constituent power as a way of embodying public autonomy. However, they also face a significant issue: they fall back on a negativistic logic (of containment

DOI: 10.4324/9781003221722-6

or contestation) that stops short of authorship, at least in the transnational domain. Agency, then, is limited to challenging and resisting the current order. The approaches discussed in this chapter are helpful, as they propose ways to frame the transformations in public authority and acknowledge that constituent power is but one way of expressing public autonomy; they also help in distinguishing public power from state power (or, more precisely, in understanding state power as but one type of public power). But they also seem to imply that abandoning foundationalism means surrendering the radical ideal of agency.

This chapter discusses three such approaches: the reinforcement of domestic constitutionalism (D. Grimm's strategy of "containment"); constituent power as a discursive resource for *pouvoir irritant* (Krisch); and constituent power as destituent power (Möller). The containment strategy seeks to rescue a sphere in which constituent power can still play a partial role in decision-making. *Pouvoir irritant* and destituent power make the distinction between foundation and contestation core to transformations in public autonomy.

The Containment Strategy[1]

The containment strategy argues that the achievements of constitutionalism cannot be reconstructed on the inter- and transnational levels, and that the second-best solution is to preserve these achievements as much as possible, either by striving for a greater accumulation of power at these levels or by limiting the erosion of statehood. The former is an unlikely path, because this would require the international order to have the potential to develop into an object capable of being constitutionalized whereas there is no model for democratic governance that is likely or convincing at that level. Limiting the erosion of statehood, then, is the best hope for constituent power and constitutionalism to regulate public power. The containment strategy seeks to rescue a sphere in which constituent power can still play a partial role in legitimating public authority.

The work of D. Grimm illustrates this approach in an exemplary way. Grimm focuses on the shrinking of the constitution to a partial order as well as on the loss of exclusivity of the primacy of constitutional law. From his point of view, the preconditions for the existence of the constitution are the public/private and the inside/outside boundaries. The public/private boundary has been eroded because private actors have gained a share in public power[2] "without being integrated into the framework of legitimation and accountability that the constitution establishes for public actors", and because "there are modes of decision making that are not submitted to the requirements prescribed by the constitution for acts of public authority" (Grimm 2010, 14). The inside/outside boundary (which is constitutive of sovereignty) is blurring because states have established international organizations to which they have transferred sovereign rights "which these organizations exercise within the states and unimpeded by their right to self-determination" (Grimm 2010, 14). Hence, the capacity of the constitution "to fulfil its claim of establishing and regulating all public power that has an impact on the territory" where it is in force is endangered (Grimm 2010, 14).

It is in Europe that the blurring between the "inside" and the "outside" has progressed the farthest. There,

> the state is no longer the exclusive source of law within its territory. Laws and acts of law enforcement claim validity within the state that emanate from external sources and prevail over domestic law. The identity of public power and state power that was implied in the notion of sovereignty and had been the basis of the national as well as the international order is thus dissolving. This development cannot leave the constitution unaffected. Since the constitution presupposed the state and referred to its power, the fragmentation of public power inevitably entails a diminution of the constitution's impact.
>
> (Grimm 2010, 15)

The achievements of constitutionalism cannot be reconstructed on the inter- and transnational levels. To deserve the name "constitutional", societal law must abide by the following criteria: it must function as a higher law that regulates the making of ordinary law; it must contain provisions that regulate the organization and procedures of global actors; it must limit the scope of action of the private global actors; and it must provide some control mechanisms "similar to constitutional adjudication that guarantee an effective review of the acts of global organisations with respect to their compliance with higher law" (Grimm 2010, 20). In the absence of a global legislator, limitation won't be guided by the common interest—whereas it must be imposed "by a public authority whose task is to keep the self-interest of the various actors of society within the limits of the common best" (Grimm 2010, 20).

Grimm assumes that the state as the consequence of a demos is a "natural" basis of integration[3]. Actually, Grimm

> holds the idea of a constitution to be hollow, or at least deficient, in the absence of certain attributes, including the idea of a democratically self-constituting and self-constituted 'people' possessing comprehensive powers of self-determination and self-legislation. These attributes [...] are ultimately contingent upon certain prior or emergent socio-cultural facts concerning identity, solidarity, and allegiance, absent of which any self-styled constitutional project is fated to be either a dead letter or a much more modest affair. Since only the modern state has known such a

> socio-cultural formation, and since even if the modern state is no longer so robust in these terms it still constitutes a standing impediment to the development of similar cultural formations at non-state sites, there can be no real prospect of a full constitutionalism beyond the state.
>
> (Walker 2010, 294)[4]

The post-state constitution is a machine deprived of the crude social energy to power itself sufficiently (Walker 2010, 296).

In the absence of a democratic origin, the gap between public power and the range of constitutional norms cannot be compensated for, at the international level. The latter is not susceptible "to the type of coherent and comprehensive regulation that characterises the constitution" (Grimm 2010, 18). Moreover, a constitution is characterized by a specific form of regulation. A mere legalization of public power is not the same as its constitutionalization (Grimm 2010, 19). A constitution is a set of legal norms that emanate from a political decision and whose purpose is to regulate the establishment and exercise of public power; such regulation is comprehensive, "in the sense that no extra-constitutional bearers of public power and no extra-constitutional ways and means to exercise this power are recognized" (Grimm 2010, 9). The function of the constitution is "to establish legitimate rule and to regulate its exercise by rulers comprehensively. A system that rejects the democratic origins of public power and is not interested in limited government does not meet the standards of the modern constitution" (Grimm 2010, 10)[5]. The democratic pedigree is fundamental: to be an act of self-determination, a legal order must either have originated in a decision made by citizens or be attributed to them (Grimm 2005, 207).

In Grimm's work, then, the increasing incongruency between state power and public power is seen as a loss. Such incongruency challenges the very possibility of embodying democratic agency (as well as of constitutionalizing public power) beyond the state. Democracy depends upon socio-cultural facts that are encountered only within the state. And because there is no prospect for a post-state constitution, we shall strive for limiting the erosion of statehood. The problem, though, is that the containment strategy allows for very limited possibilities as to the democratic authorization of some of the actual forms of public authority in the current context. It *a priori* excludes the possibility that the conditions conducive to democracy (and constitutionalization) can be met in non- or post-state polities. They actually may not, but by making democratic authorization dependent upon characteristics that are deemed unique to statehood, the containment strategy *a priori* excludes the possibility that in different settings democratic iteration may build on specific grounds. It also neglects the fact that "domestic" constitutionalism risks being both underinclusive and insufficiently effective (Krisch 2016): it risks being underinclusive because of the lack of congruence between nation-state boundaries and the range of those affected by political decisions; and it risks being insufficiently effective because realizing democracy requires sufficient public power to implement self-legislation (Krisch 2011, 21).

Destituent Power and *"Pouvoir Irritant"*

Approaches focusing on destituent power and *pouvoir irritant* also stress the growing incongruency between state power and public power. But rather than arguing for a containment strategy (a fall back upon the state as the only sphere eligible to constitutionalization), they focus on contestation as a possible trigger for constitutional or public law change. As the notions of destituent power and *pouvoir irritant* are very close[6], I will first propose some general observations about the general category of destituent power. These observations build on Patberg's analysis of destituent power in both its juridical and anti-juridical versions. K. Möller and N. Krisch both belong with the juridical conception of destituent power[7], and they both suggest to recast constituent power as a negative device in the polycentric setting of governance. Möller argues that constituent power always has been about contestation, and that it can be reconstructed "as a communicative mechanism which allows for revocatory scenarios 'from below' [...]" (Möller 2018, 50). Krisch argues that constituent power was about comprehensive founding through self-government but that this idea must be forsaken in the transnational domain: constituent power can survive as a normative ascription providing the ideational basis for resistance against global institutions, but it cannot claim to be the source of legitimacy of the transnational order. Both types of claims should be distinguished from anti-juridical conceptions of destituent power, since the latter argue for an outright rejection of sovereignty and law. I will argue that a focus on contestation can contribute a fruitful insight to the debate about constituent power beyond the state since it points to a post-constituent power. But approaches focusing on destituent power (or *pouvoir irritant*) may also foster a sense of powerlessness—of facing institutions designed by forces that are out of reach of democratic authorship.

Destituent power is "a category according to which opposition or withdrawal from the regulatory grasp of public authority can function as a legitimate trigger for constitutional change" (Patberg 2019, 83). More precisely, it "stands for forms of political action that seek to escape the regulatory grasp of public authority, to render political institutions inoperative and to dismantle constitutional orders. At the same time, it is usually introduced as a category of democratic theory that provides (or is at least compatible with) normative standards as to which acts of contestation can be deemed justifiable" (Patberg 2019, 86). Hence, destituent power also carries a transformative ambition and democratic orientation; it "is a useful addition to the vocabulary of democratic theory because it allows us to explicate potential strategies that may seem purely 'disruptive' at first sight as meaningful and potentially legitimate acts of contestation that aim at reversing democratic decline or at removing obstacles for progressive reforms" (Patberg 2019, 95). Such a transformative ambition stops short of foundation, though. I do not deny that contestation actually is a significant component of any process of democratization. The issue raised in this chapter is whether a negativistic logic of contestation is sufficient to ground public autonomy and democratic authorization.

Juridical and Anti-juridical Conceptions of Destituent Power

Patberg makes a useful, and important, distinction between juridical and anti-juridical conceptions of destituent power. The basic distinction between juridical and anti-juridical conceptions turns upon "whether theories endorse or reject the legal institutionalisation of (democratic) politics" (Patberg 2019, 96). Let me first briefly explain the main distinction between juridical and anti-juridical conceptions of destituent power, before turning to Krisch's and Möller's approaches of constituent power as destituent power—which as I said are both juridical conceptions.

Whereas juridical conceptions ascribe a positive potential to sovereignty and law (Patberg 2019, 89), the anti-juridical conception "rests on an outright rejection of sovereignty and law and thus promotes withdrawal from conventional forms of constitutional order" (Patberg 2019, 83). The anti-juridical conception argues for the creation "of new forms of (democratic) politics that operate outside legal-institutional frameworks" (Patberg 2019, 86). From this perspective, the juridical form of collectively binding decision-making is a form of violence[8] that is first and foremost concerned with its own reproduction; hence, the goal of anti-juridical perspectives "is to render public authority inoperative and to establish self-organised and non-institutionalized forms of political action" (Patberg 2019, 86). In other words, the withdrawal of consent is a way to undermine the capacity to rule (Patberg 2019, 86)[9]. If there is no withdrawal from sovereignty and law, a power that will have been knocked down with a constituent violence will resurge in another form (Patberg 2019; Newman 2017).

The important thing for the purposes of this chapter is that from this (anti-juridical) point of view, destituent power is not a reinterpretation of constituent power, because the latter is seen as belonging with a framework built upon violence and that aims mainly at its own reproduction. In other words, constituent power belongs with the paradigm of sovereignty (Patberg 2019, 87; Newman 2017, 289), whereas destituent power is "meant to result in something new [...] The goal is to reorganize political life in forms that do not rely on legal and institutional mechanisms [...]" (Patberg 2019, 87). The main problem with such approaches, from my point of view, is that they merge the critique of state sovereignty and representative democracy with a general rejection of all forms of institutionalized politics. As I explained in

Chapter 1 when discussing approaches arguing that constituent power carries a public law bias, such approaches cannot allow for a systematic understanding of how claims translate into lasting transformations of the political. Hence, they remain purely negativistic and formless, unable to frame a sound conception of collective political agency and democratic authorization[10].

The juridical conceptions rather targets "legitimacy problems that arise in specific contexts and aims at constitutional reordering" (Patberg 2019, 83)[11]. The core idea "is that structures of public authority can be transformed through acts of opposition and withdrawal" (Patberg 2019, 89). Hence, a positive potential is ascribed to law (and sometimes to sovereignty as well). Juridical conceptions include accounts of destituent power as state civil disobedience and accounts of destituent power as an expression of popular sovereignty. Only the latter conceives of destituent power as a dimension of constituent power; hence I won't discuss the former[12]. From the point of view of accounts of destituent power as an expression of popular sovereignty, the category of destituent power belongs "with the people's right to establish and reorganise structures of public authority" (Patberg 2019, 89). It is juridical because it relies on law as a medium of expression (Patberg 2019, 89); and it allows for transformative ambitions, rather than merely restorative ones (Patberg 2019, 93). The focus on a transformative ambition is significant because its aim is broader than the one of approaches that do not allow for framing reconstructive ambitions: it claims the people's right to reorganize structures of public authority, although it stops short of the codification of new constitutional norms (see, e.g., Patberg 2019, 94)[13].

I will come back in Chapter 6 on approaches focusing on "narratives of protest" (more precisely, Patberg's and Niesen's ones). They deserve a discussion of their own because they emphasize the basic role of contestation in identifying (new) narratives that can account for *constituent* power in a polycentric setting; therefore, they also aim at justifying a jurisgenerative capacity that would be core to democratic authorization, whereas approaches discussed in this chapter, although they can ground a transformative intent, in a sense renounce authorization by focusing on the destabilization of existing orders. In this chapter, then, I wish to focus on approaches that emphasize destituent power as "irritations" of constituted power. As I have done in the last three chapters, I will first explain their argument in order to make explicit the difficulties conveyed by these theories and to explain how these difficulties contribute to frame my own argument about public autonomy and democratic authorization beyond the state.

A "Pouvoir Irritant"

The idea of a *pouvoir irritant* as a second-best solution to constituent power is grounded in a description of the current context that emphasizes both the fragmented, polycentric order, on the one hand, and the absence of a defined locus of constituent power, on the other one. Krisch highlights two main aspects of the current transnational sphere. First, the political and the state have become incongruent: public power[14] has moved to a plurality of transnational sites (Krisch 2010, 245). The global polity is divided and characterized by a polycentric setting of governance. Second, there has been a transformation in models of authority. The global context includes forms of authority that are characterized by a lower degree of consolidation and a significant dynamism in the configuration of authority structures, when compared to the state's forms of authority (Krisch 2017, 238). These forms of authority are more "liquid" than "solid". They blur the boundaries between the domestic and the international, between the public and the private, and between formally binding norms and other norms. "Solid" authority is difficult to create in the global realm because it depends on the consensual action of governments and entails sovereignty costs. But there nonetheless is a high demand for some form of authority: actors need authority "to further their substantive goals and tackle transboundary problems [...] Governments often choose informal institutions and soft law; regulators create networks and define best practices, sometimes competing with already existing ones; and private actors seek to establish and implement norms where public regulation is missing or regarded as insufficient" (Krisch 2017, 245). The "command" model of authority (namely, the exercise of binding powers to create formal obligations) is inappropriate in the global context. Krisch stresses that the high degree of consolidation reached by the modern state always has been challenged in some ways, and that in recent decades domestic settings also have turned to greater "liquidity". As I will stress in Chapter 7, this implies that a focus on delegation and formal legal power (as, e.g., in Loughlin's work) introduces a bias in the investigation of forms of authority characteristic of the current context; it actually "misreads the way in which authority is created and maintained" (Krisch 2017, 249). Being more "liquid" than "solid" does not mean that these forms of authority are weak (Krisch 2017). However, "liquid" authority is much more difficult to grasp because it is harder to locate and in constant flux (Krisch 2017, 243). It therefore also represents a particular challenge for law.

In this context, conceiving of the postnational order as grounded in constituent power would require a recasting of the concept that would empty it of the content that has generated its historical appeal. It would also risk legitimating the postnational order by wrongly evoking a continuity with the modern democratic state. The claim of a political and legal order to be grounded in the constituent power of the people depends upon three conditions: a degree of cohesion and collective identity that makes a claim to common representation possible (Krisch 2016, 676); a congruence between boundaries and the range of those affected (Krisch 2011, 21); and a monocentric setting of governance. None of these conditions applies in the transnational order[15]. Hence, Krisch agrees with the advocates of the containment strategy "that in postnational governance continuity with key political traditions is difficult, if not impossible" (Krisch 2011, 17). He also agrees with proponents of the transfer approach (e.g., Walker) that the idea of returning to domestic constitutionalism "is neither practically possible nor normatively desirable" (Krisch 2011, 17). Actually, in the postnational order, we cannot keep true to the central pillars of constitutionalism; and attempts that loosen the link with the domestic origins risk adjusting too easily the concept to the circumstances of the postnational order (Krisch 2011, 38). The postnational order is a sphere of fate, not of constitution. It is better understood as post-constituent because of adverse institutional and societal conditions. Ascribing the origins of such an order to a constituent power "would be to misunderstand the core of the concept, or to misconceive the distance at which this order travels from potential reconstruction as 'founded by the people'" (Krisch 2016, 678).

The postnational order actually poses two sets of challenges for constituent power. First, there is a multiplication of potential constituent powers (a multiplication of "publics"). This issue is not a new one. It has been consistently raised in multinational states; and in liberal societies, the growing recognition of diversity has led to an imagery of constituent power as a discursive structure (Krisch 2016, 661). The political force of such a reflexive account is precarious, though, because the idea of constituent power is then diluted, as "acts are only recognized as acts of constituent power if they can make a claim to include a multiplicity of (individual) actors in a normatively satisfactorily process" (Krisch 2016, 661). In the global arena, it raises two main issues: first, subnational and national constituencies cannot fully respond to the needs and interests of outsiders affected by their decisions; second, regional levels are not fully inclusive, and their democratic structures are not sufficiently deep. In other words, in the global arena, the locus of constituent power "is too undefined for the concept to have traction at all" (Krisch 2016, 666). The second set of challenges rests with the dispersion of authority, that embodies the "lack of a center". This "makes it much more difficult to relate to a single legitimating subject or process" (Krisch 2010, 667).

Krisch argues that in such a setting, claims to constituent power will keep arising, either into national frames of ascription or sometimes by referring to a transnational collective, but that they will remain "merely political irritants" (Krisch 2016, 677). In other words, they would still draw their power from narratives of popular sovereignty, but they would not underlie the political order. So rather than reimagining the transnational polity or recasting the notion of constituent power to make it more amenable to the current conditions, Krisch focuses on the "irritating" element that (according to him) "has characterized the relationship between (national) constituent power and the global order for a long time" (Krisch 2016, 674). This element is "irritating" because "instances of fundamental domestic change are not construed as constituent power in the system. They act only as political challenges to broader law-making processes" (Krisch 2016, 675). When there is a recourse to a broader (transnational) representation of the acting collective (as, e.g., in resistance against the WTO), "the supposed constituent power [...] does not enter the stage itself: it operates through representation or ascription, and it is invoked to destabilize the claims of constituted powers and to justify resistance against them" (Krisch 2016, 675). In the postnational order, "all these instances appear primarily as acts of resistance—connecting at best to conceptions of constituent power that predates the modern, evolutionary tradition and place contestation, rather than foundation, at their center" (Krisch 2016, 676). Therefore, they cannot be seen as claims to be at the origin of the postnational order itself; we cannot regard the latter as being legitimated by some form of constituent power, for we cannot see it as traceable to an act succeeding in representing its addressees as a group.

The same line of argument explains why Krisch challenges the fitness of constitutionalism *per se* for the postnational order (as well as for diverse societies)[16]. He argues that the assumption that the postnational order ought to be structured in a way that continued on the constitutionalist path is misguided. The legitimacy constitutionalism provides in domestic politics depends upon the foundational tradition (Krisch 2011, 53). As I have already stressed in Chapter 3, "foundational constitutionalism would pose high, perhaps radical demands, on the existing structure and institutions of postnational governance, and would go further than most proposals of postnational constitutionalism to date" (Krisch 2011, 53). Krisch also argues that "neither the delegatory relationship nor domestic implantation can guarantee significant national control over postnational governance beyond the state. This significantly conditions the viability of the domestic constitutional route [...]" (Krisch 2011, 20). He makes a stark contrast between postnational constitutionalism, on the one hand, and pluralism, on the other one. The former "attempts to provide continuity with the domestic constitutionalist tradition by construing an overarching legal framework that determines the relationships of the different levels of law and the distribution of powers among their institutions" (Krisch 2011, 23). It thereby seeks "to redeem the modern, revolutionary promise of a human-made constitution as an antidote to the forces of history, power and chance" (Krisch 2011, 23). But as I said above, Krisch argues that a return to the classical picture is both unlikely and undesirable, since domestic constitutionalism risks being at once underinclusive and insufficiently effective (Krisch 2011, 21). Pluralism rather "sees such an overarching framework as neither practically possible nor normatively desirable and seeks to discern a model of order that relies less on unity and more on the heterarchical interaction of the various layers of law" (Krisch 2011, 23). Pluralism "eschews the hope of building one common, overarching legal framework that would integrate postnational governance, distribute powers, and provide for means of solving disputes between the various layers of law and politics. It is based on the heterarchical interplay of these layers according to rules ultimately set by each layer for itself" (Krisch 2011, 69). Krisch actually argues for systemic pluralism, namely one in which there is no common point of reference within the legal or institutional rules[17]. He also has contributed a great deal to the Global Administrative Law (GAL) project, which focuses on the accountability of global administrative bodies. The GAL project is of a more modest reach than constitutionalism, and hence more suitable for political reform than constitutionalism's holistic vision (Krisch 2010, 245). It "starts from the insight that much of global governance can be understood in administrative terms [...]" (Krisch 2010, 255)[18]. It seeks to map existing and emerging accountability practices in a framework borrowed from administrative law (Krisch 2010, 256). It focuses on particular elements of global governance and the realization of narrower political ideals (Krisch 2010, 246).

Even if Krisch challenges the very desirability of modern constitutionalism and constituent power in the postnational order, there is an unambiguous sense of a loss in Krisch's argument about *pouvoir irritant*. Constituent power embodied the ambition to a comprehensive founding through self-government and allowed to conceive of public power as an exercise of public and private autonomy. This is what we must renounce to in the postnational order by refocusing on *pouvoir irritant*, systemic pluralism, and accountability practices. As I said, from Krisch's perspective the postnational is a sphere of fate, not of constitution. Under the conditions of the polycentric setting of global governance, it is difficult to explain how public power can be regarded as an exercise of public and private autonomy; "[t]he distance between ambition and reality, however, can feed a *pouvoir irritant* that keeps reminding us of what we have lost" (Krisch 2016, 679). In other words, constituent power may survive "as a normative ascription which can, under certain conditions, provide the ideational basis for resistance against global institutions with truncated legitimacy. The *pouvoir constituant* then becomes a discursive resource for the operation of a *pouvoir irritant* in social reality, but it has lost its claim to being the source of legitimacy of the existing—post-constituent—order" (Krisch 2016, 678). In Krisch's work, therefore, the impossibility of making sense of foundational constitutionalism in the postnational order implies challenging the radical promise of agency embodied in constituent power. In other words, it is the radicality of the promise core to constituent power—a comprehensive founding through self-government—that we must forsake. In the postnational sphere, agency is limited to challenging the current order and resisting it (at best, destabilizing it). Renouncing foundationalism means renouncing framing constituencies as the origin of the postnational order.

A similar line of argument is to be found in Möller's analysis of destituent power. In transnational contexts, as there is no clearly demarcated people on a given territory (which is for Möller the inherited point of reference of constituent power), we should reframe constituent power as a negative device and countervailing power—as "a matter of revocatory scenarios which open up avenues for a re-negotiation of existing orders" (Möller 2018, 36). Constituent power conceived as destituent power "provides ample resources for the critique of existing hegemonies within transnational constitutionalism" (Möller 2018, 35). Möller stresses that constituent power "has always been about contestation and even the destitution of already constituted power as well. By invoking constituent power those who were dominated de-legitimised the mode of rule and opened up avenues to re-negotiate the existing order" (Möller 2018, 48). He focuses, then, on a contestatory logic that he holds to be inherent within the concept (rather than on comprehensive founding through self-government). The aim is to "make a strategic use of revocatory scenarios [from below] with a view to undermine hegemonic projects *within* transnational contexts" (Möller 2018, 50). Destituent power aims at overcoming asymmetrical relations of power in specific contexts.

Yet, not anything can count as destituent power: the latter "must urge towards overcoming asymmetrical relations of power (instead of exacerbating them) and it would have to show an internal reflectivity in terms of self-questioning. Otherwise, destituent movements undermine their own promise" (Möller 2018, 53). Such a view, though, stops short from proposing a new constitutional order. Möller acknowledges that contestatory processes "will have to come back to legal formalism in order to self-organize and not to collapse into a mere gesture of total politicization or into an exodus that immunizes itself against critique and reflexivity" (Möller 2018, 54). However, it is far from obvious how such acts of contestation can "translate into collectively binding decisions nor generate democratic legitimacy for them" (Patberg 2019, 96). This is why Patberg argues that destituent power "can complement but not replace the constructive side of constituent power" (Patberg 2019, 96).

A Post-Constituent Order?

So where does that leave us in terms of democratic authorization and collective political agency in the polycentric setting of global governance? What would a post-constituent order mean, from that point of view (assuming that destituent power cannot stand on its own, for it lacks a constructive side)? Would that mean returning to conceptions that predate the modern tradition, and if so, what would be the consequences of such a move?

The focus on contestation contributes a fruitful insight to the debate about constituent power beyond the state. One reason for this is that it rightly emphasizes that constituent power is part to a theory of government belonging with very specific types of polities in which a constitution attributes (*a posteriori*) to a people the foundation of an order, making the people the source of authority within a regime. The scholars discussed in this chapter rightly acknowledge that the postnational order is no such comprehensive order, and that in the postnational domain there is no comprehensive claim to authority to which a people as constituent power can be related. Another reason why their contributions are helpful is that notions of *pouvoir irritant* and destituent power nonetheless try to rescue a role for publics as triggers of constitutional (or public law, in Krisch's case) change, and to reassert the people's right to claim the reorganization of the structures of public authority. They also point to significant transformations in forms of authority; as I will claim in Chapter 7, an accurate analysis of the transformations in the forms of authority is key to framing a conception of collective political agency that may ground democratic authorization in a polycentric setting.

Krisch and Möller both point to a post-constituent order—an order in which claims to constituent power will keep arising (drawing their power from narratives of popular sovereignty), yet remain mere political irritants unsuitable to ground public autonomy. In Krisch's work, constituent power becomes a discursive resource for *pouvoir irritant* but cannot claim to be the source of legitimacy of the political order; a combination of *pouvoir irritant* and administrative law would allow to rescue some (limited) sense of democratic agency (driven by a logic of contestation) in a sphere of fate. Möller makes the critique of existing hegemonies core to destituent power within transnational constitutionalism, because in the transnational sphere there is no clearly demarcated people on a given territory. In both cases, agency is limited to challenging and resisting the current order. One can only hope for piecemeal reforms aiming at ensuring greater accountability.

From my point of view, containment, destituent power, and *pouvoir irritant* are but second-best options aiming, at best, at destabilizing hegemonies. They are fallback solutions built on the assumption that without the possibility or promise of the foundation of a whole new and comprehensive order, the expression of public autonomy is inescapably limited. In other words, it is as if renouncing foundationalism also implies giving up the radical sense of agency that embodied the promise that institutions are for us to build and rebuild; it is to go back to a state of mind in which institutions are driven by forces that are beyond the reach of purposeful institutional design by citizens. This stance risks fostering a sense of powerlessness and resignation. Moreover, some may interpret it as falling back on an idea of resistance which is actually quite different from constituent power. Discussing I. Maus's argument about such a difference, P. Niesen explains that from the latter's point of view,

> Claims to resistance derive their legitimacy not from the horizontal social contract or *pactum unionis* proposed by authors like Hobbes, Rousseau, or Kant, but from a very different and additional vertical contract retained by authors such as Pufendorf or Achenwall. This is a contract of subjection (*pactum suiectionis*), specifying the respective rights and duties of rulers and citizens, violations of which can be redressed via

> a right to resistance [...] Moving on from vertical contracts of subjection to the modern horizontal social contract allows replacing appeals to resistance with appeals to popular sovereignty, that is, the control of constituent power and all other legislative power by the people.
>
> (Niesen 2019a, 33)[19]

However, in a perspective such as Maus's, popular sovereignty is necessarily geared to the nation-state. Hence, although she rightly points to basic differences between resistance and constituent power, reaffirming the classical notion of constituent power is not helpful when trying to frame public autonomy in the post- or transnational sphere. In other words, I agree that acts of contestation are not sufficient to ground constituent power, because they cannot translate into collectively binding decisions, although they contribute to frame alternative narratives of collective agency related to democratic authorization. But falling back on the nation-state and a strategy of containment is not helpful either, for reasons I have explained.

Conclusion

Stances such as Möller and Krisch do not intend to fall back on a mere idea of resistance. It is true that destituent power and *pouvoir irritant* stop short of authorship. Yet, they are still intended to act as triggers of constitutional or public law change. It is also important to stress that Krisch acknowledges that constituent power is but one way of expressing public autonomy. From my point of view, there are sound reasons to believe that agency can still play a significant part if we rather look both at transformations in forms of authority (namely, if we reframe our conception of public power to take into account actual sites and mechanisms of authority) and at how the democratization of public politics actually is driven by contention—and then propose new conceptualizations of the symbolic poles of democratic authorization in such a context. A basic issue is the one of the governing relationships to which people are subjected. There may not be uncontested collectives such as those that were made possible by the comprehensive reach of the sovereign state. Yet, there are publics, constituencies, and governmental capacities that are post- or non-state; there are self-founding regimes to which people are subjected (just as they have been subjected to states as self-founding orders of public power). Since the basic fact of the political is the claim to authority, if we cannot frame these into a systematic approach of the power relationships they embody, then we won't be able to ground appropriately democratic authorization either. Actually, this (along with "our limits of imagination") explains why many people fall back on containment strategies.

One last issue needs to be discussed before turning to narratives of protest. It is the issue of the difference between the notion of *pouvoir irritant* (and destituent power more generally), on the one hand, and Teubner's reformulation of the QOT principle, on the other one. This clarification is necessary, since Krisch's use of the term *pouvoir irritant* is inspired by Teubner's work. Let me first recall that Teubner argues for a reformulation of the QOT principle focusing on the self-contestation of transnational regimes in diverse context-adequate forms (Teubner 2018). From this perspective, transnational institutions must focus on the dissensus element, because they are poor candidates for identitarian consensus building. Teubner puts forward the idea of "organized dissent", namely, the ability "to challenge the decisions of power holders effectively" (Teubner 2018, 13). From his point of view, this idea "concentrates on the problem-solving capacity of democratic institutions" (Teubner 2018, 13), just as epistemic and deliberative theories of democracy do. However, contrary to the latter theories, the concept of organized dissent is skeptical of claims to normative truth. It does not strive for the rightness of political decisions, but rather concentrate "on a 'right to contingency' which opens alternative world constructions" (Teubner 2018, 13); it focuses on the confrontation with alternative world views, rather than on the one best solution (Teubner 2018, 13).

Krisch's use of the term *pouvoir irritant* relates to Teubner's claim that in the context of a (societally and institutionally) fragmented postnational order, "invocations of constituent power are no longer easily connected to the order in its entirety" (Krisch 2016, 673). As I have already explained, Krisch argues that Teubner's account is conceptually problematic because it "downplays the holistic nature of constituent power's ambition" (Krisch 2016, 673). But he nonetheless takes Teubner to rightly acknowledge that invocations of constituent power are "confined to a much smaller scope in terms of possible achievement" (Krisch 2016, 673), hence appearing "as 'irritants' of the broader *pouvoir constitué* of global governance" (Krisch 2016, 673).

However, there seems to me to be a significant difference between Teubner's multiplication of constituent powers and reformulation of the QOT principle, on the one hand, and Krisch's notion of *pouvoir irritant*, on the other one. As I just said, Krisch rightly stresses that Teubner's societal constitutionalism downplays the holistic nature of constituent power's ambition (Krisch 2016, 673). By severing the link between agency, foundation, and holism, Teubner actually distorts the meaning of the notion of constituent power and neglects its nested relationship with the state. One could at first sight think that because he multiplies constituent powers, Teubner also multiplies the points of entry for democratic authorization within the fragmented order of global governance. But as I have explained, the impact rather is to multiply the possibilities for subjecting the capacity for self-rule. Krisch chooses to fall back on a capacity for dissent that still builds on claims that politically challenge governing relationships. He argues that claims to constituent power would still build on narratives of popular sovereignty but that they would not underlie the political order. Correlatively, this also allows to stress that, contrary to Krisch, Teubner at once depoliticizes constitutions and neglects the basic political issue—the one of the enforcement of collectively binding decisions. The multiplication of constituent powers goes along with the dilution of the significance of collective (democratic) authorship of basic norms regulating regimes.

Constituent power can be equated neither with consent nor with dissent. Addressing the challenges of the current polycentric setting of governance from the perspective of public autonomy and democratic authorization requires reaching beyond both foundation and contestation. It requires that we think outside the box of foundational constitutionalism because the latter is not appropriate to the polycentric setting of global governance[20]. It requires that we reach beyond contestation because neither resistance nor mere consent is enough to provide a sound framing of democratic authorization, in such a context. Destituent power needs to work in combination with a constructive dimension[21]. Contention and contestation are a significant part of the framing of democratic authorization, for in framing their claims as to governance relationships, people also frame their identities as political actors, in the course of their interactions with each other as well as with rulers. So let us turn now to approaches that focus on narratives of protest and assess how far the attempts to relate contention with specific narratives of public authority can contribute to re-frame democratic authorization and collective political agency.

Notes

1 The term is used by Krisch's (2016) to designate Grimm's approach.

2 "Public power" denotes the various forms of regulatory activity in general: political power, regulatory powers, the legal conditions for political rules, rule-making, governmental behaviour, rulers' power, laws and acts of law enforcement claiming validity, and acts of public authority (Grimm 2010, 15–19). In the aftermaths of the Reformation, public power was no longer limited to law enforcement. It came to include "the right to create a legal order that was independent of the competing faiths and secular in nature" (Grimm 2010, 6). The prince claimed the monopoly of the legitimate use of force in order to enforce the law against resisting groups. This led both to the privatization of civil society and to the rise of the state, whose most important attribute is sovereignty (the highest and indivisible authority over all subjects). State power is "a concentration of all prerogatives on a certain territory" (Grimm 2010, 11); the specific feature of the state as a political entity is "the concentration of public power in a given territory and the fact that this power was not submitted to any external will" (Grimm 2010, 13). So, in this process, the state actually claimed "the entire public power and the monopoly of legitimate force" (Grimm 2010, 12). The constitution limits the purpose for which, and the conditions under which, it might be used.

3 See, e.g., Grimm (2005, 204). An entity such as the EU has no such basis.

4 See also Walker (2012, 66–7). From such a perspective, the concept of the modern state is a consequence of these socio-cultural facts, rather than their cause (Walker 2012, 67).

5 Constitutionalism hence is "a special and particularly ambitious form of legislation", one that is not identical with the legalization of public power (Grimm 2010, 9). Only a constitution that comprises both democracy and the rule of law "is capable of fulfilling the expectations of constitutionalism fully" (Grimm 2010, 10). Constitutions have a normative function, but they are subject to expectations that extend beyond that function because they are expected to unify a society, to be a guarantee of the fundamental consensus necessary to social cohesion. They do this because they are to enable political power to be exercised according to a set of rules, to exclude certain fundamental values and procedures from day-to-day political debate, and to reconcile continuity and change (Grimm 2005, 195).

6 In both cases constituent power is reinscribed into a (negativistic) logic of contestation, either as a discursive resource or as a critique of existing hegemonies. A potential difference between Möller's destituent power and Krisch's *pouvoir irritant* rests with the part played by constitutionalism itself. But this is not the focus of this chapter (nor of this book).

7 As I said, Krisch rather designates it as *pouvoir irritant*.

8 Because it results in binding norms "that are reinforced, if necessary, through the coercive means of the state" (Patberg 2019, 87).

9 G. Agamben, for example, holds that constituent power recreates new forms of law, whereas destituent power deposes law once and for all, making up for a new reality (Patberg 2019, 87).

10 As I also explained in Chapter 1, I (following Føllesdal) take institutions to play a basic part in sustaining reciprocity, in socializing individuals so that they comply with norms involving unconditional cooperation, and in limiting free-riding. This does not mean, though, that democracy should be limited to its current institutional mechanisms nor that these cannot be redesigned in order to fare better as to democratic authorization.

11 In the case of Krisch, though, it aims at public law reordering rather than at a post-state constitutionalism. Krisch actually argues for pluralism as the alternative to constitutionalism in the context of the global polycentric polity. But public law is core to his approach.

12 Discussions of state civil disobedience as destituent power revolve around the justifiability of illegal state action "as a response to particular defects of existing constitutional orders" (Patberg 2019, 92).

13 Patberg assumes that in the context of the EU, destituent power can take a purely negativistic form because even if the EU were to be completely dissolved, states would still be there. But he also argues that the appeal of a destituent power grounded in popular sovereignty lies in a lure towards the jurisgenerative dimension of constituent power—namely, constructive projects.

14 "Public power" designates governance institutions, political decisions, ultimate responsibility for regulatory responses to political challenges, the problem-solving capacity of public actors, and the provision of public goods by institutions (Krisch 2010).

15 In the absence of the circumstances that made a claim to common representation plausible, "other forms of legitimation will have to be sought [...] ranging from the technocratic to visions of democracy that rely more on contestation and participation than on foundation" (Krisch 2016, 676).

16 He is the only scholar discussed in this book to do so. Walker argues for a *constitutional* pluralism. Krisch argues that three main understandings of constitutionalism shape both the debate on the European project and debates as to the postnational order: a focus on checks, with an emphasis on human rights and legalization (the submission of politics to a process of law); a focus on structural issues (the constitution as a unitary, hierarchically ordered political structure); and a discursive strand (the constitution as a process) (Krisch 2011, 34–5). From his point of view, "translating constitutionalism to

the postnational sphere is likely to alter its appearance significantly, ushering in fragmented reconceptualization or at least tilting the balance in favour of a liberal model that emphasizes the rule of law over democratic concerns" (Krisch 2016, 678).

17 He distinguishes systemic pluralism, on the one hand, from institutional pluralism, on the other one. The latter allows for a common point of reference and is a continuation of constitutionalist themes.

18 The GAL project focuses on "the limitation of power, the requirement of justification and proportionality, the procedural mechanisms for deliberate decision-making, and the protection of human rights" (Kuo 2012). It carries an idea of inclusiveness and deliberation.

19 From this perspective, narratives of resistance (and those of civil disobedience) impose conformity with the constitutional order, making it difficult to see "how those subjected to a constitutional order can possibly claim to want to transcend it" (Niesen 2019a, 33). They also obstruct a clear view of the grounds of non-compliance, since resistance can never be a coercive claim (it can only be an ideal one). And they express a civil mindset, insofar as "the strategy of symbolic rule violations does not constitute a trigger for processes of democratic will-formation, leading to a comprehensive change in law, but restricts itself to seeking legal recourse" (Niesen 2019a, 33, quoting Maus 1992, 37).

20 I mean both that it cannot adequately capture the challenges related to public authority that are raised by such a setting and that it is not normatively desirable. As I have explained earlier, it already was challenged in the "domestic" context. Globalization has made these intrinsic tensions and paradoxes more visible.

21 I hereby rephrase Patberg's claim that destituent power must ultimately work in combination with "a constructive exercise of constituent power" (Patberg 2019, 95). He stresses that constituent power includes the idea "that political orders should be established and reformed on the initiative of free and equal persons", as well as the idea "that constituted powers should be excluded from constitutional politics to prevent the danger that public authority takes a life of its own through the self-referential distribution of competences [...]" (Patberg 2018, 264). Destituent power, therefore, "is not a free-standing, independent normative concept" (Patberg 2019, 95). I agree with him that "Ultimately, the potential of a purely negativistic logic of constitutional politics is limited" (Patberg 2019, 83–4). But I argue that we need to reframe this constructive ambition because the notion of constituent power is too dependent upon statehood to allow for a sound grounding of democratic authorization in the current setting. Krisch agrees that the postnational space demands "new, different answers to the question of how to structure governance" (Krisch 2011, 69); however, his argument allows only for a limited recasting of the constructive dimension associated with constituent power.

References

Grimm, Dieter. 2005. "Integration by Constitution." *International Journal of Constitutional Law* 3, no. 2-3: 193–208.

Grimm, Dieter. 2010. "The Achievement of Constitutionalism and Its Prospects in a Changed World." In *The Twilight of Constitutionalism?*, edited by Petra Dobner and Martin Loughlin, 3–22. Oxford: Oxford University Press.

Krisch, Nico. 2010. "Global Administrative Law and the Constitutional Ambition." In *The Twilight of Constitutionalism?*, edited by Petra Dobner and Martin Loughlin, 245–266. Oxford: Oxford University Press.

Krisch, Nico. 2011. *Beyond Constitutionalism. The Pluralist Structure of Postnational Law.* Oxford: Oxford University Press.

Krisch, Nico. 2016. "*Pouvoir Constituant* and *Pouvoir Irritant* in the Postnational Order." *International Journal of Constitutional Law* 14, no. 3: 657–679.

Krisch, Nico. 2017. "Liquid Authority in Global Governance." *International Theory* 9, no. 2: 237–260.

Kuo, Ming-Sung. 2012. "Interpublic Legality or Post-Public Legitimacy? Global Governance and the Curious Case of Global Administrative Law as a New Paradigm of Law." *International Journal of Constitutional Law* 10, no. 4: 1050–1075.

Möller, Kolja. 2018. "From Constituent to Destituent Power beyond the State." *Transnational Legal Theory* 9, no. 1: 32–55.

Newman, Saul. 2017. "What Is an Insurrection? Destituent Power and Ontological Anarchy in Agamben and Stirner." *Political Studies* 65, no. 2: 284–299.

Niesen, Peter. 2019a. "Reframing Civil Disobedience: Constituent Power as a Language of Transnational Protest." *Journal of International Political Theory* 15, no. 1: 31–48.

Patberg, Markus. 2018. "Challenging the Masters of the Treaties: Emerging Narratives of Constituent Power in the European Union." *Global Constitutionalism* 7, no. 2: 263–293.

Patberg, Markus. 2019. "Destituent Power in the European Union: On the Limits of a Negativistic Logic of Constitutional Politics." *Journal of International Political Theory* 15, no. 1: 82–99.

Teubner, Gunther. 2018. "*Quod omnes tangit*: Transnational Constitutions Without Democracy?" *Journal of Law and Society* 45, special issue 1: S5–S29.

Walker, Neil. 2010. "Beyond the Holistic Constitution?" In *The Twilight of Constitutionalism?*, edited by Petra Dobner and Martin Loughlin, 291–308. Oxford: Oxford University Press.

Walker, Neil. 2012. "Postnational Constitutionalism and Postnational Public Law: A Tale of Two Neologisms." *Transnational Legal Theory* 3, no. 1: 61–85.

6

CONSTITUENT POWER AND "NARRATIVES OF PROTEST"

So far, approaches that recast or translate constituent power in ways that seem up to the expectations associated with the modern notion of constituent power continue to abide by the basics of foundationalism—which is problematic in the current polycentric setting. And approaches that renounce foundationalism seem to have a hard time in framing a conception of democratic authorization—an idea of collective political agency that extends beyond consent or dissent. Notions of destituent power and *pouvoir irritant* are mainly negativistic: they convey the sense of an irreplaceable lost; they do not really frame a constructive side that could complement contestation and dissent. They hence make it difficult to conceive of how public autonomy can be framed and embodied in the current context. In some cases (although not necessarily in the ones I have discussed), they may bring us back to an assessment of rule by non-democratic criteria (or criteria that are neutral vis-à-vis a government's democratic credential) (Niesen 2019a, 32–3). Consent, after all, does not equate with democratic authorization.

However, notions of destituent power and *pouvoir irritant* open the way for a discussion of how "narratives of protest" can contribute to reframe collective political agency in the current, polycentric setting of governance. Narratives of protest play a significant part in any discussion about constituent power in the current context. They do so because in contestation and contention, people frame their claims as to public authority in specific discourses ("narratives"), and because the mechanisms and processes through which they interact with each other and with rulers also shape their political identities. More broadly speaking, they also are significant because democratization depends on contentious politics (although the latter is not always conducive to democratization)[1]. Approaches that focus on narratives of protest raise three significant issues: are the assumptions of an open composition

DOI: 10.4324/9781003221722-7

of constituent power that is a by-product of processes of constitutionalization and of an always available pre-institutional self-activation consistent with the radical promise embodied in the modern notion of constituent power? Is this still constituent power? And if it is not, what is it (in other words, how do we frame it so as to embody public autonomy)?

Some approaches relate narratives of protest to a sense of political agency akin to the one that was core to constituent power, yet still try to capture what it may means in a quite different (post-Westphalian) context. They do so by focusing on a transformative ambition and by connecting it to a narrative of agency; they explicitly aim at framing the conception and representation of a collective political agent. Their contribution hence is significant as to the purposes of this book. As Blokker has stressed, there has been little systematic research on "how legal mobilization and the rights claims of social movements are related to the more general forms of constitutional claim-making, inclusionary calls, and forms of (radical) critique" (Blokker 2018, 54). In the main views of constitutions in scholarly debates, the democratic role of citizens and civil society is marginalized or limited. Approaches discussed in this chapter focus on such a role while trying to connect it with theoretical approaches that can allow for a constructive dimension related to democratic authorization of post-state regimes.

More specifically, two such approaches will be discussed in this chapter: Niesen's charting of a third path between foundation and contestation, and Patberg's analysis of public narratives revealing latent notions of constituent power in the EU. I am aware that most of their discussion deals with the case of the EU. I have argued earlier that the latter is a *sui generis* case, one from which we cannot necessarily generalize. Moreover, discussing constituent power in the EU case does not necessarily require us to depart significantly from the classical notion of constituent power. However, I still take their contributions to be significantly useful inasmuch as they attempt to rescue the constructive side of constituent power in a conception more appropriate to a mixed polity and that does not necessarily build on foundationalism. In Niesen's case, for example, a focus on the transformative function of the ascription (or claim) to constituent power allows to cast aside the foundational tradition without renouncing the empowering side of constituent power. Protest narratives are seen as a way to connect the category of constituent power with political agency in post- or non-state polities.

Transformative Protests and the Language of Constituent Power in Processes of Constitutionalization Beyond the State

Niesen is interested in whether the language of constituent power can offer a normative basis for transformative protests beyond the state. He also stresses the need for a revised notion of constituent power that can provide critical purchase on processes of constitutionalization beyond the state. He is interested both in the usefulness of the notion of constituent power in understanding transnational protests and in the part it plays in the reconstruction of claims to authority in processes of constitutionalization in non-state contexts. Let us start with the former claim, namely, the one related to the understanding, analysis, and justification of transnational protest.

According to Niesen, protest narratives are a way of connecting the category of constituent power with political agency. Narratives of protest "have strategic and justificatory dimensions that can be discussed with a view to their functionality and appropriateness" (Niesen 2019b, 3). He takes the vocabularies of constituent power and civil disobedience to be complementary, with the latter having the potential of expressing a transformative intent. From his point of view, "tying constituent power to civil disobedience may help to clear up the function of the former for protest practices as it can serve to formulate a fundamental qualification" (Niesen 2019b, 6). Civil disobedience has a specific communicative intent; "[i]t admits to speaking from a particular point of view and attempts to persuade the mainstream citizenry" (Niesen 2019b, 6). Invoking constituent power in civil disobedience "is based on an exclusively communicative authority: a claim to rights to swing public opinion in order to enable a constitutional politics, not a claim to pre-empt that politics, much less execute constitutional change unilaterally" (Niesen 2019b, 6). Concepts of resistance and disobedience, on the one hand, and concepts of popular sovereignty and constituent power, on the other one, are not opposed to each other: the former are types of political action, while the latter are "Hohfeldian powers"[2]. Hence, "it is possible that the former types of activity draw on, contribute to, or instantiate exercises of the latter type of powers. The central conflict between the narratives of resistance and disobedience and the narrative of constituent power may lie in their scope, extension, advantages, and disadvantages as justificatory languages" (Niesen 2019a, 35). There is no internal connection between protest and constituent power, though; and Niesen acknowledges that it is not clear "whether civil disobedience and constituent power can be successfully transnationalized", as both "were specifically tailored for statist polities" (Niesen 2019a, 37).

Niesen's discussion of narratives of protest focuses on DiEM25[3] and on the role of the notion of constituent power in the strategy of this movement. He relates constituent power to some (intentional) transformative purpose. In Europe, illegal protests acting as if federal institutions were already in place "can hardly be justified as purely defensive acts of resistance. They cannot exclusively rely for their justification on the integrity of an already existing institutional setup. Instead, they must refer to a transformative authority: in other words, a *pouvoir constituant*, which is assumed and *articulated* in at least some acts of disobedience" (Niesen 2019a, 40). However, claims of articulating constituent power shall be distinguished from claims of activating it. Protests activate constituent power, for they are "a political activity that brings about a change in [the] allocation [of constituent power], such that for a given polity, there occurs a shift in the holders of constituent power" (Niesen 2019a, 41). Although transformative civil disobedience in processes of self-determination "can be framed as the articulation of constituent power" (Niesen 2019a, 41), such articulation is inconclusive, for protest activities do not claim authority in attempting to bring a fundamental change in the law (Niesen 2019a, 42). Actually,

> [t]he articulation of constituent power provides an empowering self-description for border-crossing protest movements, especially where their activism involves law-breaking, but it does not invest them with conclusive entitlements to the formation or exercise of a *pouvoir constituant.* The limits of a constituent power-based approach to civil disobedience lie in unilateral attempts at effectively shaping or exercising such power. Constituent power gives protest movements a deep and broad basis for advocating change, not for pre-empting it.
>
> (Niesen 2019a, 46)

Niesen rightly stresses that resistance as a language of protest allows to focus on the fact that in resisting, those subject to rule "prove the existence of relations of domination" (Niesen 2019b, 4)[4]. Resistance hence manifests "the fact that the people are endowed with constituent power in permanence—they are always free to change, amend, remake the political order at will" (Niesen 2019b, 5–6)[5].

Yet, resistance as a language of protest suffers from two flaws. First, it is "indeterminate vis-à-vis the type of political system it opposes, or the political ideals it invokes, especially as regards their democratic or rule-of-law credentials. Resistance is thus too broad a notion to specify the strategies of current democratically minded protest movements" (Niesen 2019b, 4)[6]. Second, resistance, at least in its origins, has "a status quo ante bias: it fights to retain what has to be taken as legitimate possession, against tyrannical encroachment. It provides a justification for repair, but not for change" (Niesen 2019b, 4–5).

The notion of constituent power can be useful for analyzing and justifying transformative protests[7]:

> One asset of the language of constituent power is that claiming it gives protest a cause, a subject, a justification and an agenda. Its *cause* is subjection to unauthorized rule or domination, brought about by past usurpation of decision-making powers. The *subject* of constituent power has traditionally been identified as 'the people', in polemical opposition against the de facto holders of political powers. Its *justificatory force* lies in the idea that all decision-making authority must be explicitly circumscribed, authorized by the people, and permanently open to change.

> No order can claim full legitimacy if it has not arisen through constituent processes in the right way and if it cannot be undone by the constituent subject. Finally, constituent power gives protest an *agenda*: in its classical version, that of a fundamental legal transformation of the present situation.
>
> (Niesen 2019b, 5)

But can it offer "a normative basis for transformative protests *beyond the state*" (Niesen 2019b, 7)? This question points to three basic issues. The first relates to the agent itself: who is to claim constituent power? States? Executives? Individuals? Collectives of individuals? The second relates to constituencies: how are we to distinguish authoritative and well-justified protests from non-authoritative and ill-justified ones? Contrary to civil disobedience (which is featured by co-citizens), in many cases of transnational protest the constituency "cannot be fixed in advance. Indeed, in most contexts, a formal institutional co-citizens status of protest participants will not be seen as decisive for distinguishing authoritative and well-justified from non-authoritative and ill-justified protests" (Niesen 2019b, 7). This difficulty can be addressed in two different ways. A first way is to reconstruct transnational protests "as expressions of constituent power with reference to an already existing legal-constitutional frame" (Niesen 2019b, 7). This is to assume, though, that the composition of the constituency is already fixed—that it is not an open question[8]. For from this perspective, "the truth about where constituent power lies is a matter of the best available interpretation of an already existing transnational polity. Protesters derive their authority from membership when acting extra-legally to transform the existing polity, and thus authoritatively exercise civil disobedience or constituent power" (Niesen 2019b, 8). A second possible way to address the need for distinguishing between authoritative and non-authoritative protests is to adopt a prospective approach that refer to an open membership condition appealing to a practice-based conception "that cannot be bound to the reconstruction of existing institutions" (Niesen 2019b, 8). In this case, the composition of the constituency is left open. It is assumed that "the truth about where constituent power lies is a matter of constituent practices and thus exposed to revision through the very protest practices they account for [...]Formal citizenship is not required in order to authorize transnational protests by non-citizens as (fallible) articulations of *pouvoir constituant*" (Niesen 2019b, 8). The third, and last, issue as to the question of whether constituent power can offer "a normative basis for transformative protests *beyond the state*" (Niesen 2019b, 7) relates to the legalistic function of constituent power: using the notion of constituent power to analyze protests is viewed by some as imposing a public law bias on protests rather than focusing on their intrinsic value as practices or forms of life, because of the legalistic understanding of constituent power. I have already discussed this issue earlier[9].

How are we to address these issues? Niesen argues that it is plausible to describe the need for popular authorization of public decision-making by keeping with the notion of constituent power, in processes of constitutionalization[10] beyond the state, but that the notion must be revised in order to do so. The post-national order features decision-making bodies that enable supra-state powers and limit domestic ones. It necessarily raises the question of constituent power because of the assumption that constituent power is a key legitimating feature of state constitutions. According to Niesen, "it is not implausible to continue to describe the need for the popular authorization of public decision-making by sticking to the notion of constituent power if we manage to sever its traditional connection to a single state demos and allow for its complex allocation to various individuals and/or collective actors" (Niesen 2017b, 231). The critical bite of such a revised notion of constituent power lies with its capacity to diagnose constituent usurpation in processes of constitutionalization beyond the state (Niesen 2017b, 231). The notion of constituent power can take on a critical function in global constitutionalism because the latter raises the issue of "who ought to be conceived of as authoritative constituting and constitution-changing actors" (Niesen 2017b, 227). Its explanatory potential "lies in its contribution to reconstructive accounts of claims to authority that are embodied in supra-state orders aspiring to constitutional status [...]" (Niesen 2017b, 227). Constitutionalization reconstructs claims to authority by relating them to constituent power, just as it did in the state context.

But what does this revised notion of constituent power look like, exactly? In Niesen's work, it has three basic characteristics. First, in the case of global constitutionalism, ascriptions of constituent power are relevant "in a transformational, not a foundational perspective" (Niesen 2017b, 223)[11]. Second, the composition of such constituent power must be conceived of as open: the issue cannot allow for a tautological answer (as it did in the state context), nor can a single definite actor capable of decision-making can be identified (Niesen 2017b, 230). Hence, in global constitutionalism, the

> logic of discovery of constituent powers is largely reactive: it traces their emergence as by-product of processes of constitutionalization. Where constitutions emerge, they create their own authorities, thereby suspending the alleged social contract or natural law basis of *pouvoirs constituants*. We can no longer assume that membership in a *pouvoir constituant* is fixed before constitution-making has been brought to a definitive end. Since we also assume that under the doctrine of constituent power, processes of constitutionalization do not allow of a definitive point of termination, this entails that global constitutionalism needs to conceive of the composition of its *pouvoirs constituants* as open in principle.
>
> (Niesen 2017b 230–1)[12]

Third, Niesen reasserts that constituent power cannot be bound by existing constitutions, nor can be restricted in its forms of expression. The creative side of the exercise of constituent power "can never be fully institutionalized" (Niesen 2017b, 231). Plausible uses of the notion of constituent power in global constitutionalism cannot be restricted "to the *ex post* empowerment of future constitution-owning actors" (Niesen 2017b, 231). From his point of view, "in contrast to the state-based understanding of constituent power, a pre-institutional self-activation is always available in global constitutionalization. No authorization is needed for people to claim that all authorization derives from them" (Niesen 2017b, 231). The language of constituent power "channels claims to eventual self-government, not just the absence of tyranny" (Niesen 2017b, 232).

Therefore, in processes of global constitutionalization, the concept of constituent power is useful because it has three functions: an explanatory one (it contributes to reconstructive accounts of claims to authority embodied in supra-state orders aspiring to constitutional status) (Niesen 2017b, 231); a critical-restrictive one (the issue of "who ought to be conceived of as authoritative constituting and constitution-changing actors") (Niesen 2017b, 227); and an empowering one (the creative side of constituent power, the "pre-institutional self-activation" aspect that cannot be fully institutionalized, and yet is not merely a claim to non-compliance to usurped authority).

By focusing on the transformative function of the ascription of (or claim to) constituent power, Niesen hopes to chart a third path between foundation and contestation. The focus on transformation seems to allow to cast aside the foundational tradition without giving up the creative and empowering side of constituent power. It reasserts the normative significance of capturing democratic (collective) agency. Niesen actually makes it more vivid because he wants to account for the actual participation of those who own constituent power. A "bootstrapping ascription" is not enough, from his point of view, since it can do without the actual participation of those who own constituent power, "as a merely formal reference to a subject to whom constitutive authority is imputed" (Niesen 2019a, 39). Combining a focus on actual participation and the narratives that frame it (and actually, the interaction between participation and the construction of narratives), on the one hand, with the notion of constituent power as a normative basis for reconstructing claims to authority, on the other one, could help rescuing a sense of democratic self-authorization in mixed polities. It is an attempt to retrieve the idea that those who are constituted as the subjects of constitutional authority should also be represented as its constituent authors[13].

However, I am not certain that the close relationship of the notion of constituent power with statehood warrants its use in other, non-state contexts, if the aim is to reconstruct claims to (public) authority so as to empower constituencies with the capacity for self-rule[14]. There may actually be a confusion, here, in the discussion of the notion of constituent power (and of constitutionalism as well, but that is a matter for constitutional theorists to decide): in post-national contexts, the cause of protests would be unauthorized rule in undefined polities[15]; in the state context, constituent power belongs with a framework aiming at the legitimation of public power in well-defined polities (constituent power belongs with constitutionalism as a theory of government developed to frame a specific type of regime, not the state itself as the condition of the unity of a people). As I explained in Chapter 1 (building on Louhglin's work), it is the authority of the constitution that derives from the construct of the people; the foundations of political authority lie in the state[16]. This does not only impact on the issue of the subject of constituent power, but also on its cause and agenda. Niesen rightly points to the transformations in patterns of authority; this is precisely why we have to build new narratives of political authority and democratic agency. Resistance actually (and significantly) proves the existence of relations of domination. It also points to the very sense that people struggle for civic freedom in widely different political and social contexts—that self-rule is (to borrow J. Tully's words) the oldest political good. But is a "constituent" power without any ground in a legal-political order—in other words, a "constituent" power conceived as open, reactive and pre-institutional, which is "up for grabs"—still constituent power in the modern sense? And if it is not, what is it exactly?

Niesen's own work does not provide for a well-defined answer to the issue of agency (who is to claim constituent power) and constituencies (the distinction between authoritative and non-authoritative protests). Let me stress that I do not mean to say that he does not contribute significantly to debates on democratic authorization in the post-national order; I merely mean to say that the notion of constituent power may not be the more appropriate tool to conveys the fruitful insights of his work. In the transnational order, there is no uncontested collective such as the one that was assumed in a state context[17]. The holistic ambition characteristic of constituent power (the claim to make and remake the entire system of government) also must be forsaken; and apart from the cases of specific entities such as the EU, it is doubtful we can expect some comprehensive founding of self-government. Let me turn, then, to Patberg's work. For Patberg explicitly focuses on the connection between public narratives and constituent power as a way of framing models of democratic decision-making.

Constituent Power in Public Narratives About the EU

I have mentioned earlier that Patberg stresses that the notion of destituent power is not a free-standing, independent normative concept[18]. It can complement the constructive side of constituent power but it cannot replace it, because acts of contestation cannot translate directly into collectively binding decisions, nor generate legitimacy for the latter (Patberg 2019, 96). Constituent power bears a "future-oriented, normative" meaning, namely, "the idea of a democratic process of constitutional politics initiated by free and equal persons" (Patberg 2018, 264). It includes two ideas: the idea "that political orders should be established and reformed on the initiative of free and equal persons" (Patberg 2018, 264); and the idea "that constituted powers should be excluded from constitutional politics to prevent the danger that public authority takes a life of its own through the self-referential distribution of competences" (Patberg 2018, 264)[19].

A significant aspect of Patberg's contribution to debates on constituent power beyond the state lies with his claim that a normative account of constituent power cannot be developed *in abstracto*. Such an account must be guided "by ideas that have already gained traction among citizens" (Patberg 2018, 264). From his point of view, models of democratic decision-making must combine the "is" and the "ought" (empirical and normative legitimacy), because the *de facto* validity of a norm varies with the addressees' belief in legitimacy, and this belief is based on the supposition that the norm can be justified. In other words, to have any practical relevance, a prescriptive account of constituent power needs to make sense "to those to whom we ascribe founding authority" (Patberg 2018, 267). Moreover, "it is a defining feature of constituent power that the *pouvoir constituant* is free to choose its own forms of expression" (Patberg 2018, 267).

Patberg elaborates this idea by discussing constituent power in the EU. Protest movements such as DiEM25, Plan B, and Eurexit represent attempts to reorganize the EU from within. According to him, "it seems promising to understand these developments in terms of destituent power" (Patberg 2019, 83), because although they aim at reforms, their strategies reflect "an attitude of opposition rather than constitution" (Patberg 2019, 83)[20]. He argues that

> [a]s past attempts to replace executive-centred treaty making with formal procedures for democratic higher lawmaking have proved difficult [...], the idea that contestatory politics could function as an informal pathway to constitutional change seems promising. Public discourse during the euro crisis has produced notions of counter-power that could inform a new mode of reorganizing the EU's structure and competence.
> (Patberg 2019, 84)

All three movements have projects as to EU constitutional politics, and "[i]n each case, the ultimate objective is to reorganize public authority" (Patberg 2019, 85)[21].

Patberg stresses that "the potential of a purely negativistic logic of constitutional politics is limited" (Patberg 2019, 84). A juridical destituent power grounded in popular sovereignty emphasizes "the right to dismantle constitutional orders without the intention to construct new ones" (Patberg 2019, 84), hence capturing the disruptive political strategies of EU protest movements. But "democratic legitimacy for new constitutional norms cannot be generated out of acts of contestation alone. As soon as jurisgenerative ambitions are involved, which seems almost inevitable, a purely negativistic logic of constitutional politics reaches its limits. [...] In the final analysis, destituent power can only work in combination with (at least the prospect of) a constructive exercise of constituent power" (Patberg 2019, 95).

According to him, "the EU could enable the exercise of constituent power if it established a procedural path for higher law-making that excludes ordinary political institutions" (Patberg 2018, 267). To get from this abstract idea "to an actual alternative to executive-centred treaty-making" (Patberg 2018, 267)—namely, to a model of democratic decision-making that bridges the gap "between facts and norms"—he analyzes public narratives in which citizens challenge the role of the states as "masters of the Treaties" in the EU[22]. He takes these ideas endorsed by citizens as actual attempts to give shape to a European constituent power. According to him, analyzing these public narratives "can reveal latent notions of constituent power in the EU that give us an indication as to which political theories have some initial plausibility as basis for the envisaged normative account because they explicate ideas that at least some of the relevant actors endorse" (Patberg 2018, 268).

These narratives present specific understandings of "who should be in charge of EU constitutional politics, how the respective subject came to find itself in that position, and how it should invoke its founding authority in the future" (Patberg 2018, 271). They are constructed by both institutional and non-institutional actors (protest movements, unions, public intellectuals, parlementarians, ...). They should be considered as emerging rather than as consolidated; in other words, "they are not sedimented in the same way in political practices, norms, and institutions as is the case with long-established stories that have already acquired a justificatory function" (Patberg 2018, 271). This might be due in part "to the fact that they potentially conflict with state-bound ideas of founding authority" (Patberg 2018, 271). They provide a potential link between facts and norms because they convey sovereignty claims that can have a real effect on practice (Patberg 2018, 271). Hence, "[a] mapping of public narratives is a way to make sure, first, that our normative considerations on constituent power in the EU tie in with ideas that are emerging in empirical practice and, second, that they do not unduly interfere with the freedom of the *pouvoir constituant* to choose its own forms of expression" (Patberg 2018, 272).

Patberg's identification of relevant narratives has been guided by two main criteria. First, the narratives challenge the authority of the "masters of the Treaties". Second, the narratives "present a proposal for how the citizens could take control of European integration on the basis of a democratic form of EU constitutional politics" (Patberg 2018, 273). On such basis, Patberg identifies four narratives that can be read as attempts to give shape to an EU constituent power. Assessing Patberg's claims requires presenting each of these narratives briefly. The first one ("We, the people of Europe") conveys the idea of a cross-border constituent power composed of European citizens. According to this narrative, the unification of Europe was a great achievement, but it was an elite project. As such, it has been undermining democracy and social justice; the euro crisis has accelerated this process. To get out of this situation, the EU must be transformed "into a supranational democracy that restores solidarity and governs the existing (economic) community of fate. Building such a new order can only be the task of all Europeans who should put their nationalities aside and establish themselves as a cross-border constituent power" (Patberg 2018, 273). DiEM25 is the most prominent proponent of this narrative. It aims at a European constituent assembly "that is to enable the citizens to give the EU a new—and this time democratic—constitution" (Patberg 2018, 274)[23]. This constitution would be the one of a supranational democracy, of one cross-border political community.

The second narrative ("We, the peoples of Europe") ascribes constituent power to the demoi of the member states[24]. The transfer of the substance of the Constitutional Treaty—rejected by people in France and the Netherlands in 2005—into a reform treaty prepared behind closed doors is seen as the bypassing of the peoples, whose demand for control over EU constitutional politics remains unheard. Yet, it is the peoples who are the EU's ultimate source of authority. The main message of this second narrative is "that the predominance of executives needs to come to an end. This demand is explicitly formulated in the terminology of *pouvoir constituant* and *pouvoirs constitués*" (Patberg 2018, 278). The focus is on a plurality of constituent powers "that have an interest in defending their respective structures of nation-state democracy" (Patberg 2018, 279).

The third narrative ("We, the citizens of Europe and of its Member States") claims that a federal union is the only way for Europe to retain its current position. This union is meant to be a non-state federation; it "could only be legitimately created through a process of constitution-making that enables the citizens to act as a dual constituent power and to determine the common good from a European as well as from a national perspective" (Patberg 2018, 279; see also p. 281)[25]. From this perspective, the basic problem of the EU is that a political union was not established alongside the monetary one. European integration must be deepened through institution building. For this order to be functional, "the citizens would have to conceive of themselves as members of two different political communities at the same time" (Patberg 2018, 281). Hence, this narrative "presents each individual as a member of two different demoi at the same time. From this perspective, the EU's constituent power consists of European and national parts [...]" (Patberg 2018, 281)[26].

The fourth narrative ("We, the multitude of Europe") does not delineate a subject and "focuses on resistance as a trigger for constitutional change" (Patberg 2018, 282). The EU, and especially the euro, are understood as instruments for the realization of a neoliberal agenda "aiming at the deregulation of markets and the privatization of public sectors. To achieve these goals, more and more constraints on nation-state democracy had to be established over time" (Patberg 2018, 282). The reinstallation of democracy requires a radical transformation. However, as "the institutional structure of the EU is specifically designed to obstruct any change that could pose a threat to the neoliberal hegemony [...] the only option for restoring popular sovereignty is a rupture that forces a renegotiation of the treaties" (Patberg 2018, 283)[27].

All of these narratives reject "executive-centred treaty making, which is seen as lacking democratic legitimacy" (Patberg 2018, 285). All of them "call into question the view that the complexity and fast growth of the EU has left intergovernmentalism as the only plausible steering mechanism of European integration. The bottom line is that 'the people' should reclaim what [...] has been illegitimately withheld from them: the right to decide on the EU's structure and competences" (Patberg 2018, 285). But these narratives offer very different views as to the subject and object of constituent power. The first one argues for a cross-border (supranational) constituent power that aims at a democratic constitution for the EU, a constitution that is to be established by a constituent assembly. The second one argues for a plurality of constituent power (with no overarching one) that have an interest in defending the structures of their respective nation-state democracy; in this narrative, the way for such constituent powers to decide upon the competences and structures of the EU would seem to be through referendum on treaty proposals. The third one argues for a mixed constituent power made of individuals as members of two demoi at the same time; the institutions and competences of the EU should be decided by a convention. The fourth one focuses on resistance as a trigger for constitutional change; it does not propose a delineated subject of constituent power.

As I have already mentioned earlier, Patberg takes such a mapping of the public narratives that challenge the role of the states as "masters of the treaties" to be useful in determining "which political theories have some initial plausibility as starting points for a normative account of constituent power in the EU [...]" (Patberg 2018, 287). Each narrative "shows an affinity to a theoretical framework developed in EU scholarship [...] These political theories could be used to develop the competing notions of constituent power—which are only vaguely articulated in the public narratives—into systematic models that could then be analyzed in a comparative perspective" (Patberg 2018, 287). The picture of a cross-border constituent power oriented towards European solidarity lends some initial plausibility to the political theory of "regional cosmopolitanism". The picture of a constituent power segmented into national parts and geared towards restoring the popular sovereignty of the national demoi in order to make sure that membership in the supranational polity does not undermine citizens' political autonomy "shows affinity to the political theory of demoi-cracy, which portrays the EU as a political system grounded on a plurality of peoples that are determined to engage in a common project of self-government" (Patberg 2018, 288). The picture of a constituent power ascribed to individuals as members of two demoi at the same time (a European one and the one of their respective nation-state) "seems to support the political theory of 'split' popular sovereignty, which conceives of the EU as a non-state federation and suggests that such a constitutional order has a dual source of democratic legitimacy [...]" (Patberg 2018, 288)[28]. The picture of a non-delineated political subject (the "multitude") shows affinity with the political theory of destituent power. Except for the latter, these approaches identify some collective political agent (in the making?) to whom constituent power can be ascribed and which is to be the source of legitimacy of the constitutional order. Matched with specific public narratives about the right of the people to reclaim the right to decide on the EU's structure and competences, they combine the activation and articulation of constituent power. Let me stress that according to Niesen, the first two types of political theories actually are monistic. The first one ascribes constituent power exclusively to European citizens-subjects (Niesen 2019a, 37)[29]. The second one ascribes constituent power exclusively to the peoples of the EU member states, so that constituent power "lies in the people severally, not collectively speaking: the aggregate of plural *pouvoirs constituants* does not create a new *pouvoir* in addition to those of the several peoples [...]" (Niesen 2017b, 228).

Patberg stresses that there is a significant difficulty as to conceiving constituent power when it is to be exercised "among (the members of) already constituted political communities which themselves go back to an act of founding" (Patberg 2017c, 203–4). The classical understanding of constituent power "does not live up to the complexity of the constellation that political communities find themselves in when they participate in EU constitutional politics" (Patberg 2017c, 206). There is a normative problem relating with the possibility that "the exercise of constituent power at the EU level might conflict with decisions that the *pouvoir constituant* has previously taken at the state level. Traditionally, constituent power is conceptualized as an unrestrained competence to establish and revise constitutional orders. But can this idea be upheld when already constituted political communities engage in a higher-level process of constitutional politics?" (Patberg 2017c, 206).

Patberg argues that in order to understand how constituent power might work, we need an analytical distinction between constituent power's different contexts of manifestation[30], as well as a systematic normative account of their relationship. The latter relates to the issue of who should be in charge of EU constitutional politics: "The member state *pouvoirs constituants* would have to authorize the installation of a higher-level constituent power but it is an open normative question what form it should take" (Patberg 2017c, 211). The practice of EU constitutional politics hence gives rise to the following questions: "To what extent should the constituent power of the EU be bound by constitutional decisions previously taken at the state level? What are the principles of democratic legitimacy that the exercise of constituent power at the EU level should conform to? And last but not least: What should be the adequate composition of EU constitutional politics?" (Patberg 2017c, 210–1). The classical account of constituent power is not appropriate nor useful in a context in which "already constituted political communities engage in a higher-level process or constitutional politics" (Patberg 2017c, 206).

Patberg recalls that in the context of the EU, apart from the classical account of constituent power, there are also (at the theoretical level) retrospective and functionalist approaches to constituent power. A retrospective approach makes constituent power "a popular self-ascription of decisions taken by others in the past" (Patberg 2018, 264)[31]; but by focusing on a singular moment of founding as the origin of a constitutional order, a retrospective approach limits the role of citizens to "reflexively appropriating decision that others made for them in the past" (Patberg 2018, 264). Let me stress that from my point of view, though, the classical understanding of constituent power mostly is a retrospective one; hence, there is no conceptual innovation here. Functionalist approaches rather use the category of constituent power to describe the forces "that de facto shape the EU constitutional order" (Patberg 2018, 265). Some make constituent power "a synonym for the treaty-making competence of sovereign nation-states" (Patberg 2018, 265); others focus on the jurisgenerative potential of court ruling. Although functionalist approaches understand EU constitutional politics as an open-ended and ongoing process, they do not provide "the means to criticize existing procedures for their democratic deficit" (Patberg 2018, 265).

Conclusion

In Patberg's work, as in Niesen's, there is an explicit and purposeful attempt at rescuing a sense of collective political agency that can ground democratic authorization in supra-state polities. They focus on the dynamics between contestation, on the one hand, and the articulation and institutionalization of democratic agency, on the other one. They acknowledge the significance of destituent power for challenging unauthorized rule. Yet, they also claim that the democratic legitimacy of new constitutional norms cannot be generated out of contestation alone. Focusing on narratives that propose how the citizens could take control of European integration on the basis of a democratic form of EU constitutional politics is fruitful because it allows to bring together activation and articulation of constituent power.

However, at the end of the day, one may wonder whether there is much conceptual innovation in what regards democratic authorization as such in these approaches. This does not mean that the scholarly contributions to these debates are not important nor interesting. They actually allow to get a clearer picture of the significant challenges raised by the issue of public autonomy and democratic authorization in a "post-Westphalian" context. But the public narratives analyzed by Patberg actually run into the very same difficulties as the approaches already discussed in previous chapters. Imageries of a cross-border constituent power are characteristic of approaches arguing for a transfer of constituent power as a building block of modern constitutionalism. As I have explained in Chapter 4, these approaches (such as, e.g., Walker's one) stand by the basics of state constitutionalism. Imageries of a plurality of constituent powers mainly fall back upon the idea of containment. Yet, the containment strategy implies falling back on a negativistic logic that stops short of authorship in what concerns the framing of authority in non-state polities. What is challenged is the very possibility of embodying democratic agency beyond the state (see Chapter 5). Approaches arguing for a non-state federation (e.g., Preuss's) may seem promising as they explicitly aim at distancing themselves from statehood; they argue that constituent power is possible at a non-state level. But as I have explained in Chapter 4, the notion of constituent power does not stand on its own, for it belongs with a specific framework—the one of statehood. We need to be able to address this close relationship to correctly understand the challenges peculiar to our age. Finally, as to imageries of a multitude (of no delineated subject) whose resistance triggers constitutional change, they do not propose a conception of *constituent* power. They rather argue for some anti-juridical version of destituent power and stop short of framing how democratic agency (including some jurisgenerative capacity) may be embodied in the transnational sphere. None of them offers an innovative conception of democratic authorization and public autonomy in polycentric settings of governance.

For the purposes of this book, I am less interested in debates about the nature of EU's constituent power and EU's constitutionalization processes than about proposals and conceptions of constituent power in post- or non-state settings in general. Debates about constituent power in the EU, though, are more systematically structured than debates about constituent power in the transnational domain in general, because of the high degree of integration of the Union. As the EU is an economic, political, and social union of democratic states, it was almost unavoidable that the issue of its direct democratic authorization by the people would be at some point be raised and debated. Yet, it is not obvious how a discussion embedded in the EU context and its (likely) processes of constitutionalization allows to overcome the limits of foundational constitutionalism. It is not because "our limits of imagination" are peculiarly blatant in this specific case. It is because the EU actually was built upon (democratic) nation-states.

I have already explained that the EU is a *sui generis* case, and that an issue with some of the theses discussed in this book is that discussing constituent power in this specific, *sui generis* context does not necessarily allows for generalization to other regimes of the current polycentric setting of governance[32]. The fact that it has been longing for a more substantial democratic authorization (one that is not merely dependent upon its member states' own democratic legitimacy) cannot conceal the fact that it is a composite polity—and one, as well, in which the democratic tradition is well anchored (even if its institutions are not always up to the democratic credentials). In other words, discussing constituent power in the EU may actually not require that we significantly depart from the classical conception of constituent power. For example, it is plausible to ascribe a founding authority (which, anyway, always is ascribed *a posteriori* and given shape in the constitutional text) to an identifiable constituency[33]. This is so because the mix of territorial and functional authority characteristic of the EU nonetheless pertains to a polity whose territorial boundaries can be quite clearly delimited. However, this is not necessarily true of other types of post-state polities that may impact upon these constituencies significantly. Yet, we still have to reframe public autonomy and democratic authorization in the broader setting of the transnational domain.

The other problem with the accounts discussed here is that they do not challenge the consistency and desirability of retaining constituent power as a normative ascription providing the ideational basis for resistance against global institutions. They actually look for evidence that it remains appropriate in post- or non-state context. This may introduce a bias when it comes to try to make new forms of public autonomy intelligible and amenable to systematic framing. Hence, in the next (and very last) chapter, I wish to focus on the framing of what is "public" and on the issue of the expression of public autonomy.

Notes

1 Whether contentious politics drives democratization depends upon specific mechanisms and processes. See Tilly (2007) and McAdam, Tarrow, and Tilly (2001).
2 Incidents that enable agents to alter primary rules (Weinar, n.d.)
3 Democracy in Europe Movement 2025.
4 Niesen argues that this assumption could give the epistemology of international politics "a 'Copernican' turn" (Niesen 2019b, 4). Tully has stressed that people are always already involved in governance relationships. I also take resistance and protest to signal the capacity of people to point to existing relationships of governance and domination. The fact that most people still address their claims to their state rather than to other regimes or polities depends upon their sense that the state is still the institutional organization on which they are keen to have a more substantial influence.
5 "The act of making a constitution does not dispel or absorb, but conforms and perpetuates constituent power" (Niesen 2019b, 6).
6 This is not specific to post- or transnational resistance, though.
7 Remember Niesen means it as the enablement to alter primary rules.

8 This, for example, is the case with Habermas's account of split constituent power in the EU.
9 See Chapters 1 and 5.
10 I won't tackle the issue of whether the assumption that there are constitutionalization processes beyond the state actually rests upon confusing legalization for constitutionalization. This issue is raised, e.g., by Loughlin. Let me just mention that according to Niesen, there are state-unbound constitutionalization processes that create comprehensive legal orders that claim constitutional status (Niesen 2017b, 226).
11 See also Niesen (2019a, 40).
12 This basically reasserts the idea that the constitution transforms a multitude into a constituent power, but in a more open-ended process than in the state context (for in the latter, the constituency is determined *a priori* by territorial boundaries).
13 See Chapter 1.
14 As I have already explained, this is also doubtful in the state context, for popular sovereignty has been subordinated to state sovereignty. But this is not what I want to focus on right now.
15 I use "undefined" to point to the fact that most of the time such entities do not recognize themselves *as polities* and to the fact, as well, that their boundaries are overlapping in a complex setting of governance.
16 Constituent power is the generative aspect of the political power relationship that bounds rulers and ruled within a constitutional order; it generates political power by converting the multitude into a form of political agency. This conversion grounds the authority of the constitution. The latter is regulative, not constitutive. See Chapter 1.
17 Once again, I do not mean to say that such a collective was not contested, amongst others by minority nations and First Nations. But there was a dominant assumption that the state embodies one people.
18 See Chapter 5.
19 See Chapter 5, note 21.
20 Let me recall that destituent power is "a category according to which opposition to or withdrawal from the regulatory grasp of public authority can function as a legitimate trigger for constitutional change" (Patberg 2019, 83). See Chapter 5.
21 Moreover, they "all claim to speak in the name of the people [...] They see themselves as opponents of an accelerating erosion of democracy emanating from European integration. This self-understanding implies that the proposed acts of contestation are meant to outline a democratic practice" (Patberg 2019, 85).
22 Public narratives are "collective stories with a normative message that are constructed in the public sphere and result from the non-coordinated contributions of various actors" (Patberg 2018, 264–5). He focuses on public narratives "that paint a picture of the constituent power from which the process of European integration needs to derive its democratic legitimacy" (Patberg 2018, 271).
23 This narrative conveys the claim that the EU cannot be reformed through the standard process of intergovernmental negotiations and treaty changes (Patberg 2018, 274–6).
24 Niesen designates it as the "demoi-cratic" account. In this account, constituent power "lies in the people severally, not collectively speaking: the aggregate of plural *pouvoirs constituants* does not create a new *pouvoir* in addition to those of the several peoples [...] The member *demoi* reflect the enlarged mind-set of their citizens, but [...] individuals figure as (suitably idealized) members of states rather than of the federative EU" (Niesen 2017b, 228).
25 To establish the federal union, a convention is needed.
26 See also Niesen (2019a, 37).
27 Integration has proceeded under the hegemony of neoliberal interests, and hence the EU is incapable of progressive reform from within. The only hope is "that a significant number of citizens decide to force a break with the existing structure" (Patberg 2018, 285).

28 Split conceptions criticize unitary ones.

29 Its advocates criticize the notion of *pouvoir constituant mixte* for putting individuals on a par with collective subjects, whereas supra-individual entities (a people, a majority, a state) "'are not self-authenticating sources of valid claims' and thus cannot figure in a conception of popular sovereignty" (Patberg 2017b, 167, quoting Eriksen 2016, 197).

30 In the context of the EU, constituent power can manifest itself at different stages. See, e.g., Patberg's discussion of Habermas's argument about levelling up constituent power (Patberg 2017c). He argues that Habermas does not provide a systematic justification "for regarding the *pouvoir constituant mixte* as the subject that should be in charge of actual processes of EU constitutional politics" (Patberg 2017a, 442), because he does not subject the processes by which the EU is shaped to a rational reconstruction (Patberg 2017c, 211). According to him, Habermas ultimately fails "to determine who is entitled to actually decide on the EU constitutional order and under what conditions" (Patberg 2017a, 442).

31 "According to this view, constituent power emerges when citizens idealize the historical genesis of their constitution and paint the picture of a democratic founding. With a view to the EU, this is seen as an ongoing, incomplete process that can potentially tie in with various norms and practices" (Patberg 2018, 265). Some scholars focus on invocations of the EU's ultimate source of authority in positive law (e.g., Walker), while others make the new possibilities generated through the establishment of the EU the basis of a reflexive appropriation of its constitution (e.g., Lindahl) (Patberg 2018, 265).

32 I of course do not mean to say that the scholars discussed here are not aware of such distinctiveness.

33 There is no consensus on whether the EU is going through a process of constitutionalization. But there is at least the possibility of common grounds on which to discuss whether or not there is such a process. This possibility demonstrates that it at least makes sense to discuss the EU as a polity in terms of constituent power and constitutionalization, even if at the end of the day we may disagree as to the conclusions of such an analysis.

References

Blokker, Paul. 2018. "Constitutional Mobilization and Contestation in the Transnational Sphere." *Journal of Law and Society* 45, special issue 1: S52–S72.

McAdam, Doug, Tarrow, Sidney, and Tilly, Charles. 2001. *Dynamics of Contention*. Cambridge: Cambridge University Press.

Niesen, Peter. 2017b. "Constituent Power in Global Constitutionalism." In *Handbook on Global Constitutionalism*, edited by Anthony F. Lang Jr. and Antje Wiener, 222–233. Cheltenham: Edward Elgar.

Niesen, Peter. 2019a. "Reframing Civil Disobedience: Constituent Power as a Language of Transnational Protest." *Journal of International Political Theory* 15, no. 1: 31–48.

Niesen, Peter. 2019b. "Introduction: Resistance, Disobedience or Constituent Power? Emerging Narratives of Transnational Protest." *Journal of International Political Theory* 15, no. 1: 2–10.

Patberg, Markus. 2017a. "A Systematic Justification for the EU's *Pouvoir Constituant Mixte*: Principles of Constitutional Politics in Supranational Polities." *European Law Journal* 23: 441–453.

Patberg, Markus. 2017b. "Introduction: the EU's *Pouvoir Constituant Mixte*—Exploring the Systematic Potential of an Innovative Category." *Journal of Common Market Studies* 55, no. 2: 165–170.

Patberg, Markus. 2017c. "The Levelling Up of Constituent Power in the European Union." *Journal of Common Market Studies* 55, no. 2: 203–212.

Patberg, Markus. 2018. "Challenging the Masters of the Treaties: Emerging Narratives of Constituent Power in the European Union." *Global Constitutionalism* 7, no. 2: 263–293.

Patberg, Markus. 2019. "Destituent Power in the European Union: On the Limits of a Negativistic Logic of Constitutional Politics." *Journal of International Political Theory* 15, no. 1: 82–99.

Tilly, Charles. 2007. *Democracy*. New York: Cambridge University Press.

Weinar, Leif. n.d. "Rights". Stanford Encyclopedia of Philosophy. Accessed April 20, 2021. https://plato.stanford.edu/entries/rights/

7

A NEW NARRATIVE OF PUBLIC AUTHORITY?

In the previous chapters, I have argued that the normative resonance of the concept of constituent power builds upon three dimensions that are dependent upon statehood. I have also assessed different attempts at recasting, translating, or somehow rescuing constituent power in the post- or transnational sphere. I have explained the difficulties they involve and the challenges they raise. In this final chapter, which also concludes this book, I wish to develop more thoroughly two core aspects that stand out of the conceptions, debates, difficulties, and challenges tackled in the previous chapters. These aspects must be addressed if we are to frame alternate ways of embodying the radical promise embodied in the notion of constituent power—ways that do not depend upon the framing of public power as state power.

The first dimension relates to the new mappings of public authority that challenge the sovereign state as embodying the autonomy of the political and as the condition of the unity of a people to whom constituent power is attributed. A core issue here is one of the standards that we shall use to account for such a transformation and to assess it. I have stressed that Loughlin rightly argues that sovereignty is the expression of a public realm conceived as autonomous. It is juridical and relates to authority, not to power. Authority is the right to be obeyed; power is the ability to control its material conditions and destiny (Loughlin 2014b, 10). From Loughlin's perspective, as long as sovereignty as the expression of an autonomously conceived public realm is not itself challenged (namely, as long as public law won't have lost its symbolic power), it is groundless to argue that we are going through a paradigmatical shift. As long as globalization's regimes cannot be considered institutions endowed with an autonomous status and having aims of a general nature (rather than performing limited and particular

DOI: 10.4324/9781003221722-8

functions), they can't be said to have displaced the political reality of the state as the "institution of institutions".

Yet, if the issue is framed in such a way that the state is paradigmatic of what is public, there is no way of thinking outside the box and of trying to sketch new ways of embodying democratic autonomy in settings that combine state and non-state entities. We are condemned to lament democratic self-rule as it was embodied in the state, and to argue for a containment strategy. However, the state should be understood as participating in a specific representation of what is public. It is more fruitful, therefore, to focus the investigation into the location of authority on the practices of recognition and deference that actually sustain authority (Krisch 2017, 249). Of course, this is a difficult exercise, for it requires us to try to move beyond "our limits of imagination". C. Tilly has explained a while ago how difficult it would have been for someone living in 14th-century Europe to predict how polities were to be structured in the following centuries, because from that person's point of view, the territorial state would have been but one amongst several possibilities (and not the more likely one), even if the processes that were to lead to its consolidation were already well underway (Tilly 1975). We probably face a similar situation, trying to grasp significant ongoing processes, yet not being able to frame and name them appropriately. S. Sassen has also made this point, stressing that

> [i]t is interesting to recall that in feudal times, the capabilities for a future formation marked by unitary authority—the territorial sovereign—were being developed through organizational modes that would have seemed incompatible with those of the territorial state. We need to ask if today we might have a similar situation of ambiguity and illegibility [...]. The nation-state remains the prevalent organizational source of authority and to variable extents the dominant one. But [...] critical components of authority deployed in the making of the territorial state are shifting toward becoming strong capabilities for detaching that authority from its exclusive territory and onto multiple bordering systems. Insofar as many of these systems are operating inside the nation-state, they may be obscuring the fact that a significant switch has happened.
>
> (Sassen 2006, 419)

The challenge, then, is the one of "theorizing public authority in global governance" (Krisch 2012, 986). I of course do not claim to address thoroughly this challenge here. I merely claim to contribute to the current debates on constituent power by emphasizing a few dimensions that are particularly significant as to the issue of democratic authorization and public autonomy.

I have argued throughout this book that the classical notion of constituent power may not be appropriate to capture democratic agency and authorization in the polycentric setting of global governance. It bears a radical promise (the one of a comprehensive founding of self-government by people as agents) but it also faces significant limitations, both because it is intertwined with statehood and because of the current transformations in regulatory activity. I have argued that the classical notion of constituent power is too much dependent upon statehood for it to have critical purchase on the new patterns of public authority. Constituent power belongs with the conceptual apparatus of a theory of government peculiar to a statist way of knowing, and being into, the world. It presupposes the state as the political unity of a people. It depends upon the idea that public power—namely, political power harnessed through the institutionalization of authority—acquires autonomy with the establishment of the modern idea of the state (Loughlin 2003, 78). It is the generative aspect of the political power relationship that bound rulers and ruled within a constitutional order (Loughlin 2003)[1].

From my point of view, the significant transformations in patterns of authority call for a reconceptualization of collective political agency correlative to the one of public authority. The two issues are closely related, because it is the sovereign state that made it possible to presume of the unity of a people, in modern constitutionalism. As I have already stressed, this also raises a normative issue, since constituent power as a modern concept belongs with a framework in which the "people-as-the-governed" are "invisible" (Nootens 2015): their constituent power is unformed and unbounded unless framed by the state[2]. It also had been challenged for a while by minority nations and First Nations, as I explained in the Introduction. Globalization has exacerbated these issues, because it has made incongruencies and incongruities more obvious. Let me tackle these two dimensions, starting with public autonomy.

Public Autonomy

The issue of public autonomy (and the related one of how it is to be embodied and expressed) is a complex one. I want to focus on the issue of whether the notion of the "public" is the right frame to think about the need for structure and guidance in an order devoid of the ordering domestic/international divide (Krisch 2012). In the latter ordering, the distinction between what is public (for the whole society, by the whole society, and hence, what raises issues of legitimacy rather than issues of mere coordination), on the one hand, and what is private, on the other one, seemed relatively well-determined[3]. The fact that we use to take for granted the equation of state power with public power is a problem, though. For example, Teubner stresses that the critique of transnational constitutionalism as a self-serving device for elites or for functional systems (although justified in its insistence on the legitimacy principle) is hypocritical

> when public lawyers and political scientists categorically declare 'private' transnational regimes as illegitimate due to their lack of publicness, but at the same time accept their legitimacy without ado if they are

> based formally on public law institutions in nation states and in international politics. They ignore empirical studies, which demonstrate that several so-called private transnational regimes [...] have a considerably better record of democratic decision making than many so-called public regimes [...] And when they criticize the undemocratic practices of transnational public regimes, they turn a blind eye and a deaf ear to the massive democratic deficit of national and international public institutions whose 'post-democratic' character again and again has been revealed and criticized.
>
> (Teubner 2018, 8)

The problem with approaches that equate the public with the state (or that equate public power with state power) is that they do not allow for an independent assessment of what is public[4]. I am aware that there is a very specific sense of the public closely associated with modernity (and particularly with the rise of the bourgeois public sphere[5]). Yet, one must allow for a more generalizable sense of what is public that can provide a critical standpoint on specific embodiments of it, that allows for the idea of a general interest (of something brought by the whole society), and that can be related to some idea of self-rule. A core issue is that the idealized structure of state power grounded a unified framework of public power, but the latter also belongs with a dualistic "society of states", namely, one built upon an assumption of a duality internal/external. The disarticulation of this framework, and particularly of the territorialization of authority peculiar to the modern state (in which a number of functions of a general reach neatly coincided with a specific territory), makes it necessary to reconceptualize the public. Hence, following scholars such as Grimm and Krisch, I argue that public power cannot be equated with state power: statehood shapes public power in a specific way, but public power is a broader category.

The problem is that there is a conventional association, in the liberal theoretical worldview, between public power and the state—and correlatively, between "private" and "non-state" (Mcdonald 2008, 44–5)[6]. Rather than being problematized or given clear articulation within democratic theory, the term "public power" "is commonly employed loosely and interchangeably with a family of related but distinct concepts—including 'authority', 'sovereignty', 'statehood', and 'governance' or 'government'" (Mcdonald 2008, 21). Public power, then, is "commonly assumed to entail a range of organizational characteristic linked to statehood" (Mcdonald 2008, 45), and more particularly the three following ones: the reliance upon law-making and law-enforcement as the central institutional vehicle for the exercise of power; a capacity to use force or violent coercion to sustain the exercise of power; and a centralized or constitutionalized structure of power (Mcdonald 2008, 45). Yet, none of these organizational characteristics are actually essential for the exercise of public power (Mcdonald 2008, 45). Hence, there must be an independent criterion for identifying the forms of power (state as well as non-state) that qualify as public. A democratic perspective would certainly require that such a criterion implies specific normative requirements as to the relations between rulers and ruled. However, the equation of state power with public power does not build on democratic assumptions. It rather rests on the pivotal role of the notion of sovereignty (Grimm 2010). I am aware that one may argue (such as, e.g., Walker does) that the operational autonomy of the political domain is precarious unless it is joined by a claim to self-authorization—a claim that, within constitutional thought, has usually been conceived in terms of the idea of constituent power. But Walker also acknowledges that a specialized political system does not necessarily imply democratic procedures of decision-making. It is public politics within states as territorially sovereign entities that has been democratized, in the West, in the 19th and 20th century, not the state itself (Nootens 2019). The distinction is crucial.

Going back briefly to T. Mcdonald, let me recall that she argues that the criteria for delineating what is public should be the problematic impact of power on the autonomous capacities of others. As she works from the perspective of liberal democratic theory, she argues that it is the value of individual autonomy that should be the normative criterion for identifying public forms of power[7]. The public, from her point of view, is any existing form of power that impacts problematically upon such autonomous capacities; this is why public power is the legitimate subject of democratic control. Although one may dispute this specific criterion[8], she rightly argues for the possibility of some non-state forms of power to qualify as public. For example, she stresses that there is a plurality of non-state agencies of public power, namely, agencies that "wield many of the forms of 'public' decision-making power [...] that democrats have traditionally sought to subject to public regulatory control" (Mcdonald 2008, 30). Hence, if we are to have any fruitful debate about non-state forms of (public) power, we need to be able to contradistinguish public power from state power, at least conceptually. Grimm, for one, allows for such a distinction. He argues that state power actually meant the concentration of public power (the various forms of regulatory activity) in a given territory. It was the notion of sovereignty that implied such an identity between state power and public power. But state power and public power are increasingly incongruent.

Many scholars frame the issue as one of legitimacy because it is increasingly difficult to disentangle questions arising in the "domestic" context and questions arising in the "international" arena, so that the long-standing assumption that the division between legitimacy and coordinating functions was feasible cannot be sustained any longer (Krisch 2012). This is what raises the issue of public autonomy and its expression (the normative production of governance). The public also has a normative meaning: it carries the idea (and ideal) of some general interest, one that at least ideally does not suffer from biases in favour of certain interests or is not captured by particular groups—in other words, of something "brought by the whole society". Public autonomy relates with the right to self-government, "to equal participation in the design of the political order" (Krisch 2006, 274). It carries an ideal of inclusiveness and deliberation (Kuo 2012, 1052). What is public, then, is what concerns the society as such; non-public means "interest-oriented". The notion is framed by specific requirements. For example, in the GAL project in which Krisch contributes, the underlying notion of publicness includes "the limitation of power, the requirement of justification and proportionality, the procedural mechanisms for deliberate decision-making, and the protection of human rights" (Kuo 2012).

From such a perspective,

> the idea of public authority might help us transcend a focus on existing institutions and their risks: it might force us to think about what kinds of institutions we would need to enable self-government in a global context, and provide us with a perspective on the *lack* of institutions in many areas and for many problems. The idea of public authority is, in a reading that emphasizes public autonomy in its positive form, also the idea of institutions by which a public hopes to assert itself.
>
> (Krisch 2012, 985)[9]

The idea of public authority

> allows us to gain traction on different problems by linking to discourses and scholarship on related phenomena in the domestic realm. In this, it provides a competing frame to classical intergovernmental frames, and it helps to break open established understandings about legitimation mechanisms beyond the state. Once this opening is created, though, we are forced to consider the differences from domestic conditions. This may lead us to take inspiration from models which are not common in, or have remained on the fringes of, domestic discourses. Some of these emphasize societal diversity in a way that may not resonate in all national polities but may fit well in a global setting characterized by strong cleavages and contestation.
>
> (Krisch 2012, 986)[10]

Krisch acknowledges that the ideal of the public "has probably never been fully achieved; any institution suffers from biases in favor of certain interests, and many are captured by particular groups. But by marking them out as public, we gain a yardstick for measuring deviation and a regulative ideal that demands not only checks and responsiveness but also actual input by a broader public –authorial, not only editorial control [...]" (Krisch 2012, 985).

What then about Loughlin's claim that sovereignty (as juridical) has not up to now been significantly challenged as the expression of an autonomously conceived public realm? I already have explained in Chapter 3 that it is difficult (although critical) to assess whether sovereignty as a legal concept is significantly challenged, because of the entanglement of forms of authority, of the blurring of boundaries, of the transformations in models of authority, and of the formation of new types of territorialities[11]. I also explained in Chapter 5 (when discussing Krisch's notion of *pouvoir irritant*) that the global context includes forms of authority that are characterized by a lower degree of consolidation and a significant dynamism in the configuration of authority structures. These forms blur the boundaries between the domestic and the international, between the public and the private, and between formally binding norms and other norms. If this is the case, then focusing on delegation from states to identify, map, and explain authority, as well as for framing questions of accountability and legitimacy, is likely to be misleading, for "[i]t might suggest that there is no authority when there is actually authority to be found [...] or it might locate authority in one place when, in fact, it resides elsewhere (or is distributed more broadly) [...]" (Krisch 2017, 249). This is why the empirical investigation into the location of authority "cannot rest on a focus on delegation and formal legal powers; it needs to center on the practices of recognition and deference that sustain authority" (Krisch 2017, 249). In other words, focusing primarily on delegation may lead us to misread "the ways in which authority actually is created and maintained. Moreover, it provides a framing for follow-on problems—legitimacy, accountability, and legality—that hides key challenges deriving from the particular character of governance on the global level" (Krisch 2017, 249). A "deference" model is more appropriate than the usual "command" one (the one focusing on the exercise of binding powers to create formal obligations) if we are to understand "liquid" authority. A focus on the command model "tends to overstate the analogy with traditional domestic government, and at the same time it obscures from view the many forms of institutional influence which, though highly consequential, do not operate through formal, legal tools" (Krisch 2017, 240–1). The deference model rather focuses on "the plurality of authority structures emerging, in the contemporary world, from social processes without an anchor in formal or legal powers and operating through informal tools" (Krisch 2017, 241). Understanding authority according to the deference model "shifts our view to sources of recognition that are not based on formal legal empowerment" (Krisch 2017, 242)—yet, still are sources of authority.

From our (modern) perspective, the transformations in the interactions and forms of the public/private and of the inside/outside appear as a blurring of boundaries that complicate the enterprise of appropriately framing public autonomy. Yet, we must get rid of the assumption that societies are closed as to the structure of public power and the structure of the agents of democratic control (Mcdonald 2008, 24). We must also get rid of the assumption that public power "is structured as an organizationally unified framework [...] to which each member of the democratic society is equally subject" (Mcdonald 2008, 24), and of the assumption that it is paradigmatically concentrated "in a state, agent, or sovereign power, which exercises public power through law-making" (Mcdonald 2008, 24)[12]. State-centred accounts actually prevent us from asking questions of accountability as to all forms of political power (Anderson 2012).

Other scholars, such as S. Sassen, have provided thorough analyses of the genesis and dynamics of these new forms of authority. Sassen's work is a particularly significant contribution to the issue of the appropriate framing of these new patterns of authority. She has explained how "disassembling" the national state takes place inside the state: the current authority structure builds upon capabilities that are present within the national state but that are relodged into assemblages that denationalize and globalize such nationally oriented capabilities. These capabilities "come from both the public and private domains as constituted in the national era. Getting relodged into denationalizing and global organizing logics not only reorients these capabilities toward objectives other than those to which they were oriented, it also reconstitutes the construction of the public and the private, and of the boundaries between these domains" (Sassen 2006, 13). As she rightly stresses,

> [t]he specificity of the global does not necessarily reside in being mutually exclusive with the national. The strategic spaces where many global processes are embedded are often national; the mechanisms through which new legal forms, necessary for globalization, are implemented are often part of state institutions. The infrastructure that enables the hypermobility of financial capital at the global scale is embedded in various national territories. But the processes that constitute this insertion partly denationalize the national.
>
> (Sassen 2006, 381)

The state is a "major locus" of this transformation, "even when this is not easily legible and seems to contradict what is legible about the current epoch [...] As the most formalized instantiation of the nation-state, the state apparatus itself is then undergoing foundational change in one or another of its critical components, making this one of the constitutive changes of the new global era" (Sassen 2006, 401).

Another important dimension of her analysis as to the purposes of this chapter revolves around emergent territorialities that evince specific features and require that we do not draw a simplistic opposition between the territorial and the functional. It is important to explain this dimension more thoroughly, because a simplistic opposition between the territorial and the functional leads to a neglect of forms of territorialities specific to the disassemblage of the national. These territorialities are "assembled out of 'national' and 'global' elements, each individual or aggregate instance evincing distinct spatio-temporal features" (Sassen 2006, 386). There are three broad types of such emergent territorialities: global networks of financial centers; global networks of localized activists and the constituting of global civil society; and new jurisdictional geographies. Emergent territorialities of the first type are denationalized in very specific and partial ways, and can be seen "as constituting the elements of a novel type of multisited territoriality, one that diverges sharply from the territoriality of the historic nation-state" (Sassen 2006, 386–7). Emergent territorialities of the second kind point to the denationalization of the subjectivities of the actors involved, rather than of their subnational space. Contrary to the global capital market, these global publics are barely institutionalized and mostly informal. The third type of emergent territorialities points to those legal frameworks for rights and guarantees that are strengthening a non-national organizing logic and alter the valence of older national state capabilities (Sassen 2006, 388).

These emergent territorialities evince specific features:

> First, they are not exclusively national or global but assemblages of elements of each. Second, in this assembling they bring together what are often different spatio-temporal orders [...] Third, this can produce an eventful engagement, including contestations and the frontier zone effect [...] Fourth, novel types of actors can emerge in this assembling [...] Finally, in the juxtaposition of the different temporal orders that come together in these novel territorialities, existing capabilities can get redeployed to domains with novel organizing logics.
>
> (Sassen 2006, 389)[13]

As these assemblages unbundle the traditional territoriality of the national, one should be careful not to draw an oversimplistic opposition between the territorial and the functional. Amongst other things, even dematerialized forms must be managed somewhere. But they nonetheless constitute a space that is "predicated on, or productive of, a disarticulation of territory and authority when compared with the case of the nation-state" (Sassen 2006, 411). This phenomenon also "alters the historically produced distinction between the private and public domains" (Sassen 2006, 411). Sovereignty "remains a systemic property but its institutional insertion and its capacity to legitimate and absorb all legitimating power, to be the source of law, have become unstable" (Sassen 2006, 415). Moreover, "prevalence is not to be confused with dominance" (Sassen 2006, 416). Hence, the historical territorial exclusivity associated with the nation-state should be conceived as but one among different possible forms of authority with territorial parameters (Sassen 2006, 419).

Another consequence of these processes is that they enable a proliferation of temporal and spatial framings, as well as a proliferation of normative orders "where once the dominant logic was toward producing unitary spatial, temporal, and normative framings" (Sassen 2006, 421). Although this development is partial, it nonetheless is of a strategic character because it signals the remixing of constitutive rules (for example, in the shifts of the public/private divide) and the multiplication of partial systems (Sassen 2006, 421). There is, therefore, a critical difference with the multiple systems of rule of the Middle Ages: the new assemblages produce a type of segmentation entailing an intersystemic inequality built into the possibility of exiting ruling normative orders, and assemblages having particular, internal normative orders (Sassen 2006, 422). A number of those constitute themselves "as private systems of justice and authority" (Sassen 2006, 423). By contradistinction, the medieval period was an era in which "there were strong broadly encompassing normative orders (the church, the empire) and the disaggregations (the feuds, the cities) each contained within them a fairly complete structure involving many if not most aspects of life" (Sassen 2006, 422). Today, the state cannot quite counteract the particularized normativities of the new assemblages; let us think, for example, of the norm-making power of the global capital market (Sassen 2006, 422)[14].

So, we cannot see (yet) that this centrifugal logic has replaced important segments of the centripetal logic of the nation-state, in part because the latter's administrative capability

> remains critical also for significant elements of the new centrifugal logic [...] and because war and militarized border controls mark the geopolitical landscape and have mostly been sharpened rather than diluted in much of the world. The ongoing prevalence of strong state politics and policies may well increasingly be a matter more of raw power than the more complex category that is authority –as the new types of wars [...] suggest. Even as the raw power of national states in many cases has increased, this may not necessarily mean that sovereign territorial authority has become more significant. [...] As the unitary character of the nation-state becomes disaggregated, even if only partially, sovereign authority is itself subject to partial disaggregations.
>
> (Sassen 2006, 423)

Therefore, the state is, or will be, "a profoundly changed entity" (Sassen 2006, 423).

I have explained Sassen's claim at length because it points to the necessity of a very nuanced discussion of the transformation of forms of authority if we are to assess the latter properly. Sassen's work emphasizes that sovereignty and state's authority are deeply transformed by some of the current processes, in ways that are not easily definable if we assess them using the traditional categories of statehood. Let me stress that Sassen's analysis at first sight seems to concur with Teubner's description of "constitutional fragments". However, whereas Teubner praises functional differentiation (and societal constitutionalism for acknowledging it), Sassen acknowledges the critical part played by the impact of the norm-making power of global capital in the differentiation process. The fact is that polycentricity does not mean that there is no core structuring process. The fragmentation praised by Teubner can actually signal the deepening of a dynamics that is core to modernity and that sustains functional differentiation itself (for example, the coercion/capital dynamics analyzed by Tilly). Hence, Sassen can offer a more accurate analysis of the inequalities involved and of the difficulties in framing democratic authorization in such a context. Hers is a nuanced analysis, which points both to the critical part still played by the administrative capability of the state and to the reorientation of some of those capabilities to another logic. I wish to stress that not being able to make such transformations legible yet, nor to name frameworks that are yet to be consolidate, should not stop us from trying to understand them. Such difficulties probably are characteristic of "tipping points". To grasp the actual substance of claims to authority in the current era, one must nonetheless try to overcome the conventional statist framework.

Democratic Authorization and Collective Political Agency in Mixed Polities

So far, I have focused on the issue of public authority. I have stressed that framing accurately the current, ongoing transformations requires that we somehow move beyond the categories and distinctions conventionally used to understand public authority. I have suggested that Krisch's, Mcdonald's, and Sassen's work provide significant benchmarks that help to understand the complex nature of public authority in the current era. This step is important because the claim to (and seizure of) authority is basic to the political. Citizens have a sense that these transformations blur the traditional categories that allowed them to negotiate with rulers. For example, some of their claims have transnational regimes as their object (even if they still most of the time address their claims to their state). But framing collective political agency and democratic authorization remains a difficult task, both because of the complexities of these transformations and because our democratic practices are deeply framed by the state institutions in which they developed. Moreover, it is not only "our limits of imagination" that are at stake; it also is the willingness of those who rule to explicitly enter into a relationship that could generate public power.

In Chapters 4–6, I have stressed the main difficulties faced by attempts to recast or rescue constituent power. As I have already explained, the conundrum, from my point of view, is the following: approaches that remain faithful to the (radical) idea of agency also tend to replicate foundationalism, which, as I have explained, can hardly apply in the post- and transnational sphere; and approaches that (rightly) appreciate the problems raised by attempts to replicate foundationalism fail in offering accounts of agency likely to support actual democratic authorization[15]. Approaches discussed in Chapter 4 try to retrieve a sense of how constituencies can self-organize in complex settings. But they ultimately fail to frame a notion of collective political agency appropriate to the transformations of public authority. Walker replicates foundational constitutionalism, whereas the latter is not appropriate in the global, polycentric setting. He makes democratic agency in non-state polities a constituent power "light", arguing that such polities (notably the EU) lack the conditions that made the sense of a political community possible within states. Preuss incorrectly downplays the significance of sovereign statehood for the conceptualization of the notion of constituent power, as he takes the relationship between constituent power and statehood to be a contingent one. He also (wrongly) seems to assume that the transnational is mostly made of horizontal and non-coercive schemes of social coordination. Teubner challenges the way foundational constitutionalism, holism, and agency relate in the statist paradigm. However, his approach faces significant issues related to the management of political conflict. These issues impact upon the recasting of democratic authorization. Teubner's work highlights the shortcomings both of a depoliticization of the constitution and of an approach of the self-constitution of social subsystems focused on dissent and self-contestation.

So basically, the approaches discussed in Chapter 4 either stand by the basics of state constitutionalism or fail to propose a narrative of collective political agency. Yet, if we are to address the issue of democratic authorization in the polycentric setting of global governance, we must tackle the very issue of the relationship between statehood and constituent power. Approaches discussed in Chapter 5 acknowledge the normative significance of constituent power, but they argue that the shift in regulatory activity that characterizes the polycentric setting of global governance does not allow for its embodiment and enactment. They rather try to retrieve a way in which democratic authorization could at least be triggered through containment or contestation; they focus on dismantling constitutional orders but not necessarily on the capacity for enacting new ones. In other words, they acknowledge that the polycentric setting of governance and the shift in regulatory activity challenge the very possibility of constituent power as a way of embodying public autonomy. But they fall back on a negativistic logic that cannot sustain authorship in the post- or transnational domain. Grimm makes democratic authorization dependent upon characteristics that are deemed unique to statehood. Moreover, his approach does not take into account the fact that domestic constitutionalism risks being both underinclusive and insufficiently effective. In Krisch's work, renouncing foundationalism means renouncing framing constituencies as the origin of the postnational order, and limiting agency to challenging and resisting such an order. The idea that destituent power or *pouvoir irritant* can trigger constitutional (or public law) change means that it is not to be equated with mere resistance. But *pouvoir irritant* can hardly be conceived of as an alternative narrative of democratic authorization, even if it opens the way for a discussion of how narratives of protest can contribute to reframing collective political agency.

Approaches discussed in Chapter 6 try to rescue the constructive side of constituent power without building on foundationalism. They rightly claim that narratives of protest play a significant part in any discussion about constituent power, because in processes of contention and contestation, people frame their claims as to public authority in specific narratives, and because these interactions (among people, and between people and rulers) also frame political identities. As I have explained, Niesen argues that in the case of global constitutionalism, ascriptions of constituent power are relevant in a transformational (rather than foundational) perspective. He also argues that the composition of such constituent power must be conceived of as open and that a pre-institutional self-activation always is available. However, one may doubt this is still *constituent power.* Patberg stresses the limited potential of a purely negativistic logic of constitutional politics. By focusing on narratives that challenge executive-centred treaty making in the EU, he provides a clearer picture of the challenges raised by the issue of public autonomy and democratic authorization in the "post-Westphalian" context. However, the public narratives analyzed by Patberg run into the very same difficulties as the approaches discussed in previous chapters. Moreover, it is not obvious how a discussion embedded in the EU context can allow to overcome the limits of foundational constitutionalism. The EU is a *sui generis* case. But it nonetheless is an entity built on (liberal democratic) national states. Discussing constituent power in the EU may not require that we significantly depart from the classical conception of constituent power. For example, although we may not agree on it, it would be plausible to ascribe a founding authority to an identifiable constituency. The case of the EU also shows that the idea of a pre-institutional activation always available does not tell much about the kind of polity in which the activation is taking place. In the EU, claims are activated *because* the EU exists. These claims may be considered "pre-institutional" in the sense that they do not require formal representative institutions to be activated (people can initiate the contention process outside existing institutions). But they definitively take place within an existing political framework. Hence, constituent power's composition actually is not open. Moreover, approaches focusing on narratives of protest start from the assumption that it is consistent and desirable to retain constituent power as a normative ascription and are looking for it in the narratives they analyze. They may thus overlook other ways of framing collective political agency.

Is there a way out of the conundrum? From my point of view, this requires a more thorough reflection on two significant issues. First, does renouncing a comprehensive founding through self-government imply renouncing a positive (active) role for collective political agency? In other words, is constituent power the only way to frame public autonomy so as to allow for the realization of self-rule? Second, how are we to conceive of democratic authorization in the polycentric order of global governance? I of course do not pretend to settle these matters here. I only wish to contribute a few insights on these issues as a way of concluding my discussion of approaches to constituent power beyond the state.

As to the first issue, I see no reason to assume that constituent power is the only way to frame public autonomy—provided we challenge the equation of state power with public power for which sovereignty is pivotal[16]. What was critical, in the development of modern constitutionalism, is the fact that it proceeded within already-defined polities (states) in which public politics was transformed by the dynamics of contention that, under specific circumstances, drove democratization. The development of constitutionalism came second to the "seizure of authority" (that is itself empirically dependent upon the interaction between coercion and capital analyzed by C. Tilly). In constitutionalism as a theory of government, the legitimacy of a regime is *a posteriori* imputed to a symbolic pole (the people) embodying a unity (out of a multitude). But this unity was made possible by the existence of the state. So constituent power belongs with an act of retroactive ascription of a capacity to generate political power within an already delimited polity[17].

Nonetheless, unless challenging sovereignty also necessarily means challenging agency, there is no reason, at least *a priori*, to argue that the fading of sovereignty requires renouncing agency as such. I am aware that sovereignty and agency basically belong with the same conceptual world; and that therefore, one must leave open the possibility that challenging the former may mean challenging also the latter. However, since state sovereignty has actually subjected such a capacity for collective political agency (shaping it through the pre-defined existence of the polity as a state), this opens the possibility for it to be recast, although it must be fundamentally reframed. This claim can be supported by normative and practical arguments related to struggles for civic freedom. These struggles point to relations of domination. Hence, the subordination of collective political agency to state sovereignty can be challenged from a normative point of view grounded in an argument about self-rule and freedom (individual and collective). And when struggles for civic freedom point to different kinds of polities (such as in transnational processes of contention), they also practically challenge the subordination of collective political agency to statehood by illustrating how new types of political identities can develop. Constituent power is not, and cannot be, the only way to frame public autonomy and democratic authorization. This also means, then, that we do not require foundationalism in order to do so. We can actually look for options that go beyond both foundation and contestation, and rather point to a radical transformation of the practices of democracy. But as I said earlier, this also depends upon our capacity to understand appropriately the regimes that currently exercise public authority.

So, (this is the second issue) how are we to conceive of (or to conceptually frame) democratic authorization in the polycentric order of global governance? I suspect that up to the point where narratives of protest will get a significant grip on the transnational sphere and lead to situations in which consent will have to be negotiated (and public politics democratized), it will be difficult to name any symbolic pole of collective political agency. Although theories of democracy have made a number of proposals as to how to institutionalize authority, I would rather not start with too specific an idea of how democracy is to be institutionalized. We shall rather focus on the mechanisms underlying the democratization of public politics in the regimes of global governance (including, of course, in states), namely, on specific processes by which people challenge the scope and nature of the governing relationships characteristic of these regimes. In the course of these processes, individuals and groups point to actual relations of domination, and they constitute themselves as political actors—hence, framing constituencies. One lesson that can be drawn from the state context is that narratives of public authority and autonomy are driven by the issue of subjection to non-authorized rule and by the social representations framing conceptions of legitimate authority. In the case of global governance, this point to several (sometimes overlapping) constituencies and public spheres, and to new types of territorialities, among other things. But this enterprise must also be led by a keen perception that our relationship with the modern state (and the way public law embodies the relationship between the public and the private) must be challenged, if we are to have, as citizens, an actual voice in decision-making processes. The ways we, as citizens, relate to post- and transnational regimes are basically political; negating this is a way of depriving people of an actual voice[18]. From this point of view, approaches focusing on narratives of protest are worthwhile considering even if they do not really provide us with an alternative narrative of agency.

But then, is it not equally true that democratic authorization is always, in a sense, reactive to existing relationships of governance? This question definitely calls for a positive answer. Yet, resistance, consent, or dissent are not the same as authorization[19]. The latter requires participation in a prospective and constructive sense, a sense faithful to the ideal that institutions are for us, as equals, to (re)build. For several reasons, some of which I explained above, approaching this ideal requires us to think beyond the state. That does not mean that in national states people have not succeeded in institutionalizing norms and practices getting us closer to such an ideal. But it certainly means we can fare (a lot) better by challenging the conventional assumptions of the statist paradigm. This, basically, is why we need to imagine democratic authorization beyond the state without resorting to the notion of constituent power.

Notes

1 This is why I prefer not to use "constituent power" in a very broad sense, one detached from constitutionalism as a theory of government in states (or state-like polities), contrary to what constitutionalism "from below" sometimes does.
2 In previous works (Nootens 2013 and 2015), I have argued that a non-state-based account of constituent power was possible and necessary. However, the thorough examination of the debates about constituent power beyond the state I went through to write this book had me reconsidered such a stance. Constituent power has a very specific meaning, related to sovereign statehood. It needs to be thought anew if we are to frame appropriately agonistic practices of freedom and self-rule in the current context.
3 I wish to focus more on the distinction itself than on the ideological frame sustaining it, although I am aware that public law is not free from oppression (see Chapter 2).
4 See, e.g., Skinner (2010, 45): he argues that we cannot talk coherently about the nature of public power without making some reference to the idea of the state as a fictional (moral) person distinct from both rulers and ruled.
5 See Habermas (1989 [1962]).
6 This of course does not mean that the conclusions reached by those who equate the public with the state are necessarily wrong. They actually may be right, but their claims should rest on an independent assessment of what is public.
7 She agrees, though, that democracy can be justified in other ways, and that if it were the case, then the criterion for delineating the scope of public power would need to differ accordingly (Mcdonald 2008, 35–6).
8 I do not mean that I intend to dispute it; I merely mean to say that one may wish to.
9 Some approaches point to significant limitations of a public authority approach. However, the critique of the public/private distinction may also mean "giving up an aspiration of collective self-government and its critical potential" (Krisch 2012, 985).
10 For example, multiculturalism, agonistic democracy, pluralist models, conflicts-of-law approaches, and the like.
11 See also below.
12 She rightly stresses that the paradigmatic unified framework of public power linked to the idealized structure of state power is also reflected in most cosmopolitan models (Mcdonald 2008, 25).
13 Geographic concepts of the border can switch into nongeographic border capabilities operating both transnationally and subnationally; "[i]n this process, particular legal protections get detached from their national territorial jurisdictions and become incorporated into a variety of often highly specialized or partial global regimes, and thereby often become transformed into far more specialized rights and obligations" (Sassen 2006, 417). Denationalized spatialities exist within the national territory.
14 These assemblages also tend to have rules for governance that are "distinct from formalized systems for governance", in that these rules are "wired into the structures of their system in a way reminiscent of how free markets functions" (Sassen 2006, 422).
15 They renounce agency in its radical sense of being the origin of the generation of political power and rather fall back on dissent or contestation.
16 In the state, the public was framed as pertaining to the neat overlapping of identity, territory, and ultimate authority, so that the public interest was deemed to be the one of the polity embodied by the sovereign state.
17 This retroactive ascription of the capacity to generate political power explains why some of the approaches discussed here argue that constituent power may be recast. This is very much in line with the classical meaning.
18 This is one (very good) reason to remain suspicious of societal constitutionalism.
19 I do not mean to downplay the significance of resistance, dissent, and consent. I only claim that they do not equate with authorization.

References

Anderson, Gavin W. 2012. "Beyond "Constitutionalism Beyond the State." *Journal of Law and Society* 39, no. 3: 359–383.

Grimm, Dieter. 2010. "The Achievement of Constitutionalism and Its Prospects in a Changed World." In *The Twilight of Constitutionalism?* edited by Petra Dobner and Martin Loughlin, 3–22. Oxford: Oxford University Press.

Habermas, Jürgen. 1989 [1962]. *The Structural Transformation of the Public Sphere: An Inquiry into a Category of Bourgeois Society*. Cambridge: MIT Press.

Krisch, Nico. 2006. "The Pluralism of Global Administrative Law." *European Journal of International Law* 17, no. 1: 247–278.

Krisch, Nico. 2012. "Global Governance as Public Authority: An Introduction." *International Journal of Constitutional Law* 10, no. 4: 976–987.

Krisch, Nico. 2017. "Liquid Authority in Global Governance." *International Theory* 9, no. 2: 237–260.

Kuo, Ming-Sung. 2012. "Interpublic Legality or Post-Public Legitimacy? Global Governance and the Curious Case of Global Administrative Law as a New Paradigm of Law." *International Journal of Constitutional Law* 10, no. 4: 1050–1075.

Loughlin, Martin. 2003. *The Idea of Public Law*. Oxford: Oxford University Press.

Loughlin, Martin. 2014b. "Constitutional Pluralism: An Oxymoron?" *Global Constitutionalism* 3, no. 1: 9–30.

Mcdonald, Terry. 2008. *Global Stakeholder Democracy: Power and Representation Beyond Liberal States*. Oxford: Oxford University Press.

Nootens, Geneviève. 2013. *Popular Sovereignty in the West. Polities, Contention, and Ideas*. London: Routledge.

Nootens, Geneviève. 2015. "Constituent Power and People-as-the-Governed: About the 'Invisible' People of Political and Legal Theory." *Global Constitutionalism* 4, no. 2: 137–156.

Nootens, Geneviève. 2019. "Légitimation démocratique et souveraineté méta-juridictionnelle de l'État." *ThéoRèmes* 15. https://journals.openedition.org/theoremes/3201

Sassen, Saskia. 2006. *Territory, Authority, Rights. From Medieval to Global Assemblages*. Princeton and Oxford: Princeton University Press.

Skinner, Quentin. 2010. "The Sovereign State: A Genealogy." In *Sovereignty in Fragments. The Past, Present and Future of a Contested Concept?* edited by Hent Kalmo and Quentin Skinner, 26–46. Cambridge: Cambridge University Press.

Teubner, Gunther. 2018. "*Quod Omnes Tangit*: Transnational Constitutions Without Democracy?" *Journal of Law and Society* 45, special issue 1: S5–S29.

Tilly, Charles. 1975. "Reflections on the History of European State-Making." In *The Formation of National States in Western Europe*, edited by Charles Tilly and Gabriel Ardant, 3–83. Princeton: Princeton University Press.

INDEX

For Product Safety Concerns and Information please contact our EU
representative GPSR@taylorandfrancis.com
Taylor & Francis Verlag GmbH, Kaufingerstraße 24, 80331 München, Germany

www.ingramcontent.com/pod-product-compliance
Ingram Content Group UK Ltd.
Pitfield, Milton Keynes, MK11 3LW, UK
UKHW022354190926
475702UK00015B/2287
9781032118321